Praise for *Home Sweet Anywhere*

"For anyone who harbors a secret fantasy of leaving everything behind to see the world, Lynne Martin is the perfect tour guide— she shows how she and her husband made that dream come true! I can't think of two 'senior gypsies' I'd rather follow as they journey to far-flung places than Lynne and Tim Martin. *Home Sweet Anywhere* is filled with adventure, humor, and heart. I loved this book!"

> —Mark Chimsky, editor, *65 Things to Do When You Retire*, named by the *Wall Street Journal* as "[one] of the year's best guides to later life"

"A delightful travel tale for anyone seeking to make their golden years sparkle."

> —Janice MacLeod, author of *Paris Letters*

"Lynne Martin and her late-in-life newlywed spouse have given new meaning to the phrase 'home free.' They sold their house, put all but the most necessary belongings into storage, and set off to live on the road. This is a book about the unthinkable made thinkable. Even if you don't follow their bliss, you will learn how it is done. The book is replete with money-saving travel tips like booking 'repositioning cruises.' Who knew? But it is far more than a how-to manual. Although told in sparky and breezy prose, don't be misled. It is about the hardest thing in the world to do. Like a reversible coat, Lynne Martin has shown us that there is another way to wear your life."

> —Samuel Jay Keyser, professor emeritus of linguistics, phonology, lexical theory, and poetics, and author of *I Married a Travel Junkie*

"Whether you are an intrepid adventurer or an armchair traveler, you will enjoy reading *Home Sweet Anywhere*. Lynne Martin has written a terrific book that inspires, informs, and gives hope to everyone who desires fun and freedom in retirement. Learn first-hand the opportunities, challenges, and foibles that selling everything and hitting the road to foreign ports can provide. I highly recommend it."

—Jeri Sedlar, co-author of *Don't Retire, REWIRE!*

"This captivating memoir is a wake-up call to anyone of any age who's ever wanted to take a significant amount of time off to explore the world. It reinforces the importance of 'postponing nothing' and living the life you have always dreamed—starting today. Their strategy of taking longer stays in rented homes provides a unique opportunity to gain a local perspective and is an inspiring tale for those seeking a deeper overall travel experience."

—Brian Sharples, founder and CEO of HomeAway, Inc.

HOME SWEET
Anywhere

How We Sold Our House, Created
a New Life, and Saw the World

LYNNE MARTIN

Published by Sourcebooks, Inc.
P.O. Box 4410, Naperville, Illinois 60567-4410
(630) 961-3900
Fax: (630) 961-2168
www.sourcebooks.com

Library of Congress Cataloging-in-Publication data is on file with the publisher.

Printed and bound in the United States of America.
VP 10 9 8 7 6 5 4 3 2 1

For Tim, my muse, my love, and my boon companion.

Contents

Introduction

S mart people do not loiter at the Colombia Bridge, nor anywhere else near the border in Laredo, Texas.

Nevertheless, this is exactly what my husband, Tim, and I found ourselves doing at dawn on a sparkling June morning as we anxiously waited for someone to come along and tell us the correct procedure for crossing the border into Mexico. Expats who often made the trip we were about to embark upon instructed us to use the bridge, not the more heavily traveled main border crossing, which is famous for delays and gunplay between drug dealers and border guards. But directions from our unlovely hotel to the bridge had been hard to acquire, and as we struck out shortly after dawn, we were still not sure if we had it right. The freeway intersecting the city was too new for our map, Google was inconclusive, and the hotel staff was clueless. Needless to say, we were a little nervous.

We'd stayed up too late the night before looking for a route, our iPhones and laptops blazing. It would be a ten-hour trip—provided there weren't any surprises. We had to time it just right, crossing the border early before the crowds, so we could arrive in the Central Mexican mountain town of San Miguel de Allende before dark. Smart people also avoid roaming around Mexico at night.

Finally some people arrived and entered the border office building. So we stopped loitering and entered as well to find the employees engaged in a lively recap of their weekend activities. We approached the desk hesitantly, clutching our customs documents.

An official, clearly annoyed at our interruption, curtly glanced at our paperwork, relieved us of several hundred dollars for the auto entry fees, banged our passports with a faded stamp, and instructed us to wait for the gate to open so that our car could also be inspected.

Once again, we found ourselves waiting anxiously for another official to arrive. When she did, the challenge of pawing through our SUV, crammed with luggage and gifts for our Mexican friends, which we had disguised to avoid hefty duty fees, proved too much for her. After a couple of desultory questions, she waved us through the last barrier standing between us and our newly minted expat lifestyle. We were on the road.

The border crossing marked our first step toward traveling internationally full time and finally living in places we longed to see. For years in our separate lives, we had just dreamed of going to all these places. Now we were finally making it a reality. But even more importantly, our ability to take on the world without a home base full of familiar things was also rooted in the joy my husband, Tim, and I experienced at finding one another again after a thirty-five-year hiatus.

Our torrid two-year relationship in the 1970s had ended painfully because our timing was wrong. Tim was a brilliant, handsome, sexy lyricist living a financially risky Hollywood existence in the unfettered style of that decade. I was a dynamic tall blond with a demanding career in public relations. We had been friends when we were married to the parents of our children, and when those marriages dissolved for different reasons, we rediscovered one another quite by accident and fell madly in love on the spot. It was a glorious two years, but with two little girls and a ranch-style house in the San Fernando Valley to take care of, I didn't have the courage or energy to marry Tim and his freewheeling lifestyle, even though I wanted desperately to be with him.

Thirty-five years later, I answered the door and welcomed Tim into my home. He had phoned a few days earlier, saying he was planning to visit Cambria, the seaside village in Central California where I had lived for fifteen years. I could not have anticipated what happened next. I thought our connection would have settled into its proper slot in my life's experience. When I accepted his offer to stop by for a brief catch-up, I told myself that he was a former lover from eons ago and now a valued friend, nothing more.

Not so. The minute I looked at him, the years disappeared. My heart knew that he was mine, I was his. That was all there was to it. We were in serious trouble.

"I'm so happy to see you, Tim," I said, smiling. Before he could answer, my husband, Guy, called, "Who's here?" from his studio downstairs.

My husband was a well-known illustrator/artist, popular with everyone. We had everything we wanted—a happy, loving marriage and comfortable life, a perfect garden, a terrific kitchen, a working art studio, and great spaces for entertaining. It was idyllic except for one monstrous reality: Guy was succumbing fast to Alzheimer's disease.

Tim had arrived on one of Guy's lucid days. The three of us chatted in the afternoon sun, enjoying the views of the Pacific through pine trees that meander down to the Cambria beach. At that point, Tim had been settled down for years and owned a small electronics manufacturing business, a far cry from his former rock-star days. He amused us with wild tales about that frantic industry. The conversation was going well, but when Tim mentioned that his marriage of twenty years was ending, I felt my carefully constructed world tilt.

When he left, we parted as old friends should—with a peck on the cheek and a fond hug. We simply could not speak of the obvious. Time would continue to rob us.

It was an impossible situation. My husband required my loyalty and devotion, and of course my heart still lay with him. We loved each other dearly, and for twenty years I had enjoyed the responsibility of making our lives run smoothly and playing the part of his muse while he pursued his active, successful career as an artist. Watching Guy's mind slip away was breaking my heart. I needed to stay focused, and yet my desire to never let Tim out of my sight again was equally compelling. I was miserable, afraid, and jubilant. I was in love.

The next few months were pure anguish. Guy lost ground every day; finally, for his own safety, our doctor told us that he needed to be in a facility for Alzheimer's patients. He had reached the point where he needed the level of supervision I couldn't provide at home. Guy said, as we walked into the common living room, "My dear, what a lovely hotel. Did you know that it's famous for its restaurant?" I was devastated. He settled in immediately and never inquired about our former life again. Three years later, he passed away—and eventually my new life began.

The notion of traveling internationally full time came to Tim and me several years later as we sipped drinks on a friend's terrace in San Miguel de Allende. We were staying in her beautiful colonial house for a month while she was away. By then, we had reunited and eventually married and settled in California's Central Coast wine country, while traveling as much as we could. A cheerful blaze crackled in the outdoor fireplace as we chatted about where we'd like to go next.

This conversation presented the perfect opportunity for me to bring up a delicate matter I'd been considering for quite some time. On my next birthday I would be seventy, a huge milestone. That was definitely past middle age (what I had always considered myself, since I was so healthy and energetic), unless I planned to live to be a hundred and forty. With the big day looming, I was feeling restless and frustrated because there were so many places I wanted to go, but not just to *go*. I wanted to experience living in these places, not only visiting for a week or two. The problem, I had realized in the months since this thought first occurred to me, was our big house, with its accompanying overhead and maintenance responsibilities. Owning it prevented us from leaving for too many months at a time. But since my relationship with Tim still felt relatively new, I'd kept my mouth shut, worried that if I mentioned my secret concerns he would think it meant I was unhappy just being with him.

But that day in San Miguel, I was so antsy about it that I couldn't contain myself anymore. I took a deep breath and said, "You know, Tim, I don't want to upset you or hurt your feelings, but I have to tell you this. I'm not happy living in Paso Robles. It's not you, God knows, but I've realized that there are a lot of places I need to see before I'm too old. I'm just not ready to quit exploring the world yet, and a three-week vacation just isn't enough travel for me. I think we need to figure out how to be away more than we're at home." I closed my eyes to avoid seeing his expression, terrified that he might misinterpret me, that he would think I was unhappy with our life together.

Instead, he roared with laughter. "Oh my God, we're on the same page! I've been thinking exactly the same thing for months, but I was afraid you'd think I'd lost my mind. I thought you wouldn't consider leaving the house and the grandkids."

I stared at him in disbelief—and with that, our plan was born. We would "unretire" and find a way to move freely around the world, soaking up the sights and places that had been gathering dust on our never-ending bucket lists. That night, we stayed up too late, gleefully chattering about short-term plans, long-term plans, how we'd get there, where we wanted to go, and on and on.

Our hearts hadn't been so light in a very long time. It felt like a miracle that we were united in this notion of fulfilling our dreams of being home free, experiencing the world. Anything seemed possible. I could imagine pawing through the tomatoes in a sun-splashed Italian street market, exploring the dark, mysterious *souks* in Marrakech, or whipping up a soufflé in a French farmhouse while Tim opened a bottle of crisp local white wine out on the terrace. It was like a dream in which we would recapture all the years we'd missed having together.

By the time we reconvened over coffee the next morning, we were armed with a long yellow legal pad. The sober financial reality of this idea had settled in overnight. It's tricky business balancing the rewarding life you have worked so hard to achieve with the harsh reality that you must conserve enough capital to live on as you get older. We aren't wealthy, but we have a smart financial guy who shepherds the little nest egg we've accumulated and sends us a monthly allowance from his careful investment of it. That allowance, combined with our Social Security, is the basis for our monthly budget.

✷ ✷ ✷

Concerned we wouldn't be able to make it stretch far enough, we made a list of every expense we could think of—and to our surprise discovered that our monthly nut was much larger than we thought. Then we compiled a detailed projection of what our overhead would be if we lived abroad in rented houses or apartments, including every conceivable expense. The numbers were exciting. They were very, very close. If we sold our house, we could live very comfortably in almost every country in the world.

Although the notion thrilled us, we were still both anxious about whether we could actually take on such a challenge. What would it be like to have no home, no place to curl up in our own bed and put our things in our own closet after a long trip? How would it feel to live for several years in other people's spaces? Where would our plan take us emotionally? Would the stress of moving every few months to a new country, starting over endlessly, strain our deeply contented marriage, a bond that so many of our friends envied? Would our four daughters, who already thought we were flighty for having moved around the country searching for the place we wanted to retire, ever speak to us again if we left the country for years? Were we ready to face an uncertain future, far away from our comfort zone and our family and friends? In the end, we reminded ourselves that we would never have a second chance to make this happen. It was now or never. We decided we were up to the challenge, to say "yes" to this groundbreaking idea.

Then came a tidal wave of details: what to do with the dog, the furniture, the cars? What could we store and what could we dump? And would our families forgive us for wanting to roam far from them for long periods of time? The thought of telling our children, with whom we were both extremely close, about this idea was so daunting that we decided to put that far down on our "to do" list. Instead, we began to talk about where we would go, how we would meet new friends, what kinds of insurance we'd need, and all the details we would spend several months identifying and sorting out. Just when I thought our list of things to consider was complete, another question occurred to me. "Oh, God, what will we do about mail? We'll have no address."

"You're absolutely right," Tim, ever the cool-minded one, replied with a careless shrug. "We'll be home free!"

With those magical words, off we went on a breathtaking adventure that would carry us into a high-rise in Buenos Aires; a peaceful country hacienda in San Miguel de Allende, Mexico;

a tiny apartment with a big view of the Blue Mosque and the
Sea of Marmara in Istanbul; a darling flat with a great kitchen a
few blocks from the Seine in Paris; a villa apartment overlooking Florence; a medieval three-story walk-up in La Charité-sur-
Loire, France; a balconied one-bedroom by the River Thames near
London, an apartment outside Dublin in a three-hundred-year-
old Georgian mansion with views of the Irish Sea; two rooms in
a colorfully tiled riad in Marrakech, Morocco; and a beach house
near Lisbon, Portugal.

Here's the best part: we are in no hurry to see the sights. By
living this way, we have the most precious commodity in the world:
time. We aren't tourists at all. We are temporary locals, wherever
we choose to park our suitcases. And now that we are "home free,"
home is wherever we are. How could we know the adventures that
awaited us?

Chapter 1
Packing Up

A fter our life-changing trip to San Miguel, we were primed to move forward with our exciting new plan when we returned to California. We just had a few decisions to make and we'd be on our way!

But wait, not so fast. Tim and I both are Librans, October babies. In astrological circles, this means it's impossibly hard for us to make decisions. And it certainly can be. Luckily though, we are both astrological anomalies, too, because big choices often are easy for us. We have bought cars in a matter of minutes and houses in an afternoon. (Is it any wonder our children would think we are flighty?) We decided to marry each another without a moment's hesitation. Likewise, we instantaneously came up with this plan to sell our house so we could kick around the world for a few years. The house obliged us. It sold in one day—during a down market. With a sign like that, we weren't about to let any astrological inclinations get in the way of our thrilling new life.

So here is the story of how we went from there to here…and here…and here:

We wanted to live in Paris, explore Ireland at our own pace, have an apartment in Florence, see what it would be like to live for a while in Portugal—in other words, be free! As I previously mentioned, we'd quickly realized that financially it would be difficult to just lock up our house and leave for months at a time. Maintenance problems would nag at us constantly, and a large house sitting empty is a target for all kinds of nefarious characters with bad intentions. Besides, the steep overhead would have severely limited our flexibility in where we could go and for how long. Converting the cash from the house into moneymaking investments was the sensible thing to do if we wanted to have the easiest lifestyle abroad.

Our financial manager perceived the logic of pulling the cash from our house so it would work in our portfolio, instead of waiting for years for the post-2007 housing bubble market to recover. Theoretically, if we'd waited, we would find ourselves too old to enjoy life on the road.

As I said, the house sold in one day. Now there was no turning back. The buyers also wanted a forty-five-day turnaround, which galvanized us into action.

The day after the house sold, I found Tim in our cozy little office, hunched over his computer at 6:00 a.m. "Honey, what's up? It's not even light outside," I croaked.

Without looking up, he responded, "Did you know that a repositioning cruise from Miami to Rome costs $2,300 for both of us? That's cheaper than airfare and we get two weeks' room and board to boot! There's one next year from Fort Lauderdale to Rome. Should we book it?"

Already awake, already in manic mode. My loving husband.

"What on earth is a repositioning cruise?" I asked, longing for my morning coffee. My head was already spinning.

"See, the cruise lines move their ships from one part of the world to another twice a year, and they offer passengers a really good deal then. As far as I can tell, all the services are the same, but the prices are about half what they normally are," he said, grinning. "Do you want to be in the bow or the stern?"

Half asleep or not, I couldn't believe what I was hearing. "Wait a minute, sweetie, you've never been on a cruise ship. You're claustrophobic, and we have zero tolerance for boredom. While we're both very friendly, we're also really choosy about our company, so what in the world makes you think we'd be happy for two weeks in a floating hotel?" This was too much for my groggy head to handle. Coffee was now a must.

Tim followed me on my coffee quest to the kitchen. "Look, I know it's a risk, but as long as we're doing this whole crazy thing, let's give it a try next spring. If we don't like it, we'll fly next time. Come look at this stateroom."

He steered me back to the computer as I continued to resist the idea of being confined to a monster motorboat until we landed in Rome. Or that we might be forced to chat pleasantly over dinner with people who had lingered too long at the cocktail hour. Not to mention that watching the Iceberg Follies or some other crazy musical production put on by the crew in the middle of the Atlantic or participating in endless bingo tournaments was not exactly my idea of fun nightly entertainment. To be honest, all of my notions of cruising came from one miserable three-day trip to Mexico full of drunken merrymakers, and I wasn't so sure I wanted to repeat the experience. Two weeks of that seemed like a *very* long time to me.

Tim gently and kindly countered me, because, as always, he had done his homework and had the answers ready before the conversation even started. (His ability to be prepared for any and all questions is a quality I am begrudgingly grateful for.) "This is a freestyle dining cruise ship, honey. We can have every meal in our stateroom if we don't want to bother with other people, or we can have a table to ourselves whenever we like. We don't have to go near any of the rollicking performances of *Joan of Arc on Ice* if we don't want to."

Meet Tim Martin, travel agent extraordinaire. He entertained me with dozens of photos of the ship: spa services, three swimming pools, gorgeous views from the dining rooms, smiling passengers being served fruity drinks in their lounge chairs. Slowly but surely, he won me over, and by midmorning, he'd booked us in an ocean-view stateroom, smack in the bow of a gleaming white behemoth of a boat. Our new life dream was becoming a reality. And with it, I realized, came a new mind-set.

Travel planning quickly became Tim's full-time job, and he's very serious about it. It's always on his mind. While standing in line at the movies, he'll nudge me and say, "Hey, did I tell you that we can rent an apartment in Portugal at the beach for less than $1,800 a month? That could take care of March." Tim still plies the Internet daily, no matter where we are, because trip planning remains an ongoing necessity. We are always balancing time, weather, our desires, and never-ending budget questions. It requires an enormous amount of his time and considerable experience to live as we do; even so, we still make occasional mistakes.

But in that moment, as we stood in the kitchen and I said yes to my first cruise in years, repositioning cruises and longtime rentals were still tomorrow's realities. More urgent matters stared us in the face. Literally. To be ready in time, not only did we have to dispose of our possessions, find a home for our dog, and arrange the mundane details of life like banking, mail, wardrobes, health checkups, and inoculations, but we also had to get our travel documents together for our first "outings," which we had decided would be to Mexico and Argentina. In short, we needed to give away, sell, store, or take every item we owned—in forty-five days. It was enough to send anyone over the brink, especially a pair of indecisive Librans.

✳ ✳ ✳

At this point, before we plunge in further, I would advise anyone who considers taking on this daring new lifestyle to prepare for some emotionally difficult moments. While indescribably reward-ing, this path is not for sissies.

Becoming home free is a lot like mature people starting a new mar-riage and moving in together. It boils down to one simple tug-of-war: "How can we get rid of your junk so we have room for my THINGS?" It's hard to let go of belongings you've treasured all your life, but you don't really need. In about a month and a half (hopefully your time would be longer!), we had to streamline our life and let go of the past, because storing all of our furniture and belongings wasn't practical. Besides, we envisioned having yet another wonderful fresh start when we finally gave up our traveling ways and did settle down again. The vision of living with light, bright, contemporary furnishings in the future made it possible for me to say good-bye to our lovely old pieces.

I said "possible," not "easy." Actually doing it was another story.

After finding each other again, we'd moved often, looking for the place where we'd feel at home forever. We tried Ohio and North Carolina before heading back to California, leaving a trail of books, clothes, and other beloved objects each time we moved.

This time, we had to get serious. Almost all of it had to go. We vowed to each other that a 10 × 15 storage space would be the maxi-mum size in which to put our belongings. A hundred fifty square feet fills up fast, which led to us becoming brutal sorters. We tried to tackle one room at a time, but soon, every part of the house lay in complete disarray, with daunting piles of "keep," "give," "toss," and "take" items requiring their own decisions. Our forty-five days were already evaporating like drizzle in Death Valley.

One afternoon, I found Tim in the garage, having a good stare into the distance, a large tape dispenser in his hand and a box at his feet. "Whatcha up to?" I asked.

He started, and then I noticed the huge piles of vintage CDs on the garage floor. Many were links to his history in the music business, and even more of them marked important moments in his life and career. Some even featured tunes he had written. "Well, I thought Alwyn [Tim's daughter who lived in Texas and shared his passion for music] might like to have these. They're all on my iPod anyway," he mumbled sadly. He forced a bright smile, but I knew as I walked away that I'd seen his lip quiver when his beloved Elvis hit the bottom of the box.

Every day, we collected bric-a-brac into boxes and bags for the AmVet charity truck. Every day, Tim horsed carloads to them and trunkfuls of paintings and kitchen equipment I knew I'd need at some point down the road to the storage space. Some days, it seemed as if things multiplied magically while we slept. A room we had cleared out would suddenly be full of more stuff. I'd sit there, scratching my head, thinking I could have sworn it was empty the last time I closed the door, while my possessions leered back at me, daring me to purge them.

But things kept flying out the door into the eager hands of our friends and neighbors. Our children claimed most of the larger furniture and antiques. We were beginning to feel pretty cocky about our progress.

But we were still left with ten thousand other decisions. Once, I trotted into the office where Tim was having an email battle with an apartment owner in Istanbul over the proposed rent, and twirled around in my gorgeous mid-calf, honey-colored, bias-cut skirt. It weighed at least ten pounds and its bulk would gobble half a suitcase. He shook his head and said, "Darling, you look sensational, but somehow I don't think you'd need that outfit in Florence in July."

Sadly, I placed it on the "donate" pile. Tim's elegant cashmere overcoat—perfect for living in Manhattan, but useless in the sizzling heat of Izmir, Turkey—joined the skirt. We never gave either another thought—until I wrote this sentence.

We were making headway, though. The garage stack dwindled, some of our travel plans began shaping up, and we brought our anxieties more or less under control. In spite of an escrow-closing drama, the irritations that accompany selling a house, and some panicked moments of insecurity and self-doubt—"Are we truly crazy to be doing this?!"—we were wildly happy at the prospect of this new adventure. Our union was already an unexpected gift, a breathtaking surprise from the heavens for me in the wake of losing Guy. But the prospect of being on the road permanently, the luxury to spend all of our time together while we explored exciting places and challenged ourselves with new experiences, was almost beyond my wildest dreams. I could hardly wait to finish this phase of drudgery.

One day, I scurried past Tim in the hallway. He was carrying an enormous armload of books and papers, and I was bustling in the other direction on some urgent errand. He caught my eye, dropped his burden, and pulled me into a delicious bear hug. We both burst into hysterical laughter out of pure exhilaration. We were actually DOING this!

Amidst all the excitement, one more enormous hurdle remained to be addressed: finding a new home for our adorable eighteen-month-old Jack Russell terrier, Sparky. Successfully finding a home for a dog was a lot like finding the right mate in human terms: the one introduced by a friend generally works out the best. We put out the word to everyone we knew, and sure enough, friends of friends made the match. The prospects owned five terriers and wanted another, something we never quite understood. Six small whirlwinds causing constant mayhem would have been too much for us, but these people seemed to thrive on the action. The instant they met, Sparky and his new owners were pals. He now lives on a fabulous twenty-acre vineyard property and spends his days happily mowing down smaller critters like lizards and snakes.

The details of departing weren't our only challenges, and saying good-bye to Sparky wasn't the only farewell we dreaded. When we finally screwed up the courage to break the news of our plan to our families, each of our four daughters had listened in stunned silence as we explained our unusual decision. We fully understood their initial wariness and concerns. But to our relief, when they had time to think about it, they became wonderfully supportive and delighted with our idea.

Our friends and other relatives were also shocked when we broke the news, but then they too began ask all the questions we had anticipated and planned for ourselves. For example, our loved ones were concerned about what would happen if we became ill or injured on the road. Without going into too much detail (because we did consider how to handle all the possible scenarios like that), the simple answer we gave was twofold: (1) we could become ill or injured in California, too, and (2) we'd do the same thing in Portugal that we would in Paso Robles: go to the doctor or the hospital and take care of it. Our well-rehearsed responses seemed to reassure them, and within a short time they were cheering us on, too, or at least they were polite enough to feign enthusiasm even if they thought it was a crazy idea.

And we weren't without our own concerns about this scheme. Although we never doubted we would experience a wonderful new life, the act of following through with the plan required a lot of vision and determination. And courage. Ambivalence was our constant companion. We wanted badly to start on this new path, but anxiety nibbled at the edge of our delight. We had to remind ourselves constantly that this was *our* life. At our ages, we would not have this chance again. We would find plenty of time to rest when forced to give up our peripatetic ways.

We also found that it was hard for people to understand how we could embark on this plan without going broke. "Look," we'd say to questioners at cocktail parties who slyly tried to ask how much money we had without saying so, "it really doesn't make any difference how much money you have if you want to live on the road. This is arithmetic, not calculus: just figure out the current overhead, do your homework about how much it costs to live in places that are of interest, add in transportation, and compare the numbers. All adjustable. If you have a lot of money, you live really well. If you have less, you might have to put up with a studio apartment and have a few picnic lunches or eat in at night more often. It's still an adventure either way."

To this day, some people we meet become defensive when they find out what we are doing, as if our choices somehow threaten theirs. They'll say, "Well, I could NEVER give up my furniture, my dog, my car, my… (fill in the blank)." We sometimes find ourselves having to explain that this unfettered life is certainly not for everyone. It just happens to work for us at this stage in our lives. After all, the point of us sharing the story of our unique lifestyle isn't to make other people feel compelled to make drastic life changes. We simply are highlighting the benefits of expanding your horizons, however you feel comfortable doing so. That may just mean a visit to the next town, joining a new club, or making a new friend.

Each time we told our plan to someone new, we would feel a little nervous about their reaction, but soon we became accustomed to how it would go: first, the disbelief, then the questions, and finally excitement and curiosity, sometimes tinged with just a little envy. Their reactions reinforced our hunch that we were on to something wonderful and helped us maintain the enthusiasm we needed to jump off the virtual cliff into our new life.

Chapter 2
On the Road

T he last day in our house finally came, so we prepared to head to another we had rented temporarily in Cambria, my former hometown. It would give us a place to wrap up final details, sort out the belongings we hadn't sold or given away, and prepare to be on the road for five months, first driving to Mexico and then flying to Argentina.

But we were so weary, we barely said good-bye, see ya later to our home of several years. Tim headed off once more to see his buddies at AmVet, the charity truck that had received many of our household belongings in the past six weeks, and I made the final walk-through and left for the rental house.

I must tell you that a woman knows moving preparations have reached the bitter end when her large purse weighs upwards of twenty pounds. The final sweep through an empty house always yields surprises, and usually the only receptacle left is the purse. Today was no different. Besides my regular load of essentials, my purse now held a pair of shoe liners, a rogue letter opener, a lone pearl earring, a book of 37-cent stamps, a plastic wine stopper, a church key, two blank CDs, a small photo album of grandchildren, and an antique bronze bookend that had been serving as a doorstop. I lugged it to my car, took one last look at the vibrant rosebush display that would greet the new owners, and drove away.

That evening Tim and I reconvened at the three-bedroom vacation rental on the beach. Our cars burst with I don't-know-what-the-hell-to-do-with-this-but-I'm-not-ready-to-part-with-it-yet items. The rental was much too big for us, but we needed space to stage our last standoff with our possessions in preparation for our final departure. Every item needed to be taken to storage, given away, or carried with us.

One day, Tim walked into the kitchen as I contemplated the fate of six little yellow plastic corn-on-the-cob holders. He waved a lone patent leather tuxedo shoe. "Honey," he frowned, "I know for sure that I've seen the other one, but I can't find it."

"It's in that horror of a room," I replied without looking up.

Soon enough, that became the guest room's new name. Sprawled across The Horror Room were cowboy boots, coats, cameras, CDs and DVDs, decks of cards, wine openers, maps, electronic gear, plastic containers full of random small things, paperwork, and shoes with uncertain futures. Every now and then, Tim or I would wander in and attempt to create order, only to leave a few minutes later, cursing under our breath, soundly defeated by the enormity of the task.

The day we cleared that room and closed the door was a milestone in our relationship.

We still faced two looming decisions: the clothes and travel equipment we would lug with us on our home-free trip.

After much debate, we determined we could manage with two large rolling duffel bags and two carry-ons. We held private fashion shows for each other as we tried to narrow down the clothes and gear. It was tedious, but our excitement about our impending adventure practically sparked off our bodies and made it fun. As the weeks before our departure ticked down to days, we barely slept. 4:00 a.m. became the new 7:00 a.m. Lists of chores swirled in our heads, complicated by a serious case of ambivalence about the joy our plan brought us and the pain we had at leaving our family.

Which presented our next huge challenge: How would we stay

in touch with friends and family and make travel arrangements and write the blog I was thinking of starting while we were on the road? We spent an inordinate amount of time at the Apple store, talking with smart salesmen who looked like children to us, and we came away with laptops, iPhones, mini-speakers, adapters, and a bag full of accessories. Enough equipment to provide us with communication and entertainment in every country we wanted to see in the next few years. The equipment was so technically advanced that we signed up for Apple classes to learn how to use our new gizmos. I noticed that most of the other students were gray-haired people, too, looking dazed and confused as they poked and bleeped their way through their electronic learning curves. We came away educated, synced, apped, and secure in the knowledge that we were indeed citizens of the twenty-first century!

✳ ✳ ✳

Even as we wrestled with wardrobe and electronic issues, Tim immersed himself for hours every day to put together eighteen months of travel plans.

One afternoon, I walked into the dining room, which Tim had commandeered as travel headquarters. The Pacific Ocean sparkled outside and a dramatic sunset was brewing, but Tim's focus was so intent and absolute that he could have been sitting in a cave for all he knew.

Suddenly, he banged his palms on the table and beamed at me with his dazzling smile. He leapt out of his chair and gave me a big smooch and a bear hug. "Wow, thank you! What's that for?" I asked.

"It's DONE!" he shouted. "I've just firmed up the reservation for the car to pick us up in Buenos Aires! It's all wrapped up. We're set for the next six months."

We crammed final belongings into the groaning storage space. We wrapped up last-minute chores and returned house keys. Our friends and family treated us to lunches, dinners, cocktails, phone calls, emails, gifts, cards, and good wishes.

Finally, Departure Day arrived.

And suddenly, we were in our car. Just the two of us. (Time to get used to that!) Silence descended as we followed Highway 101 toward Los Angeles, two hundred fifty miles to the south. We retreated into our own heads, each considering the enormity of the step we had taken. We had finally made our plan a reality, which left us exhilarated. And terrified.

To break the tension, Tim turned on the iPod and hit "shuffle." Folk-country singer Guy Clark's "L.A. Freeway" filled the car and sent us into fits of laughter. We high-fived each other, shared a quick kiss, and at that moment, we knew we would be more than okay. Our ambivalence fled, replaced by the certainty that we'd made the right move and we were ready for whatever happened next.

Chapter 3
Mexico

A week later, weary from lack of sleep and the long cross-country drive, we reached the border at the Colombia Bridge. When the guard waved us through, we were enormously relieved. At last, we began the ten-hour drive for which we'd been preparing for months. And dreading.

For the first few miles, our nervousness steadily mounted. We saw nothing on the two-lane road but cactus and barbed wire. We were truly on our own. What if something happened to us out here? We were elated when other cars appeared. It seemed less likely that banditos would try to molest us with other people in plain sight. About thirty miles later, we paid the toll and rejoiced as we turned onto a large, secure highway. Even though the point of this was to "broaden our horizons," it was still nice to see something familiar, at least to start off the journey.

Ironically, the most dramatic part of our experience driving through Mexico had nothing to do with roaming criminals—and everything to do with the locals' complete disregard for traffic laws. In Mexico, the speed limit is meaningless. People blast by each other at terrifying speeds without the slightest hesitation. It seemed to us that Mexicans, like Italians, must go to Mass daily so that none of them will fear dying when hurtling past huge trucks on blind curves. Needless to say, we stuck to the slow lane, or what there was of one.

Our Mexican highway cut straight through a wide valley framed by stark, knife-edged mountains. It skirted Nuevo Laredo, Saltillo, and San Luis Potosi, three cities our advisors warned us to avoid at all cost. We saw two police/military barricades on the opposite side of the highway. The police were inspecting all vehicles. We felt safer. Only later did we learn that fake police/military checkpoints were a favorite ploy for kidnapping rings.

Sometimes ignorance really is bliss.

We pressed on, the scenery continuing to improve from the dusty mudcake of Laredo. Vast Joshua tree forests and stands of cactus erupted everywhere. We passed farms, ranchos, small towns, and half-built melancholy concrete projects that looked like some architect's heartbreak. The skies were luminous and limitless, the Mexico we loved. What was there to be afraid about? We listened to music, laughed, chatted, snacked, told stories—and got lost at the turn to Saltillo, the spot everyone warned us about. We took a wrong turn and found ourselves at a toll booth in a desolate spot, the very kind of place we did NOT want to be.

A pretty young woman climbed down from her perch in the little building. She used gestures and Spanish that was basic enough for me to understand to slowly explain how to make a U-turn on a gravel cart track up the way and reenter the tollway in the correct direction. She then charged us for taking the wrong exit, of course. "*Adiós!*" she called as we beat it back to the freeway.

As we continued, the terrain grew familiar. Green fields replaced cactus forests. The little villages began to appear with their BIG *topes* (speed bumps) and minuscule stores that sell everything. We grew happy at the sight of makeshift kitchens dishing out tamales, tacos, and corn on the cob to the locals sitting at long tables covered with colorful oilcloth.

At last, we came upon a San Miguel roundabout that featured a heartfelt but badly wrought heroic *caballero* statue in its center. Tim ratcheted up the Mexican rancho music on the iPod, and we danced in our seats. We rolled down the windows to inhale that unique Mexican aroma of tortillas cooked in lard, chopped and fried chilies, garlic, and onions, and a dash of Tabasco diesel smoke thrown in for added kick.

We had made it!

★ ★ ★

We were kicking off our worldwide escapade with three months in San Miguel de Allende, one of our favorite haunts. We had owned a house there at one time, so we had friends and a comfortable familiarity with the city of eighty thousand. Again, even though we wanted to venture out of our comfort zone, we thought it would be good to start with something a bit more recognizable. Sort of a dry run for the adventures that awaited us elsewhere.

The evening we arrived, we negotiated the first traffic circle and joined the ring road, which traces the top of a neighborhood that cascades into the town. Typical San Miguel—tile-roofed houses clinging to the sides of the hills, each capitalizing on the view. Tiny family-owned *tiendas* are on almost every block. They are dark little warrens, some without any signs at all, crammed with a hodgepodge of things neighbors might need in a hurry: bottled water, mops, snacks, sewing needles, motor oil, milk, a few limes, beer. The road is punctuated with car and tire repair shops, plant nurseries, brickyards, little Mexican houses behind tall adobe walls, and a few half-filled condominium complexes.

The vista stuns us every time we turn the first corner. In the afternoon, the lake that lays below the hills of the town several miles away shimmers, the central cathedral glimmers like a pink monarch's crown. La Parroquia, as it is known, is the symbol of the town, a church with a façade remade in the nineteenth century by a local builder who put his own spin on the gothic style he'd seen only in photographs. There's nothing else like it in Mexico. Shades of pink, gold, terra-cotta, and mustard glance off the domes of other venerable churches dotting San Miguel. Red tile and verdant rooftop gardens with bougainvillea dripping down their railings tie the whole view together.

Tim handles most of the international driving while I "nagrivate," the term we invented for my explaining what I'm seeing on the screen by saying calmly and quietly (or, well, sometimes not so quietly) things like, "At the next junction you'll make a dogleg and continue through a small lane, then make an immediate right." To which I'll get a grunt indicating the driver's understanding. I act as the color commentator and operate Victoria, our GPS, who speaks with an upper-class British accent. As you'll soon see, she was destined to become the third most important character in this book.

Although drivers in San Miguel are courteous and move slowly, anything can happen on the bigger roads. A bicyclist, dog, family of five, horse, or cow can suddenly appear out of nowhere on the highway. More than once, trucks, ignoring the light, have headed right for us, and at any moment a Mexico City hotshot in a big SUV may bolt from his driveway and squeal out in front of us without ever glancing in our direction.

I have learned not to gasp or scream in these instances, because my histrionics worsen Tim's heart palpitations. My alarmed noises are one of very few habits that make him snap at me. (When we got together again, it didn't take me long to learn to control my impulses.) In Mexico—and, as we would find out, in a lot of countries—it's also a good idea to drive sober and in daylight whenever possible. Praying probably helps, too.

The ring road ended at a T intersection that would make even champion race car driver Mario Andretti cringe. Its elaborate turn-ing lanes were not designed very well, and the left turn gives us a thrill every time as our heads swivel trying to see cars, trucks, and motorcycles hurtling in our direction, unaware of the newly installed traffic lights. We survived it again, and were soon greeted by the guard at the gate of the private community where our friend Sally Gibson lives.

Sally had invited us to mind her gorgeous art-filled colonial home with its astounding views, luscious garden, and a full-time staff of three. We had considered house-sitting as one of the options we might employ as we moved around the world, so we thought this would be a great way to try it out. It was an ideal situation, a luxurious place of peace and respite, where we could relax and plan our future. It promised us tranquility after so much excitement. And it was free!

There was one minor catch: Sally has five huge exotic parrots, fourteen canaries, six cats, and Webber, her big, sweet golden retriever. The staff thankfully attended to the waste products of the menagerie, but we were their temporary masters, in charge of their emotional welfare and physical safety. Not an easy feat. We had visited Sally on many occasions, attending her sophisticated parties and admiring her pets from the distance of a couple glasses of wine. Still, since we're both very fond of animals, we looked forward to performing our duties.

As night fell, we climbed Sally's driveway to assume our new roles as their guardians. We found the key and opened the huge carved wood doors into the courtyard. It was awash in lush plants, anchored by a murmuring fountain splashing into a miniature river that ran the length of the aromatic garden. Sally, who is a com-pletely charming Southern belle, had lived in San Miguel for almost thirty years. She seemed accustomed to living in such luxury, as do most Americans who have moved their lives to Mexico. Living well in San Miguel costs much, much less than it does in other parts of the world!

Under the overhang, comfortable woven wood and leather lounges decorated with colorful pillows and throws were arranged with carved tables and filigreed iron lamps to accommodate conversation groups. Large lighted antique paintings with bird themes accented the recesses around the patio. I sighed, "Oh, darling, we're here at last. We've done the right thing. This is heaven. We're free!"

Then all hell broke loose. Webber, seventy pounds of panting, barking enthusiasm, very nearly knocked me off my feet. Two black-and-white cats sped past us and disappeared into the pitch-blackness of a country road. The feathered community jumped in as well. Five enormous parrots screeched their disapproval at our invasion, while fourteen canaries, divided into five cages scattered around the house, played backup singers for the cacophony.

Tim enticed the escapees to come inside using the cat-wrangler's age-old trick of tapping on a cat food can, while I covered up the canaries for the night and secured the other felines. It took both of us to drape the heavy serapes over the huge parrot cages, their signal to go to sleep. Chickie, the oldest, wiliest, and most verbal, acted like a three-year-old resisting bedtime. As Tim reached up to throw the serape over the top of the cage, Chickie poked his large, sharp beak between the bars, grabbed the fabric, and held on tight. The ensuing struggle might have been amusing to someone neither exhausted nor in need of a drink, as we desperately were. After proffering a diversionary banana, we finally succeeded in covering up the noisy devil. As we left the atrium, he was grumbling, "Chickie, Chickie, *hola*! Chickie *¿cómo está?*"

At last, we poured ourselves a drink and settled into our suite with its canopied bed, big bath, and private terrace, ready to enjoy a few weeks of pure pleasure and a break from the pressures of the last six months. This was a great time and place to celebrate our new life and start making concrete plans about the next couple of years.

On our first full day, we fell into our routine easily. First, there was the grocery run to the big store, so we'd have the essentials that make us feel at home—good coffee, wine, lunch goodies, soup, pasta, and condiments we particularly liked. Several years before, a big chain had opened the huge supermarket outside the city center. Practically everyone in town showed up on opening day to gawk at the big-screen TVs, browse the clothing department, and marvel at vast vegetable, dairy, and meat displays. The store departed remarkably from traditional Mexican shopping, in which one stops at the chicken store, the fish store, and the downtown vegetable market several times a week. They don't pile purchases in large grocery carts and drag home a week's worth of groceries south of the border. The convenience of a large store offering so many choices has probably eroded the bottom line of the tiny *tiendas* that provide handy access to household necessities, but I suppose that old habits and deep loyalties, along with the paucity of cars, probably protect those little stores from financial ruin.

Our favorite shopping venue, though, was still the local Tuesday market. Held in a big dusty parking lot behind a warehouse, it combined a tented flea market, farmers' market, and a black market of pirated CDs and DVDs. Its vendors sold fresh chicken, meat, and fish, and gorgeous veggies, fruits, herbs, and flowers. Those guys can bone a chicken or a fish in a flash while carrying on a rapid-fire conversation with the guy in the next stall and never miss beat. You're especially in luck if you're in the market for a kitchen table or a dresser, a bridle for your mule, some new underwear, or a pair of imitation Chanel sunglasses. There is very little you can't find.

Our last stop was always a stall where a woman from the *campos* wielded a knife the size of a scythe, whanging leftover *carnitas* (suc-culent hunks of rotisseried pork) into tiny pieces. She would grab a fat corn cake, which resembled a pita bread but without any health-ful attributes. (Warning for the diet-conscious: there is lard involved here. A lot of lard.) She would slash the bread, fill the *gordita* with the pig meat and the diabolical salsa of your choice, wrapped it in grease paper, and hand it over. She charged about 20 pesos (about $1.50) a pop for the *gorditas de migajas*. We would gently nestle them into big shopping bags that sport Frida Kahlo, Diego Rivera's wildly colorful wife with the unibrow, or Our Lady of Guadalupe, and scurry home to wolf them down with a cold beer.

While we're on the topic of domestic details, I should tell you that it took us some time to become accustomed to the way many North Americans live in San Miguel. We learned that going to the market was no longer one of our "regular" chores, as it had been for us when we lived there years ago. I found this to be one of the most attractive aspects of our new luxurious situation, because while I love planning menus and cooking, going to the market regularly becomes tedious after doing it day after day. But those are necessary steps that must be taken before the fun part, cooking, begins. However, Sally's staff more or less handled that while we were there. It was sheer luxury to have another person take charge of that routine for a change, and we were grateful to them for it.

In addition, since Mexican water can wreck a *gringo*'s stomach, and vegetables are grown in that water, all uncooked food must first be treated with disinfectant. This involves soaking lettuce, tomatoes, onions, herbs, and anything else eaten fresh or unpeeled in a sanitiz-ing solution. It's a time-consuming, drippy process, but essential. The little brown disinfectant drops do not affect the food's flavor, but they guarantee that the diner will avoid a long, unpleasant rela-tionship with his or her toilet. Using only bottled water for drinking in Mexico goes without saying. Using it for brushing teeth is also a smart habit.

Almost all the North Americans hire local cleaning and gardening help at least once or twice a week, as Sally did and as we had when we owned a house there. Not only is it inexpensive, it's almost considered obligatory for anyone who can afford it to do so, because many Mexicans need the work to feed their families. Mexico is a poor country, and in a tourist town like San Miguel, most local families depend on domestic or hospitality industry jobs because there is really no other industry to support the town. Many expats like Sally have staff who come every day.

The second morning of our stay, the dignified Angelica, in her correct beige slacks and crisp white shirt, arrived promptly at 9:00 a.m. She made the coffee, fed the dog, and sent Lupe, her assistant, to her own domain in the laundry area with instructions for the day.

Soon, we heard a gentle rap at our door. Angelica asked me, in Spanish modified for my limited abilities, what we would like for breakfast and where we should be served. We asked for cereal, fruit, and coffee on the terrace. On this beautiful day, we felt very special when our Wheaties and bananas appeared, beautifully arranged on a nicely set table near the fragrant garden backgrounded by views of the Mexican hills. Ponciano, the majordomo of the house, rhythmically clipped a hedge near the graceful bronze statue that served as a fountain.

When Tim had finished his breakfast, he rose, picked up his bowl, and took a step toward the kitchen. Angelica, who was straightening a cabinet nearby, turned, looked at him, and shook her head slowly. Nooo. He learned an instant lesson in how Mexicans protect their jobs. He cleared his throat nervously, put down the bowl, excused himself, and casually sauntered away for a garden stroll as if he had been expecting to do that all along.

I controlled myself just long enough to get to the other part of the house before collapsing in laughter at his surprised face. Our training in gracious living had begun.

It always takes us a day or two to get into the rhythm of San Miguel, a pace that agrees with us. The warm terra-cotta colors are comforting and relaxing. Lingering over lunch and taking a little siesta some afternoons changes us from busy travelers into people who are pleased when we can accomplish just one errand a day. Life seems to get in the way of progress down there.

But I was determined not to let that happen this time. "Tim, I think we should get a move on this morning," I chirped over breakfast the second day. We were munching Angelica's breakfast tacos: creamy scrambled eggs and fresh salsa rolled into corn tortillas with chorizo and fresh mangoes on the side. "We need to drop off some prescriptions at Chelo's, and then I know you'd like to say hi to Marcia. She emailed me about some new skirts and tops she has in the store. We should check out what new movies Juan has, and it would be great if we could run into the *mercado* for a big bunch of fresh flowers! Oh, and we need some candles from the mortuary."

He peered over his sunglasses and smiled at me. "Sure, baby, sounds fine to me, but don't you think your list is a little long for one day?"

He did have a point. Not only is San Miguel's *mañana* syndrome infectious (if it's not urgent, it can wait until tomorrow; if it is urgent...it can wait until tomorrow), but its 6,500-foot elevation augmented our sea level torpor considerably in the first few days. We offer that cautionary note to first-timers considering a trip here.

"Well, maybe you're right, but could we at least try?" I countered, my voice muffled by a big bite of chorizo.

Tim shrugged in compliance.

We moved fast by our standards, said good-bye to Angelica and company, and crunched down the driveway by 10:30, heading for town. Once there, we ran into a stately parade heading for El Centro. Dozens of taxis, buses, and cars rattled along on the cobblestoned streets, harmoniously taking turns at the four-way intersections and graciously allowing one another to turn as necessary. No one honked. Pedestrians took their time. It was amazing! The only ones we had to look out for were other Americans who hadn't caught on to the courtesy and kindness of their host country. The Mexican way is hard for some *gringos* to understand.

The Mexican government declared San Miguel a national monument in the 1920s, and its charm has been preserved. There are no traffic lights, neon signs, or chain stores. The place looks as it did four hundred fifty years ago, and the courteous behavior of most of its inhabitants makes one think of more gracious times. In fact, during the mid-nineteenth century, the Mexican government instituted *Las Cortesías*, a plan for civil behavior, which every well-bred Mexican is taught from childhood. For instance, it would be unthinkable to not say good morning or good afternoon to a shopkeeper, or fail to say "*gracias*" when departing the store, whether or not there was a transaction. All conversations must begin with inquiries about the health of family, and gentlemen still open doors for ladies and rise when one enters the room. It's all part of the slower pace. We have to relearn that cadence every time we arrive in San Miguel, but we are grateful for it.

Tim wheeled into the parking lot, where a large black Labrador with a neon pink collar was deep in the uninterrupted nap he seemed to enjoy every time we came here. An enormous, garish, four-foot glazed pottery chicken sat atop the rudimentary carport. It's a colorful town.

We struck out at a brisk pace, a dangerous thing to do on four-hundred-year-old uneven stone streets with foot-high flagstone curbs that dip and rise without warning. I have been among the casualties of San Miguel's curbs, spending half my vacation limping around town with an ugly bright blue brace, the kneecap cut out. From that experience, I learned two cardinal survival rules for this town I love: Never look up from the ground when walking, and leave the high heels at home. Of course, gorgeous local girls prance around San Miguel in five-inch stilettos as if they were strutting down a runway. It's maddening to me, clomping along in my sensible sandals, bent over to watch my step like a soldier looking for land mines. But I'd rather forego the heels than risk another stint in the blue brace.

Our first stop: candles. Everyone in town buys their candles at the mortuary because they are an appealing honey color, they burn for a long time, and they do not drip. I found it a little disconcerting to count out pesos over a tiny white satin coffin, but you get used to it. After a lively conversation with the owner about the fine day, the health of our families and ourselves, and the new restaurant opening on Insurgentes, we eventually completed the transaction. Observing these courtesies is one reason we find it hard to accomplish more than one or two tasks a day, but again, they make us appreciate life more.

We continued our march up the hill to Juan's, the local coffee hangout populated mostly by Americans and Canadians. Tim was anxious to say hello and also to check out the latest crop of movies on DVD. Juan, the popular Mexican man who presides over the place, serves great coffee and provides San Miguel's *gringo* population with an essential supply of movies, TV series, foreign films, and other normally unavailable entertainment opportunities. Over the years, he and Tim have struck up a jocular relationship, bonding over obscure movies. "*Señor* Teeeem," Juan shouted at us above the din of caffeine-fueled conversation and a strumming James Taylor.

"You're back!" The two launched into one of their esoteric exchanges about past and present movie trivia, while I gazed longingly at the customers' delicious food and drink, wondering how long it would be until we stopped for lunch.

Tim wrapped up his private film festival and added a handful of DVDs to the candle purchases in our bag featuring Frida Kahlo's unibrowed face. We walked purposefully down the street, headed for Chelo's, the downtown drugstore a few blocks up the hill. By now, the sun rode high in the sky. As we passed Harry's Bar, Tim said casually, "I'm really thirsty. Want to take a little break?"

I hesitated, my brain foggy from the heat. Let's see…first day back in San Miguel…hot…thirsty… Harry's. I've got it! Margaritas! "Thank you, sir, don't mind if I do," I giggled.

We stepped past the shiny brass antique shoeshine chair that marks the entrance to a San Miguel institution where *gringos* and Mexicans mingle in a New Orleans-like atmosphere for drinks, conversation, and a good lunch, dinner, or Sunday brunch.

Bob, the owner, was perched at his regular table. He was debonair as always, dressed in a poplin jacket, a silk tie loose at his neck, and expensive loafers perfectly shined. A fresh hangover encircled him like a halo. He was engrossed in deep conversation with a local land developer and a lawyer we vaguely recognized. Bob seemed to have lots of lawyer conversations. His real-estate escapades, restaurant activities, and other high-profile hijinks were hot topics in the expat gossip mill in San Miguel. He was always good fun and a source of the latest news in the community.

When he saw us, he pumped Tim's hand and pecked my cheek. Apparently, the business meeting was over, so we settled in for a drink and a chat.

Friends stopped at the table, passing along tales and local updates. An hour evaporated. When he saw us, Don Julio, our charming favorite waiter who had once worked for the snazziest hotel in town, performed his ritual hand kissing, which always amused both of us. He asked if we wanted a table. By then, we were famished, and we repaired with two friends, Merry and Ben Calderoni (whom we'd run into while chatting with Bob) to a table in the red dining room with its high ceilings and crown molding. The dining room was exquisite, its huge paintings and sparkling white linens reflective of the grand old-world Spanish influence here, and its long windows with louvered shutters keeping the noise and heat of the street away from diners.

Merry is an artist whose colorful, expressive paintings and collages are internationally popular. She and her husband, Ben, a real-estate executive, were the first people we had met on our first trip to San Miguel years ago. We had stayed at their bed and breakfast, and Ben joined us at breakfast, entertaining us with hilarious tales of San Miguel lore that only a longtime local can spin. To give us a sense of what Merry did, he suggested we visit La Aurora and see Merry's studio at the back of the building. We went that very day and were taken with the huge, brick-walled space. It was at least sixty feet long and forty feet wide, with twenty-foot ceilings. Since Merry worked on huge canvases, it suited her perfectly. After admiring her paintings, Tim said, "Merry, Ben said this morning that when you two were in college in Texas, you used him in your bullwhip act."

She laughed. "I was doing my bullwhip show, which was how I paid for college tuition, and he offered to be my assistant. He gave me a drink before we went on. The trouble was that I didn't tell him that I'd never even had a beer before, because I wanted him to think I was sophisticated. There he stood, twelve feet away, posed sideways with a cigarette in his mouth. I had done this hundreds of times before, but not with a shot of tequila under my belt.

"I damned near cut his nose off. There wasn't much blood. It was just a nick, and he healed up nicely, but he never offered to be my subject again."

As she finished her story, she stepped into her office and returned with a bullwhip in each hand. WHACK! WHACK! WHACK! Tim and I jumped as those thin pieces of leather cracked eleven feet across her studio; an empty tin paint can clattered to the floor. I wondered what their marriage was really like.

Bullwhips aside, years later, we were still good friends. As we sat down with them, Tim and I ordered *arrachera*, marinated skirt steak. When prepared properly, *arrachera* is so tender that a knife isn't necessary. We once took a prominent chef to Harry's for dinner, and he actually made snuffling noises as he plowed through a huge plateful of the stuff. We enjoyed it this time, too, but managed to avoid the piglike sound effects. When Don Julio presented our plates, he murmured, "*Buen provecho*," another part of *Las Cortesías* culture. It means more than *bon appétit*. It literally wishes the diner good use of the food.

As we sipped the last of our coffee, Merry and Ben invited us to join them for dinner at the hottest new spot in town—a restaurant within the local bullring. I do not do bullfights—ever. However, when they assured and then reassured me that the restaurant offered a great view of the city, terrific food, and no bullfighting the day we were going, I agreed. We made a plan for later that week.

After a commotion of good-byes and promises to come back soon, we stepped out into the warm lull of the afternoon *siesta*. We stood there a moment and looked up the hill toward Chelo's. "You know, we COULD drop off those prescriptions tomorrow, and I'll bet Marcia is closed for *siesta* by now," I said. "I can cut a few flowers from Sally's garden, so we don't have to go all the way down to the flower market, but I do feel like a bum. We didn't get ANYTHING done today."

Tim smiled.

I sighed. "We just played."

Tim turned in the direction of the car park, jingling his keys, and started down the hill. "Nonsense, we did TWO things, which is twice as much as usual!" he said over his shoulder. I followed him down the street, laughing all the way back to the big chicken guarding the car. *Mañana* is always good enough in Mexico.

It's not that Mexicans are lazy. In truth, most Mexican people work terribly hard. But they simply value family and respect more than money and power, so their timetables are not always as precise or rushed as those of some other cultures. Their priorities are much more European than American, and that attitude is one of the things that draws us back to San Miguel repeatedly.

We spent the rest of the day lolling on Sally's wonderful terrace, peacefully watching the sunset while we carried on our private conversation, focusing on our plans for spending seven months in Europe following our two-month stay in Buenos Aires. We were still glowing with pleasure because we had made the big leap into the world, and we were eager to explore all the possibilities that had opened up to us.

We talked excitedly about the next day, too, when we would see our Mexican "family." Our friend Maribel Barrios had invited us to join in their semiannual tamale-making event. The family befriended us when we lived in San Miguel originally, and through the years we had been privileged to share both the joy of celebration and pain of profound loss with them. Maribel was also our property manager when we first arrived here. Soon we dubbed her our fifth daughter. As our friendship grew, she introduced us to her family and their traditions, most of which involved food, like every culture in the world.

This family, though, has raised humble food to a fine art. Twice each year, everyone—from Lidia, the matriarch of the Hernandez Vilchis family, who is about my age, to Regina, her youngest granddaughter—gathers at Lidia's pink adobe house for the complicated, labor-intensive production of hundreds of tamales. A crowd of women—cousins, aunts, daughters, and sometimes a lucky outsider like me—performs a graceful dance in the kitchen known as a "gang cook." Some form of built-in radar allows us to work together easily and seamlessly in close quarters, stepping out of the way when someone passes from one part of the room to the other carrying a big bowl of chicken, or one of us quickly washing a bowl and handing it to the person who's been charged with mixing up a little salsa, without bumping into anyone else. In Lidia's kitchen, we laugh a LOT, even though one of us (yours truly) doesn't speak very good Spanish. Usually, my poor Spanish causes the most uproarious giggles. They're so sweet, though, that I don't mind at all being the butt of the joke.

Lidia's culinary talents are amazing. Everything she makes, from red sauce to *flan* to *pozole*, is the best I've ever had. But the red sauce is truly ambrosial. It's used over enchiladas, poured around chicken parts and baked, drizzled on tamales, anywhere an intense chili flavor with a pop of heat is required. Although she has given me specific instructions for producing it, my rendition has never come close to equaling hers. I'm convinced that Lidia's red sauce poured over anything is a religious experience.

The men in the family are involved, too, though much of their contributions run along the lines of drinking beer, watching soccer on television, and passing through the kitchen to sneak a few tortilla chips with fresh guacamole or salsa. Tim excels in this area of male solidarity, and his lack of Spanish does not interfere with his male bonding skills in the least. In fairness, masculine brawn is necessary for toting the enormous pots, which have been carefully layered with hundreds of tamales and filled with hot water. Since the pots are so big, Lidia's small stove can't accommodate them, and they are distributed among neighbors' kitchens around the *barrio*, or community. The men lug them to their destinations and check them regularly as the tamales simmer to perfection. Then they tote them back to Lidia's for distribution among the family. Each nuclear group receives Ziploc bags for their freezers, filled with enough tamales to last until the next session in another six months.

Tamales combine *masa* (milled corn), lard, and seasonings— three of the major food groups, as far as I'm concerned. The dough is flavored to complement the filling, so Lidia's kitchen usually contains four cauldrons of the fluffy mixture: one sweet, two medium, and one blazing with chiles and spices. The tamale maker spreads a wet corn silk in her palm, plops a big spoonful of *masa* onto the leaf, and *slap!*, presses it flat, and adds a smaller spoonful of chicken, beef, fruit, or fiery chiles in the middle. Then, she skillfully folds the edges together and ties up the whole thing into a neat little package with raffia string bow.

Before long Lidia's table groaned with tidy rows of tamales, grouped by filling type. How beautiful to behold all of this handmade food. The kitchen mirth increased as we toasted each other with my most valuable contribution: a decent tequila.

✱ ✱ ✱

That afternoon, after the men horsed the last pot of tamales down the street, it was time for dinner and more cooking. Seriously! Lidia's kitchen, with its high ceilings and a hodgepodge of tables that serve as work surfaces, kept on humming the entire day. We immediately began the monumental cleanup process. With few cabinets, she creatively tucked and stacked pots, pans, dishes, and food here and there in scrupulously clean chaos. The floral oilcloth covering the table for eight (or up to ten if little kids share a big person's lap) in the center of the room was sprayed and wiped constantly. Practiced hands hurriedly dispatched the dirty pots and pans. Out came the dinner ingredients. Lidia's famous red sauce, crumbly Mexican cheese, carrots, onions, potatoes, and a huge stack of tortillas appeared. She banged heavy skillets onto the burners. I watched all of this in amazement.

Maribel, chatting with me at the table, hardly looked at her hands as she worked on an onion. As I watched her chopping away, I gasped and grabbed her arm. "Stop it, Maribel, you're making me crazy!"

She looked at me as if I was crazy. "What on earth are you talking about?" she asked in alarm and dropped the onion, perfectly diced in quarter-inch squares, onto the plate in front of her. I pointed at her knife in horror. Using a small flimsy, plastic handled, razor-sharp knife (like those that run three for a buck at The Dollar Store), she cradled a whole onion in her left hand and sawed furiously up and down, barely missing her palm and fingers with each stroke. I was terrified that one little slip would lop off her beautiful fingers.

Maribel patiently explained that her method is just how it's done in Mexico. There's none of that Emeril-style technique, tucking fingers into your palm to guide a knife with your knuckles and spare your fingers any unwanted slices. Mexican cooks are the real deal. Each potato, carrot, and onion becomes tiny uniform squares with their hair-raising technique.

Maribel continued, but I couldn't watch.

A food production quartet formed on the stove side of the kitchen. Lidia played first chair as she stood over the huge iron frying pan full of bubbling red sauce. She coated a tortilla with sauce, drained it for a second, and moved it onto a plate with tongs.

Anna, Maribel's architect sister-in-law who had driven in for tamale day from Guanajuato, fifty miles away, oversaw the cheese-filling station, crumbling a fat line of cheese down the middle of the tortilla and rolling it into a log. After another scoop of red sauce from Lidia, the plate shifted to Maribel. She anointed the log with a big spoonful of diced veggies sautéed in butter. Auriella, sitting roughly in the fourth chair, added a chicken leg. She delivered the plate to the table where eight expectant diners waited eagerly among supersize Coke bottles, cold beer, bowls filled with various salsas, and piles of chopped cilantro.

There were so many of us that new diners had to trade places with those who had finished to get at the food. Finally, Lidia sat down across from me to enjoy her composition. As we laughed and talked about our grandchildren, her deep brown eyes sparkled. Her talents extend far beyond the kitchen. She worked terribly hard to give all six of her children the education she feels they deserve, ensuring that every one of them graduated from high school and got a college education. (Not an easy feat for most people in San Miguel in Lidia's family's economic situation.) This is what we love about connecting with people from all walks of life here. Our Mexican friends are like their sauces: richly nuanced with depth and subtlety, spice and warmth. They are imbued with a secret ingredient, a kindness that they spread to us with generosity every time we are lucky enough to be with them.

The curious thing about us is that Lidia and I share no common language besides my rudimentary Spanish. Through the years we have learned that loving our children and grandchildren, sharing the same ideas that family comes first, and taking pleasure in feeding people are the wordless ties that bind us together. The joy of being with friends who accept us as we are and crave our company transcends the need for a common language. Seeing the gorgeous food those women produce in Lidia's rudimentary kitchen with simple tools (not a fancy-dancy kitchen gadget to be seen) reminds me that money, position, and acquired things have little to do with the satisfaction that the bonds of family, tradition, and affection bring to people in every culture. Lidia and her family produce world-class food in a kitchen with almost no counter space, no dishwasher or garbage disposal, and no cabinets, self-closing or otherwise. Her refrigerator is elderly, and every wall plug bristles with extra adapters. On this visit we brought a big KitchenAid mixer as a gift to the family. By the next day, when we came to visit for a minute, Lidia had sewn an elaborate cover, complete with zipper, to keep the hulking appliance clean and safe, and I know it's whipped up a hundred batches of tamale dough since it took up residence.

We left that night with two dozen tamales nestled in their plastic freezer bags and jars of the magic red sauce to slather on everything. (Of course, we managed to gobble up every one of those tamales before we left town!) But more importantly, we left with our friendship even more deeply embedded, secured by the closeness of family and the international language of food.

✱ ✱ ✱

The next morning, Tim continued working on our complicated plans for the next year, beyond the first six months that we'd already finalized. We had been in Mexico for three days at this point, and he had reserved cruises from Miami to Rome in May and from Barcelona to Miami in November. These were the bookends for our projected seven months in Europe. We wanted to visit France, Italy, Spain, Portugal, and England, too, and we had already sent housing deposits for June in Paris and July and August in Florence. We searched the Internet every day for apartments in Spain and Portugal while simultaneously gathering information about European plane connections, car rentals, interim hotel stays, and all the rest of the minutiae that must be addressed. Overall, we were feeling pretty confident about our impending year abroad—until a new friend threw a curveball even Sandy Koufax would be proud of.

Judy Butcher, an American traveler whom we had recently met through mutual friends, joined us for cocktails one afternoon. We were enjoying her lively company and entertaining stories as we lounged in Sally's fragrant summer garden. Originally from the East Coast, Judy had lived in England, France, and Alaska, and had spent time in Africa. She was an independent woman who traveled the world, and we quickly found her to be a kindred spirit. Art classes had recently lured her to San Miguel for several months.

"So then, we thought we'd spend September in Spain," I was explaining to Judy, after divulging our plan for living internationally full-time. "Tim hasn't spent any time in Spain and I think he'd be crazy about it. In October we could go to Portugal, which Tim likes and I haven't seen. It'd be easy to get back to Barcelona to catch our ship home from there."

"Sounds great, but what will you do about the Schengen Agreement?" Judy asked.

"The what?" we said simultaneously.

"The Schengen Treaty—you know, the ninety-day rule."

Tim and I exchanged glances. What ninety-day rule? In all our careful planning, was there something we had missed? "No, we don't know anything about it. What is it?" Tim asked after a pause, a hint of alarm in his voice.

"Oh. Well, it's something you should probably look into before you firm up any more of your plans," Judy explained lightly. "Most of the European countries are participants. It limits the time U.S. citizens can be in the EU to ninety days out of each one hundred eighty days. It's a real pain because there's no way around it except for a long-term residential visa, or maybe a student or a work visa."

"Well, what happens if you just ignore it and tell them you didn't know about it?" I asked, as always looking for a plan B.

"I think people do that and get away with it, but I've also heard that they can refuse you reentry for years if you violate the law, and if they're really having a bad day, they can fine you or even jail you," Judy replied seriously.

We were incredulous. This couldn't be true! How could we possibly have missed this important information? Why would they want to kick tourists out, especially ones like us who wanted to support the local economies?

That night, computers blazed in San Miguel. To our dismay, everything Judy had told us was correct. The accord was signed in 1985, and its main objective was to allow free trade and travel for EU citizens across the borders of European countries. The rules pertaining to U.S. citizens were incontrovertible, however. The EU is trying to discourage non-EU foreigners from coming to visit and remaining to seek jobs or welfare, so they implemented a ninety-day tourist visa policy. A regular U.S. visa is good for ninety days in European countries. When that visa's ninety days are used (not necessarily consecutively), the foreigner must leave the EU for a full ninety consecutive days before returning. It's easy for border personnel to track one's movements using the dates on the passport stamps. We searched for a loophole for days and consulted everyone we could think of who might have a solution. But the fact remained that unless we could get long-term visitor's visas, we would have to get out of Europe after three months. Finally, we saw capitulation was the only course and we started altering our plans.

Great Britain, Ireland, Turkey, and Morocco aren't part of the Schengen Agreement, meaning that time spent there does not count in the ninety-day restriction, so we included them, skipping Spain and Portugal, which are a part of it. By making arrangements to fly to Istanbul, Turkey, the same day we docked in Rome, we would waste only one of our precious ninety days on traveling. We would spend the last two weeks of May in Turkey, then our month in Paris, less than two months in Italy, and hightail it for England in late August to stop the clock; stay there for September, and live in an apartment in Marrakech, Morocco, in October. Our plan left enough time for us to fly to Barcelona for a night before sailing back to the United States, plus a couple of days to spare in case there was an unforeseen emergency.

Thanks to Judy we had avoided making arrangements for air transportation, housing, cars, and hotels, which could have cost us a bundle to cancel. As we quickly discovered, our best teachers are other travelers.

After she helped us avoid this crisis, we saw a lot of Judy in San Miguel and learned more of her story. She'd once left an influential job in the corporate world, bought a camper, and taken herself to Alaska where she had a job cooking on a boat—a radical departure from her former corporate buttoned-down life. She had lived in France with her former husband and had a daughter and her family who lived in California and a handful of stepchildren and step-families scattered around Europe. She had done volunteer work in Africa for several years, helping to build wells for rural communities. She was truly a renaissance woman.

As I mentioned, Judy had been attracted to San Miguel, like so many of its inhabitants, because of its active art scene. Choice boutique art galleries dot every street in El Centro, but home base for commercial artistic wares and professional art studios is Fábrica La Aurora, the huge white textile factory located on a few acres on the edge of town. Built in 1901 and abandoned in the 1930s, it found new purpose in 1991 as a sophisticated showroom for working artists, photographers, sculptors, jewelers, and antiques and textile dealers. We gravitated there often because of a charming restaurant and because Merry, our friend famous for her bullwhips and large canvases, and another friend, sculptress/painter Mary Rapp, maintain studios there. Mary Rapp lives on the property in a gracious apartment of heroically proportioned rooms full of art, light, and international style. "I love my commute," she said one day as she dug her thumbs deep into a lump of clay. "It's about three hundred steps and there's very little traffic!"

The next day, we followed a pattern that had become a tradition on our trips to San Miguel over the years: visiting "the Marys" on our first Thursday in town and celebrating our return to San Miguel with a gourmet lunch and a bottle of excellent Mexican wine. As the women waved good-bye from the graceful archway of the building and Merry called, "Don't forget—we'll see you at the ring at 7:00 tomorrow night!" I smiled and nodded, remembering the promise we'd made to her and Ben on our first day here.

The next evening we saw the venerable gray arena for the first time. It was built of local stone, featuring entrance arches at regular intervals. As we made our way up an incline to the restaurant attached to the outside of the ring, we passed several men talking animatedly near one of the entrances. Two of them, in business attire, were clearly not *toreador* material, while the other two, wiry and graceful even when they were slouched against the wall watching the suited ones talk, were definitely the bullfighter type. Glancing at them as we walked by, I supposed that they were wrangling over contract details or the fate of a particular bull for a future fight night.

The wall of the bullring formed the back of the restaurant and offered a breathtaking view of San Miguel de Allende, bathed in its pink late-afternoon glow, seen through huge windows. Raul, a powerful-looking cattleman who owned the restaurant, seated us and took our drink orders. Merry, who is always drop-dead gorgeous, wore denim and lots of antique turquoise. Her accessories did not include bullwhips this time, much to our relief.

"We're going to be testing some young bulls in the ring tonight, just to see what they've got," Raul said. "You're welcome to sit out there and I'll have someone bring your drinks to you. You'll enjoy it!"

I recoiled at the suggestion. The idea of men sticking sharp objects into an animal held no appeal for me. "Oh no…I don't think so, Raul, but thank you."

"*Señora*, this will just be a little cape work, nothing more. I promise there will be nothing but fun!" he exclaimed. Tim and our friends nodded in agreement. I was trapped.

He led our quartet back down the hill, and we stepped into the stands. The stone bleachers reminded me of ancient Roman arenas, like one we found in Verona where they now perform operas. (Tim had been looking into tickets for us to see *Turandot* and *Aida* there the following summer.) For me, scenes of murder, suicide, and bloody battles came to mind.

As we were seated, Raul said, "*Señor* Tim, if you'd like to try a pass with the bull, please feel free!"

I know my darling Tim very well and instantly caught the excited gleam in his eye, even though he tried to hide it. I looked straight ahead but said under my breath to him, "If you do this, I will divorce you. We are leaving for Argentina soon and I am not going to drag someone wearing a cast on his leg to Buenos Aires, buddy."

Tim said nothing, but when I finally stole a glance at him, an irresistibly eager nine-year-old Tim looked back at me. I knew I'd lost the battle.

The men we had seen outside were now in the ring, the wiry ones holding colorful capes. They laughed and teased one another. One of the suited men had shed his jacket and held a baby in his arms. I was horrified to see he, too, had a cape in his free hand. Several women had draped themselves over the wall of the ring and were casually chatting. I'm sure the baby belonged to one of them.

Suddenly, a bull emerged from a chute across the arena. He ambled a few feet, paused, and surveyed the scene. Without warning, he started to run. He didn't seem very big, but he was really fast.

He aimed at the closest man, who held his cape away from his body with one arm, loosely cradling the baby with the other. The little bull hurled his body at him and shot through the cape. Everyone laughed and clapped. Obviously, this wasn't a big deal to the denizens of the ring, but it surprised me so much my hands shot in the air as if I were at a rock concert. Only quick thinking kept me from spilling my frosty margarita.

Just then, one of the men beckoned to Tim. He wiggled eagerly like a little boy desperate to use the bathroom. Twitching with desire, he looked at me plaintively and said, "Oh, for God's sake, if a guy with a baby can do that, I certainly can."

I sighed. "Oh, go on, you old fool."

Before "old" was out of my mouth, he was halfway down the stairs.

As Tim's feet hit the dirt, one of the matadors started kidding around with his pals, his cape dangling beside him. He turned around just in time for that little black bull to head-butt him in the groin. He staggered but remained standing. I could barely watch.

But even that mishap did not deter my hero, *Señor* Tim, who marched smartly around the injured fellow to meet his caped destiny. He proceeded to the man with the baby, who handed him a red cape and gave him instructions using charades. (Tim doesn't speak Spanish, if you recall.)

I downed the rest of my margarita and signaled for another while I adjusted my camera. I knew if I didn't record Tim's one shot at bullfighting, our wonderful relationship could quickly go the way of the tip of Ben's nose under Merry's bullwhip. It would probably be the only time in his life when he'd have his moment in the bullring, and not having a record of it would break his heart. Plus, after loving him enough to let him go down there in the first place, I didn't want to hear about my failure to record such a pivotal moment in cocktail party conversation for the rest of my life!

Señor Tim waited politely as a couple of his *compadres* took their turns. Finally, his instructor indicated that he should step to the center of the ring. Merry, Ben, and I rose, as I've seen people do at bullfights in the movies. I steadied my camera and held my breath as that little beast hurtled himself toward my husband. The bull suddenly looked a *lot* bigger to me. I wanted to scream for Tim to run like hell, but I gritted my teeth and clicked instead.

As the bull passed him, *Señor* Tim rose on his toes, arched his back gracefully, and lifted the cape. He was *gorgeous*—and I got the shot! Husband and marriage saved.

We left the owners and their performers to their negotiations and strolled back up the cobblestoned walkway to the restaurant. San Miguel's lights twinkled and so did the eyes of the newly minted matador. "I'm so proud of you, honey," I said. "You were very brave and graceful."

Tim puffed out his chest. "Well, you know, that sucker was a lot bigger than he appeared to be from up in the stands. And he was really fast!"

I laughed. "Well, I suppose we should add 'Retired Bullfighter' next to 'Clio Award-Winning Lyricist' on your résumé."

A couple of weeks later, as we admired the photographic evidence of his exploits between packing sessions at Sally's house, I secretly offered up thanks that crutches or casts would not be part of the baggage we'd lug to Argentina the following week. As I'd soon find out, the adventure in Argentina would provide enough of a challenge without having a limping ex-matador for my companion.

Chapter 4
Buenos Aires

Tim perched on the edge of a cast-iron bench as he gestured to a slender blond woman sitting next to him. As usual, he was alive with excitement. As I walked down the wide stairs under the shade of a fiery bougainvillea to meet them, he leaped up and cried, "Honey, come and meet Felicia. She's amazing, and she speaks English!"

I didn't trust this woman for a minute and greeted his new "friend" coldly in Spanish. "*Buenas tardes, Señora. Cómo está usted?*" I asked suspiciously.

Felicia's outfit of tight white jeans and a low-cut colorful blouse, which barely covered her push-up-bra-enhanced bosom, was accented by long silver rhinestone-studded earrings sparkling in the sunshine. She appeared to have lived hard for every minute of her forty-plus years and she had been sitting much too close to my husband for my taste. "Very well, thank you," she purred in English.

"She told me that this racetrack has been here for years. You know how Argentineans love their horses," Tim said with a goofy smile.

I understood his glee. We hadn't talked with anyone who wasn't serving food or selling us something for days. We were starving for companionship, but not THIS kind!

I said sweetly, "Honey, I see a cab over there. Excuse us, Felicia, but we have an appointment and really must get back to Buenos Aires."

Tim glared at me but complied. As the cab doors slammed, he

grumbled, "Well, that was rude. Not like you at all. She was very informative, and I was enjoying myself a lot. What's your problem?"

"Sweetheart, she was a hooker. Why do you think she was practically in your lap? I mean, you are adorable, but it was a pretty obvious come-on."

He did an embarrassed double take. "Well, that does it! This country has finally turned me into a lunatic. How could I have missed that?"

Within five seconds, he was laughing. And soon I was, too. We howled so loudly that the dour taxi driver glanced over his shoulder to look at us. His brief smile revealed two gold eyeteeth, which made us laugh even harder.

After he caught his breath, Tim said, "Seriously, this is the last straw. I'm calling Continental this afternoon and we're outta here next weekend."

Six weeks before, the ten-hour flight from Los Angeles had worn us out, and from the moment we arrived in Argentina, we never recovered. I could not understand one word of Spanish the taxi driver or anyone at the airport spoke, which added to our confusion. At first, I put it down to exhaustion. I was certain that after a little rest, my limited Spanish skills would return. Sometimes, however, reality does not always reward a positive attitude.

On the wild taxi ride from the airport (Argentineans drive like the central and southern Italians most of them are!), we could see why many call Buenos Aires the Paris of South America. Its physical resemblance to our favorite city is uncanny at times, and in certain neighborhoods it was easy to forget we were in South America. As it turned out, that was a good thing sometimes.

Palermo, the neighborhood where we would be staying, pleased us when we arrived. It was a beautiful, tree-lined area with well-kept buildings and a wide range of restaurants, pastry shops, small stores, and services. It was also in a non-tourist area, which is where we like to be.

Marina, our apartment owner's agent, was waiting for us in the lobby. She was young, gorgeous, sweet, and in a hurry. She kissed both of us on each cheek—not Beverly Hills or French air-kisses, but full-on smooches—and led the way upstairs. It took five trips to get our belongings up the minuscule elevator, which only accommodated one bag. (Our packing skills weren't honed yet, so in this first phase of the adventure, we had too many clothes and too much equipment.)

Marina dashed through the apartment, chattering in her fractured English about light switches, Wi-Fi connections, and keys as we struggled to keep up with her. The space was small, but light and airy. It featured a two-story living room, a decent little kitchen, and a guest bath on the first level. The loft bedroom had a private bath and a small desk tucked in the corner. A fancy electric contraption lowered a huge room-darkening shade over the two-story window. The tiny balcony included two little French bistro chairs and a miniature table. Marina stood on the balcony and pointed vaguely in the direction of the subway entrance and grocery store. Then she gave us a dazzling smile, glanced at her watch, and said something about her *novio*, her boyfriend. She kissed Tim and me again on both cheeks. "*Hasta luego.*" Then she squeezed herself into the elevator, which was not much bigger than she, and disappeared. We were left in the doorway, rubbing lipstick marks off our cheeks as we wondered what to do first.

The Argentinean kissing ritual is tantamount to the accepted Mexican *cortesías*. From our experiences in Europe, we knew people practice the two-cheek kiss, usually among social friends. Still, the full-on bussing in Argentina took some getting used to. The first time I visited a manicurist in Buenos Aires and she approached me with pursed lips, I jumped back. I dodged her advances until I recognized the ritual and then started returning her greeting.

We noticed that as people arrived for work in stores, banks, or even the subway, kisses flew around. Everyone got two smacks, just as they do in many European countries. We eventually caught on. It tickled me to see Tim kissing other men's cheeks, something American men would never be caught dead doing to each other. I was proud of Tim and his confidence in adopting this tradition. Real men participate in local customs!

✷ ✷ ✷

"So, here we are," Tim said to me after Marina's departure. "Let's get some lunch before we try to get settled." He fiddled with the coffeemaker, which had been a relief for my tired eyes to see when we first walked in. A coffeepot is essential to our happy dispositions. My saint of a husband takes care of the caffeine jolt we both need before we croak our first words of the day.

I was reading the tenant's instruction notebook, looking for Internet codes. "Sure," I muttered, opening my computer. Tim started impatiently tapping the espresso machine. "Damn! Neither one of these works. We need a coffeepot before tomorrow. Call Marina, please, and ask her what we're supposed to do."

I picked up the phone, dialed the number she had scribbled, and heard a recorded person speaking rapid Spanish. I couldn't understand a thing. The "Y" sound for a double "L" is replaced with a "sh," so a word like *calle*, which would sound out as "kai-yay" in Mexico or Spain, becomes "kah-shay" in Argentina. Their cadence of speaking also isn't derivative of Spanish but rather Italian, which further complicates things for visitors attempting to understand them. These and other unusual linguistic challenges would almost drive me over the edge in the ensuing weeks.

I didn't hear the beep to leave a message, so I hung up. Clearly, I hadn't understood Marina when she instructed us on phone use, and I never did learn exactly how to use the telephone there, so we resorted to other means of communication.

I sent an email SOS to Marina about the coffeepots and then we set out to find food. Lacy jacaranda trees, ready to burst into exquisite purple bloom, filled the esplanade below our apartment and jolted us out of our moodiness. The urban bustle of cars, taxis, bikes, school kids, and shoppers delighted us, and we saw our first professional dog walker, who had impressive control over all twelve pooches he was walking at once. At sidewalk cafes, gorgeous tall European and American-looking people draped their long, slender bodies over black and tan woven bistro chairs as they indulged in heavily foamed coffees and flaky pastries. These people looked as if they belonged in the West Village, but when they spoke what sounded like Spantalian, it reminded us that we were in the opposite hemisphere. Our tired, troubled brains struggled to sort out whether we were in Paris, Rome, Buenos Aires, or Manhattan.

When we finally chose a restaurant, our confusion increased. Dark wood paneling, lots of polished brass, and a black-and-white checked tile floor said Italy. The tables and their authentically uncomfortable French bistro chairs jammed next to each other and an impressive wine list suggested Paris.

This couldn't be France or Italy. The menus were in Spanish! Plus, the portions sailing past on waiters' trays were gargantuan, making me feel like we were in an American version of some multinational hodgepodge of a restaurant. But when the waiter gave me an extremely heavy wine pour, I knew for sure I wasn't in Europe. The gorgeous red liquid shimmered to the brim of a big wineglass, not halfway up the short chubby one they usually present in other countries. He had served me Malbec, the delicious Argentine wine that straddles somewhere between a Cabernet Sauvignon and a Merlot on the taste scale. I wouldn't be surprised to learn that, because of my consumption of that particular brand over the next six weeks, Trapiche Vineyards had added a few extra rows of vines.

Tim ordered a hamburger, which may sound unadventurous but actually made sense. Argentina brings to mind Ricardo Montalban, the wildly handsome Latino actor in those ancient Lincoln commercials, riding the *estancia* range on a fine Corinthian leather saddle, herding Texas-size steaks-on-the-hoof.

My spouse smiled expectantly as the waiter delivered a mountain of food. "Oh, my God," he exclaimed, inspecting the steaming plate. With his fork, he lifted slices of pancetta, glistening with fat, to reveal beneath them a pile of thin, crisp waffle-shaped potatoes. "Look at these gorgeous things," he said, his voice muffled with the first irresistible morsel. Eventually, he found the meat patty, at least two inches thick. It sat on a ciabatta bun, topped with a slab of melting cheddar.

I laughed. "I can't believe that they put a fried egg on top of the whole thing. But look, they gave you some lettuce and tomato, so it can't be all bad."

Meanwhile, I attacked my plate of ethereally light homemade pasta, tossed with arugula pesto and dusted with an enormous amount of fluffy shaved parmesan cheese. Perhaps Argentina wasn't quite so bad.

We rolled back to our building, half-lost in a food coma. We noticed a pastry shop with glass cases displaying empanadas and pastries, diabolically located on the ground floor of our building. Clouds of fragrant baking aromas wafted into our apartment each time they fired up the ovens. Resistance was futile; I knew right away that this visit was going to cost more in self-esteem than money.

But the culinary temptations didn't stop there. Within waddling distance of our apartment—we're talking two blocks—we had also passed eight restaurants, three bakeries, six fresh fruit and vegetable stands, flower and news kiosks, and two pasta factories. Both of those feature homemade dishes slathered with the customer's choice of rich, authentic Italian sauces, topped by mountains of freshly grated Parmigiana Reggiano. Clerks packaged up customers' choices in oven-proof containers. We're quick learners, and we hauled many steaming bags home with us during our stay.

At the front door of the building, I fumbled in my overweight purse for the keys Marina had breezily demonstrated during her whirlwind tour of our accommodations.

There were three thick, ornate keys on the ring. They reminded me of fairy castles and old-time jails. (Within a few days, I noticed that every set of keys looked exactly like ours: one regular and two medieval. Does Buenos Aires only have one manufacturer that works in cahoots with all the builders? I'll never know.) The short key carried a familiar size and shape. It opened the building's front door. No problem. The other two were about three inches long, thick, and heavy with big notches at the business end, and we had no idea which opened what. After a week or so, we figured out that the key with the rounded top belonged to the apartment. That took care of half our battle. The other half was trying to open the door. The key rattled around the enormous hole in the door, while the operator (Tim or me) searched for its invisible slot by feel. The light in the hall outside the elevator operated on a timer switch, so when the end of the key connected with the slot, the timer shut off the interior hallway light and shrouded us in pitch blackness. Of course!

When this happened the first few times, we tried to enter the apartment blind. Naturally, we dropped the bags of shopping, the purse, umbrella, jacket, and whatever else we toted. The key then often fell out of the door and clattered to the floor, locking us out.

We'd begin the procedure again, trying to select the right key, and swearing and fumbling for the light switch as we tripped over the belongings we'd dropped in the first place.

We never did find out what the other key was supposed to open.

* * *

From our experience in Buenos Aires, we established a first-day routine in a strange city that still works for us. Tim always arranges transportation at our arrival point to avoid a panic situation over language, traffic, or other unexpected problems. Once we've reached the apartment, paid and tipped the driver, and greeted whoever is meeting us, we shut the door on the world long enough to regroup and catch our breath. This is really important to us, especially because we are no longer as young as we used to be. We need time to acclimate when faced with exhaustion, linguistic challenges, and new surroundings.

We have also created our own checklist of essential items to inspect, like testing air conditioning and heating, how the appliances work, and other details. That checklist has grown very detailed the longer we have been on the road, and I expect we'll add to it all the years we will be home free. We learn something new with every move-in. Experience eventually taught us to review that checklist with the manager before we let him or her out of our sight. But when we first arrived in Buenos Aires, we hadn't learned that trick yet, and it cost us dearly in time and frustration.

Next, we inspect apartment storage and equipment, and read the owner's manual provided by management. It usually contains essential information about the apartment, neighborhood, and city.

In our routine, I inspect kitchen supplies and start the shopping list. Usually, we find random necessities are lacking: no scissors, no pads for lists, only a couple of limp tea towels, a kitchen sponge used for far too long (and located in another room), and a lack of washcloths for the bath.

We also try to figure out how everything works. Anything with switches and knobs tends to be taxing to learn in another language. For instance, I noticed that the air-conditioning unit in our Buenos Aires apartment was located about twelve feet up the two-story wall in the living room, unreachable from either the floor or loft bedroom. The AC's motor gobbled up about half of our little outside balcony. I briefly searched for a thermostat, but since it was early spring, we didn't need air conditioning. I quit looking and went on to the light switch challenge. Down the road, that would become a big mistake.

Then we usually have few tense moments over tech stuff like TVs, cable, DVD players, and Internet connections. As the screen flashes "*Aucun Signal,*" "*No Señal,*" or "*Belirsiz*" in the upper left corner of the black screen, Tim will ask through clenched teeth, "Did you touch this remote?"

"No Signal" looks and sounds the same in any language. It means the user could be facing the next few minutes—or hours—engaged in fruitless electronic sleuthing, trying to figure out what the problem is and where through trial and error. The situation grows even more maddening when one is stumbling around in another language.

One of the great advantages of spending at least a month in a city is that we don't need to hurry to see the sights. Thus, on the first day, we usually don't stray far from the apartment, instead contenting ourselves with a tour of our immediate neighborhood so we can pick up groceries, find an ATM, and spot some local restaurants.

On the second day of a stay, we try to go a little farther afield and figure out the transportation system. In Buenos Aires, there are cabs everywhere. However, as in most metropolitan cities (Buenos Aires has thirteen million people), traffic is snarled often and public transportation works best. It's a *lot* cheaper, too.

The first time we left our immediate neighborhood and headed for the more populated area to the east of us in Buenos Aires, we learned that strolling at our pace wouldn't work. After I'd been poked by several elbows and prodded by people who wanted to cross before the light changed, we smartened up our stride and fell in with the rest of the pedestrians. The Argentineans took no prisoners. It's a rough-and-tumble kind of town, sort of like Manhattan but with even more attitude.

We found the subway entrance and clattered down the stairs with the rest of the crowd. Once underground, we stepped back against the wall to observe the action. Local people in subway stations know what they're doing, and a smart newbie stays out of the way of the daily riders. We have found that on day one in a new city, whether we're mastering a subway system, catching a cab, getting a beer, or buying groceries, we save time and humiliation by observing how the regulars handle daily life before we jump in.

We bought *subte* passes, which allowed ten trips on the system, studied the map, and took ourselves to La Recoleta Cemetery, where almost five thousand vaults sit aboveground inside fourteen walled acres, creating a small city of mausoleums. It reminded us of New Orleans' Cities of the Dead, which Anne Rice so richly describes in her Vampire Chronicles books. It's eerie to walk down tree-lined streets full of elaborate houses built for dead people. The juxtaposition of ornate gothic spires on miniature chapels fascinated us, especially as they stood against a backdrop of modern apartment and office buildings. A gigantic upscale shopping center bordered one side. Quiet streets frozen in time in the midst of a frantic city have a chilling effect on the visitor's equilibrium.

We searched the cemetery for familiar names and quickly found former Argentinean First Lady Eva Perón, subject of the smash Broadway musical *Evita*! Her surprisingly simple shrine stands among famous writers, musicians, actors, and other notables. As we sat on a bench to rest and compare notes, Tim said, "Did you notice how many of these things honor heavy-duty military guys? There's definitely a martial atmosphere in this country. They must have paid generals really well to afford this real estate."

"Maybe they gave them a discount because they controlled everything anyway, huh?" I replied half-jokingly.

The turbulent, disturbing history of Argentina aroused our curiosity. The nation's politics and economy haven't been stable for most of the country's existence. Even during our short stay, we could sense the dramatic, moody, temperamental elements of its history through its citizens. On a single Saturday afternoon, we watched a wild and wonderful gay and lesbian pride parade and street fair with people of every persuasion adorned in breathtakingly exotic attire; fifteen minutes later on the Avenida Constitución, hundreds of women chanted, wept, and demanded justice for people "disappeared" by their government between 1976 and 1983. Our take on the Argentinean people is summed up with the joke about the definition of an Argentinean: a person who looks Italian, speaks Spanish, dresses like the French, but thinks he is English. No wonder they seem to be a confused, melancholy people! (We developed a theory that their notoriously unpredictable economy might have something to do with it, too.)

When that strange afternoon ended, we were happy to collapse on our little balcony, have a cool drink, and see what the neighbors were up to. We were unaccustomed to high-rise apartment living where people lived their lives in full view of us. In the neighboring buildings across the way, they closed their drapes only when they were undressing or sleeping. We got to know their habits quickly. One couple's red walls, decorated with Italian paintings and colorful pottery, fascinated us. We couldn't resist glancing at them as they watched TV from their big chairs, enjoyed cocktails in their living room, or huddled together reviewing their budget. It was like watching *Rear Window*, only without the murder.

Overall, we didn't witness too much drama, but one evening we did see an animated discussion between a man and a woman in another apartment. It got so heated that we were alarmed.

"My God, Tim, what will we do if he knocks her across the room?" I asked as the guy got out of his chair, waving his arms at the woman.

"I have no idea," Tim whispered. "We don't even know where the front door of that building is, and we sure as hell can't speak enough Spantalian to call the cops and make ourselves understood."

We exhaled with relief when he reached her side of the table, put his arms around her, and kissed her in reconciliation. She kissed him back, thank God. By the time we had gotten ourselves together, he could have thrown her off the balcony if he wanted to! This urban intimacy was startlingly different from our suburban California life, where waving at the neighbors while they waited for the garage door to open might constitute our only contact with them. We certainly wouldn't have known the color of their dining room walls.

As the days grew warmer, the jacaranda trees threw a mantle of purple blooms across the city. The blossoms carpeted the sidewalks with beauty, and the locals seemed a little less hostile and melancholy, which cheered us up considerably.

By then, we had discovered there are separate rates for travel within Argentina, a lesson that forced us to determine what was truly important to us to see. For instance, airfare cost about half price for citizens as it does for foreigners; unfortunately, that meant we couldn't afford to see the other side of the large country (roughly one-third the size of the United States). Our alternative was an overnight bus, which didn't appeal to us for many reasons. We also learned that if we went to Iguazu Falls, about which everyone raves, we'd have to enter Chile, a country that charges tourists $160 each for a visa. Our desire to see the falls didn't overcome our budget constraints, so we had to skip that trip. Between the visa, transportation, lodging, and food, we would have spent an enormous amount of money and effort to see that spectacular sight.

We decided to content ourselves by visiting places in our adopted city, starting with the Teatro Colón, considered to be one of the world's top five opera houses because of its near-perfect acoustics. Virtually every significant classical performer in the world has appeared in the hundred years of its history. The opera house, which had just reopened after its three-year $100 million renovation, is an ode to classical French and Italian decoration. Walking up the impressive, graceful staircase toward the auditorium, surrounded by glorious gilded opulence, made us want to be more than afternoon visitors. It thrilled us so much that we bought tickets for the ballet, just so we could sit in the red velvet seats.

We tarted up for the evening. Tim looked handsome in his tie and coat, and I swanned around in my basic black three-piece outfit and pearls, so we didn't embarrass ourselves among BA's cultural elite. The ballet performance was forgettable, but the setting and sublime acoustics made up for it. We were ecstatic to be out and about among the locals.

As we descended the opera house steps and slipped away into the luscious spring night, Tim asked, "Hey, baby, how about some real dancin'?" Off we headed to San Telmo, the funky-groovy part of BA, where the best bars, dives, and vintage stores are found. Tim lost the tie, and we watched muscular young couples tango until the small hours. (Oh, all right, stop smirking: you know we didn't stay up till the small hours. We were home by midnight.) It was great fun to watch the beautiful girls pout and stamp their feet, then eventually capitulate and drape themselves over their partners, allowing them to dominate the situation. Any brief desire to join in the fun was quelled by the sure and certain knowledge that one or both of us would end up in the emergency room if we tried to emulate their sexy contortions.

Another morning, we took a half-hour train ride to Tigre (named for the jaguars that were hunted there in its early years), a delta created by several streams and rivers. The delta rivers are lazily brown and wide, lined with boats of all sizes, and picturesque little towns full of restaurants and shops and countless marinas. There are English-style rowing clubs, humble dwellings, and elegant mansions from the gracious period before World War I, the "Belle Époque," to see. The tremendous influx of Germans and Italians clearly marked Argentina as different from all other South American countries, so during our entire stay we found ourselves confused about exactly where we were.

We found a luncheon cruise and indulged in a little more voy-euristic fun looking into the peoples' houses, which faced the river. We scored a table in the stern of the boat, where it was lovely to sip wine and watch the water slide by all afternoon. It was the most peaceful, relaxed day we had experienced in our entire visit, and Tim and I are both really happy whenever we are on or near water. That day we felt as if we'd really settled in.

Soon, we became almost proficient at living like *porteños*, the local people of Buenos Aires. (Translation: "people of the port.") We made friends with the women who ran the local fluff-and-fold operation across the boulevard, after Tim used his considerable charm to penetrate their stern facades. At last, we received smiles and attempts at conversation when we dumped our duds. We began to know where to look for things we needed in the local grocery, and also acquired a bright green two-wheel rolling cart in which to bring them home. By now, negotiating the subway system was second nature, and we put the key the right spot in our apartment door about 80 percent of the time. We enjoyed bountiful servings of meat, cheese, and wine—too much for our waistlines—and swore we would eat better the next day.

Our outings continued. Every day, the temperature rose a bit more. We strolled the gorgeous parks and took in the excellent art museums, which offered some real surprises. During the past one hundred fifty years, many Europeans immigrated to Argentina and brought their art with them. We marveled at a number of rare works by some of my favorite painters at Las Bellas Artes Museum, many of which I had never seen even in catalogs or books.

Our occasional visits to Puerto Madero, where fancy hotels and restaurants line a wide boardwalk, sabotaged our intermittent resolve to behave ourselves dietetically. We enjoyed some epic lunches and dinners in world-class seafood restaurants, the Malbec flowing in a ceaseless cascade down my willing throat—and directly to my hips.

As we began to feel more comfortable in the city, we still felt rather lonely. We quickly were learning that when you live in 500 square feet in fairly unfriendly surroundings, you'd better really like your partner. Although we were doing fine ourselves, situations with the Argentineans themselves kept arising that puzzled and challenged us.

"I just don't get it, honey," Tim said one evening as we sat, knees touching, on our apartment's little outcropping having a cocktail while surreptitiously watching our neighbors dine in that red room. It was pork chop night for them, and they were enjoying themselves. "I can't figure out why these people are so mean to us. I mean, being a nice person is really easy for you, but I have been working really hard to hide my basic contempt for everyone, and the Argentines still treat me like crap." He smiled wryly and continued, "Remember the other day when you asked the waitress at that Chinese restaurant for a glass of red wine and she refused you? I still can't figure out what the hell that was about."

He referred to our visit to Buenos Aires' Chinatown for lunch. I had asked a harried waitress for a glass of red wine, using my best Spanish coupled with a submissive smile, but she looked at me with narrowed eyes. "No," she said emphatically. She spun on her heel and disappeared behind the beaded curtain leading to the kitchen as I looked on astonished.

"Beats me," I said. "I mean, why wouldn't she ask if I'd like a beer, or offer a half bottle, anything but just saying 'no.' It was almost as crazy as that taxi driver you wanted to punch."

During that incident, Tim had proffered a large Argentine bill to a cab driver. The guy claimed he had no change; clearly he intended to take the whole bill and drive away. When Tim tried politely to talk sense, the driver crossed his arms, leaned against his car, and refused to budge. We then offered to buy some magazines from a guy who had been watching the scene from his news kiosk on the curb beside the cab so we could get change, but he took an oddly malicious delight in declining to sell them to us. None of the grim-faced shop owners nearby would help us either, even when we offered to buy their products. Finally, Tim gave the driver the only other currency we had, twenty American dollars, twice what we owed him, just to make him go away.

After he paid the cabbie, I grabbed his arm and firmly steered him away from the scene. He was steaming over the incident, waving his arms and venting his frustrations so loudly that I was afraid someone might call a cop. It took several blocks to talk him down. Usually tall, broad-shouldered Tim is kind and affable. But on the very rare occasions when he gets riled up, he can be, well, a little intimidating.

I understood his departure from his normal behavior. After several weeks of unnecessary roughness, like young men purposely bumping into me on the sidewalk, and our being told "no" repeatedly by locals before we even finished a question, Tim had just had enough. "You were so furious that I thought you might throw a punch," I reflected.

Tim shook his head in dismayed agreement.

"There's something going on in this culture that we're just not getting. Do you understand why everything is so uphill here? Could it be that we are not adaptable anymore? Dear God, maybe we're too set in our ways and too old to be out here living in the world."

"I hope you're wrong," I replied. "The thing is, we've traveled a lot and I think we're really pretty flexible, but I've certainly never run into a culture quite like this. It's going to be interesting to see if we feel this way in other places. By the way, I thought you were wonderful!"

By week four, we definitely needed an American fix—something familiar to orient us in this foreign place where we were floundering. One afternoon, as Tim sat at his computer making a car pickup reservation for our arrival in Paris the following June, he announced that we could watch the classic Alabama vs. LSU football grudge game at a bar downtown. I was delighted. My dad had been a lifelong active Alabama alum, so these games are always of special interest to us. We hoped we could enjoy a little schmoozing with other American tourists or expats by way of this good old-fashioned Southern sports rivalry.

On game day we walked a few blocks from the subway station, and when Tim opened the door, the racket hit us like a wall. Everyone was screaming, which sounded normal except for one small detail: the game hadn't even started. Clearly, something had happened to bar culture in the years since we were active participants. People didn't talk to one another anymore; they bellowed. Or perhaps the dialed-up music made everyone shout to be heard.

Or maybe, just maybe, we were simply growing old and crotchety.

It also became apparent that not only were we the oldest people in the room by at least thirty years, but also part of a very small minority of Alabama boosters. The young American professionals in the house, casually dressed in their Ralph Lauren Polo gear, were LSU Tiger devotees. Our Crimson Tide cheering section, made up of three mature traveling businessmen from Mobile, plus the Martins, congregated in a booth near the front door. We huddled together and tried to communicate over the LSU fans' screeching. Chicken wings, barbecued ribs, and beer contributed to the down-home atmosphere, and we were delighted with the tastes and aromas of home. We watched, but did not hear, LSU tear into Alabama. The bloodbath on the field was more demoralizing than the deafening roar, which rose by several decibels every time one of their guys maimed one of our gentlemen. We were getting really tired of their rude, crazy behavior.

Sometime in the third quarter, as the numbers on the big screens became more disheartening and the mood of the liquor-fueled crowd even more boisterous, a scuffle broke out at the bar. Limbs flailed, and a different type of Southern cry pierced the room. Now, I have spent a respectable amount of time in drinking establishments in my life, but somehow never witnessed a bar fight.

The fight was thrilling…and quick. Almost as soon as we became aware of the conflict, two big guys at the front door managed to part the crowd and reach the bar. Within seconds, the bouncers carried a young man aloft through the crowd, right over our heads. They pitched him out the door and slammed it. For a nanosecond, we actually heard the TV announcers. Then the roar resumed at exactly the same pitch as before the drama. But we were speechless. Seeing your first bar fight after age sixty-five is not an insignificant event.

✳ ✳ ✳

By November, the temperature was rising a little uncomfortably in the afternoon. Since our apartment faced south, we couldn't delay learning about the air conditioner any longer. We started seriously searching for the answer, peeking around corners, following electrical lines, and playing with wall switches. We minutely inspected the compressor unit on the balcony, trying to find a switch. No success.

Since I still didn't know to use the telephone (despite numerous attempts!), I sent an email to Marina, hoping she would reply this time.

Miraculously, she got right back to me. Her message verbatim:

The air conditioning turn on with the blue button. Then press the button "mode" and put the symbol of could (snow) if the air conditioning stay in hot (sun). If you cant, Eduardo is in the front door. call Eduardo for help- :)

Confirm me that.

besos

m

The hunt was on. Tim and I retraced every step of our previous searches and considered taking up the floorboards. Once more, we failed. We saw no blue button anywhere in the apartment. I emailed again:

Where is the blue button?

She replied at once:

It is on the remote.

Remote? What remote?

We found the remote. In fact, we'd never lost it. Of course it was there. We had shoved the small clicker aside because we thought it belonged to the clunky CD player that hogged valuable space on a kitchen shelf. It had a blue button, as well as a "mode" button that displayed the above-mentioned snowflake. The machine started as instructed. Life was good!

A few days later, Marina accepted our invitation for wine and hors d'oeuvres. She looked darling in her high spindly heels and filmy summer top. We stood on our balcony, and for the first time, the red wall people looked at us. Of course, it was the fetching Marina who caught their interest, but we waved and smiled anyway. This time they waved back. I'm sure that the beautiful Marina was more wave-worthy than two older tourists!

Marina told us about her work as an assistant to a mid-level poli-tician. She also shared about her boyfriend, who was still in school pursuing an advanced degree, and she told us about her parents. Later in the evening, after several large glasses of Malbec, Marina favored us with a song. We had no idea she could sing, and her a cappella performance thrilled us, just as people who routinely pres-ent after-dinner "party pieces" without embarrassment had always delighted me when I lived in Ireland in the nineties. Marina told us that her mother had written the mournful tune that she sang in her husky alto voice. The girl was full of surprises; we were so smitten that she became daughter number six for us, after the lovely Maribel in Mexico. Her giggling acceptance to be one of our own made us homesick for our brood. If we kept this up, we'd end up with dozens of adopted daughters, but we were pleased to finally have a friend in this city.

Tim took the floor. "Marina, before you go I have a very serious question for you. We've been here for many weeks, and we have tried very hard to assimilate, to understand the culture, to be good guests, flexible visitors, but somehow we seem to miss the mark."

He told her about the cabbie incident, the Chinese wine fiasco, and the Disco Disaster. He even mentioned the blue button incident, all examples of an overall communication problem.

She listened carefully, thought about it for a minute, and smiled. "I know what the problem is. You are asking the wrong questions."

We glanced at each other. "What?" we said in unison.

"Okay, let me explain: it is true that the first response from an Argentine to any question will be 'no.' It's just part of the culture. And it's also part of our culture for women to look so unhappy. They pout all the time because they are all waiting for some man to come along and make them happy—buy the woman a gift, a meal, an apartment!" she laughed.

We expressed disbelief, but she swore it was true. It accounted for the surly looks I had interpreted as personal dislike. Now we were getting somewhere.

"Now, about the questions. Here's an example: with the cabbie, the right question, before you got into the cab, would have been, 'Do you have change for one hundred pesos?' If he said 'no,' then you move on to the next cabbie."

We stared at her. Suddenly, things began to make sense. We had been making assumptions the whole time based on the way we were used to doing things in America.

"So, let me try this out," Tim said. "If Lynne had asked the Chinese restaurant waitress if they sold wine by the glass, instead of assuming that they did, she might have gotten further?"

Marina nodded.

After she left, we reviewed other situations in which we had been frustrated and thwarted. In all cases, we realized the outcome could have been different had we known to take that approach. We swore that we'd remember this lesson and apply it.

Marina's explanation proved to be the lesson that would make our life abroad much easier overall. Invariably, when we find ourselves struggling in a new environment, we realize we are failing to ask the right question in the first place.

It also relieved us to realize that we weren't too old or inflexible to take on the world. We simply needed to let go of any assumptions or expectations we had and change our perspective.

However, when we set out the next day for the racetrack, expecting a fun-filled afternoon among excited people cheering on their chosen nags, enjoying their companions and maybe even smiling at us, we were let down again. The gamblers proved to be quiet and dead-pan, their women clearly hoping to frown and growl their way to riches, and the food servers apparently alumni of the same training school as the Chinese restaurant lady. Our re-phrasing questions and attempts at charm didn't seem to warm any hearts at the racetrack. We were truly disappointed that our newly minted skills didn't produce the outcome we hoped for.

We left the track early, lonely and frustrated. No matter what we did, we didn't seem to be able to make Argentina work. This is when my darling, so desperate for conversation that he chatted up a "lady of the evening," announced we were leaving the country two weeks early. In two days, we had learned two valuable lessons. The first was to stop and ask the right questions. The second was that we don't have time to waste in places where we were struggling to be happy.

We called Alexandra, one of my California daughters, and announced our new plan: to return to the United States for Thanksgiving. We heard delight on the other end and a promise to buy a bigger turkey. We started packing up our gear that very day. And for better or worse, we didn't regret it.

Naturally, Argentina "spoke" the last word. As we left the country, Tim deposited me in the executive lounge (we have found that belonging to these is worth the dough when you're on the road all the time) and walked into the airport's main lobby to exchange our remaining Argentine pesos for American dollars. He came back much later and plunked down next to me, where I sat in a circle of chairs, listening to other travelers' harrowing experiences in Buenos Aires, some much more disturbing than ours.

Tim gritted his teeth. "They would NOT give me dollars."

"You've got to be kidding. How can that be?"

"They claim I must have a receipt for the pesos from a bank," he said. "That's crazy…nobody keeps those things. Besides, it's only a hundred bucks! It must be because the peso is falling so fast again that nobody wants them now."

A beautifully dressed and coifed Argentinean woman sitting across from us heard our conversation. "I'll be coming home to BA in a couple of weeks," she said. "I'll buy the pesos from you if that will help."

Tim thanked her and agreed on an exchange rate. They exchanged currencies.

Hours later on the plane, I said, just to make conversation, "Wasn't it nice of that woman to take the pesos?"

Without looking at me, he said out of the corner of his mouth,

"Sure it was. She charged me about twice what the guy at the *cambio* was offering! It was Argentina's last little joke on us!"

I sighed. "Let's go back to Cambria and have some turkey."

It was time for a fresh start.

Chapter 5
Transatlantic Crossing

We retreated from Buenos Aires to California, where we rented a house, regrouped, and prepared for seven months in Europe, putting the final touches on the plan and fussing over wardrobe choices. Neither of us slept much as departure time grew near. My interior conversation, usually held at two or three in the morning, was repetitive: What if we hate being on a ship for fourteen days? What if our stateroom is claustrophobic? Do I have enough blouses and sweaters? Did I pack that little clothesline? Is he going to HATE me after seven months on the road? Am I going to hate HIM? Will the children and grandchildren forgive us for taking off this way?

Finally, we flew to Florida to board the ship that would take us to Rome. We stayed with Amandah and Jason, our Florida family, who patiently endured our jumpy nerves and constant chatter, our need for printers, phones, FedExes, and excursions for last-minute necessities. I am certain that they were glad to help unload our luggage at the pier as we took our slightly frenetic show on the road.

The instant they drove away, we were swept up in a congenial atmosphere. Everyone was happy. Everything was easy! The porter smiled, joked with us, and made our luggage disappear.

We strolled into the port terminal trying to look sophisticated, amused, and slightly bored. In truth, we were wobbly with anticipation, dread, and relief. Tim whispered, "I have never been so excited in my entire life."

"Me neither," I muttered through my small, tight smile. Then I dropped my attempt at nonchalance. "Oh my God; it's enormous!" I gasped. There was the *Mariner of the Seas*, the 1,000-foot behemoth that would take us from Miami to Rome. We were like kids arriving at Disneyland. We peered around. Guests in the short check-in line were excited, relaxed, and happy. The desk clerk beamed, handily finishing the paperwork and handing us our precious plastic identification cards, the only currency we'd need for two weeks. The background music was benign. No babies screamed, people didn't smack us with their carry-ons, no beeping carts toting wheelchairs and walkers ran us down. All of the airport madness was missing, and we felt no need to make decisions: there was only one gate available. The passengers and crew were pleasant and polite. As everyone glowed with happiness, our reflexes from Argentina kicked in and our excitement turned to suspicion. Why was everyone so happy? Were these people on drugs? What was going on here?

But more jovial people welcomed us aboard, and our cool facades crumbled quickly into naked glee as we inspected our new home. The common areas glittered in the gorgeous, faux Las Vegas style, their brightness and spaciousness conveying a sense of glamour and fun. On our initial exploration, we found pools, bars, restaurants, library, a computer room, a spa with a beauty salon, and a fabulous sea-view gym complete with yoga, spinning, sauna, and Jacuzzi, just as advertised. We walked along an appealing, cheerful "main street" with shops, cafes, and bars. A jazz group provided live music. Everyone smiled, with good reason.

"So, what do you think so far?" Tim asked as we walked along a freshly vacuumed wide corridor in search of our stateroom, his desire for my approval evident. I glanced at him and suddenly realized that he was anxious to reach the stateroom. When we had talked about his being in charge of the arrangements, I had told him, "She who does not make the plans is not allowed to complain," but my glib remark didn't absolve his concern. So now I was determined to put him at ease and reward him for the enormous effort he'd made, although I felt a little apprehensive myself.

"It's fantastic, honey, and I know that our cabin is going to be just fine. It was lovely in the photos and you were so smart to book us in the bow so we'll have a fabulous view," I said encouragingly.

Just then, we reached a short hallway, with three doors at the end. Two were marked "crew." The third was 2308: our new lodging. Our room was the first on the curve before the ship angles to its point in the bow, so we were tucked into a private little nook.

As I opened the door and looked in, the love seat in front of a big porthole delighted me, as did an inviting king-size bed. "Oh, Tim, this is extraordinary," I shouted as I ran around the small stateroom like a child, inspecting the innovative tricks that make living aboard ship feel like playing house. Things slide away, fold up, and scoot under other things. Everything is multi-functional. It's difficult to be uncomfortable, especially since a steward shows up numerous times a day to tidy, sparkle up, replenish, bring ice, and make hilarious towel art while we and other occupants fritter away our time elsewhere in the bar, at the pool, gambling, playing bridge in the card room, or knocking the ball around on a miniature golf course. A miniature golf course on a ship, for crying out loud. What's not to like?

The loudspeaker in our petite hallway crackled. The captain informed us, in an uber-happy Norwegian accent, that everyone on the ship was required to attend an evacuation drill. During the drill, I noticed that passengers had already begun the social do-si-do; by dinner, jockeying for position in a group would be in full swing everywhere on the ship. It was like a high school popularity contest, and there were a lot of people vying for the king and queen spots.

Afterward, we stopped on the way "home" for a pre-voyage cocktail. "It's a strange thing, but I noticed just now that people were already huddling up to form packs," I said.

"I saw that, too. This is like a little village of three thousand people. Humans can't help themselves, though. They hook up naturally and then want their little crowd to be exclusive. Chickens do it, too. Did you know that? If you bring new chickens into the flock, the others will attack them. I guess chickens aren't the only bird-brained creatures."

"Well, I say you and I try to maintain a little distance and don't date anybody until we're sure we want to be pals, okay? Two weeks is a long time to avoid eye contact if you make a mistake."

He smiled. "Good plan."

All kinds of cliques emerge on a big cruise. The gay guys sport better haircuts, hipper clothes, and seem to have more fun than everyone else, and professional cruisers enjoy one-upping each other about the number of times they've sailed. These people congregate before dinner in the special room reserved for the cruise line's pets, and come down for dinner more dressed up than everyone else. They are usually a little tight from indulging in the free booze upstairs. There is the exercise bunch who obviously hang out in the gym, while those of us who are occasional visitors to the sweatorium wait our turn to use the treadmills. The exhibitionist crowd wears Speedos and micro-kinis, bouncing around the jogging path with their body parts keeping time to their stride. The gambling geezers spend their time in the casino with machines that don't talk back, while the fancy crowd, who brought (or rented onboard) tuxes and gowns, participated in every formal evening. Perhaps one day we'll go on vacation and dress up, too, but for us the cruise was transportation. We positioned ourselves on fancy nights in the main street bar where we could observe the show of all the cliques marching in their little clusters on the way to outshine each other in the dining room.

The first evening, we dined with a group of eight. One couple, Pat and George Mauch, Canadians who eventually became our good friends, had cruised often, so they gave us excellent tips about the subtleties of life aboard. As our salads arrived, the powerful engines changed pitch, and I glanced out as the docks slid past the white lights of the warehouses blinking as we made our stately procession.

Then I felt the engines intensify. We were at sea! I realized we wouldn't see land for nine days...a thrilling thought.

After dinner, Tim and I stood at the railing in silence, watching the moon play over the water, listening to the slap of waves against the majestic hull of the ship. I'd brought the last of my wine with me, and I felt terribly *soigné* sipping it on deck. The ghosts of Deborah Kerr, Cary Grant, William Powell, Myrna Loy, and their glamorous contemporaries joined us. All of those romantic, dramatic cinema moments we'd seen over the years resurfaced from where they lay embedded in our minds, right next to one of my favorites, Fred Astaire and Ginger kicking it up in Paris. This was bliss.

We learned another valuable lesson on the cruise, one that we take with us to this day. One night, we had dinner with Gerry and Lorraine Singer, people we had met that afternoon. Gerry has Parkinson's disease and uses a walker, but it didn't appear to slow them down at all. Those two bright, well-read, entertaining people had traveled everywhere for over fifty years. No matter where we went on shore excursions—crawling around ruins, dining in a port, or wandering through narrow streets—we'd find Gerry and Lorraine laughing, seeing everything, as he progressed on his walker over cobblestones and gravel paths, slowly but steadily. One day, as Lorraine and I were emailing back and forth after the cruise had ended, she wrote, "Oh, Gerry says to send his love and remind you, 'Postpone nothing.'" It was profound advice from a courageous person.

POSTPONE NOTHING now sits in large type on my computer desktop and serves as our motto. We try to remember it when we are tempted to put off doing something because it's a little out of our budget or we think it too difficult, or we fall into that abyss of saying, "Maybe we're too old." If Gerry can do it, so can we!

After nine days of being enraptured by the romance of endless sea, I saw a smudge on the horizon. The whole ship was buzzing with excitement, but I was filled with ambivalence. I was so ready to get on with the rest of our life, but the cruise had been so delightful that I hated to leave our blue cocoon. The smudge grew bigger and became Tenerife, the largest of the Spanish Canary Islands, which sits off the coast of Morocco. From there we sailed through the Straits of Gibraltar, hopscotched along the coast of Spain, and made for Rome.

As we began to gather our belongings from their hiding places in our stateroom, it occurred to me that the end of a transatlantic cruise is oddly melancholy. During those long days at sea, it's easy to be so lulled by the ocean, routine, and the sheer pleasure of complete leisure that it seems it will never end. I felt sorry that it would soon be over, but quickly became intoxicated with anticipation of what was to come.

We slept badly the last night because we were so excited. When we debarked, we would begin our next seven-month adventure living home free. This would serve as the true test of Tim's hundreds of hours of meticulous planning.

A bus from the ship took us to the airport. The bustle was startling after being sequestered for so long on what had become such a familiar haven. The airport was crowded, and our flight was delayed forever. When we finally boarded, Tim, my dear claustrophobe, was jammed in a tiny seat against the side of the plane…without a window. He was so miserable that I could barely look at him. Our night grew more complicated thanks to excruciatingly slow immigration and customs lines. It was almost 1:30 a.m. when we emerged from the customs area in Istanbul, bedraggled, exhausted, and just a little scared in this utterly foreign country. As in any international airport, the travelers are separated from the greeters by a hall or corridor that ends in a sliding door. When the door opens, I always feel as if I'm on the stage when the curtain lifts: a sudden burst of light, noise, people waving and calling to their friends and family, and a bunch of fellows holding papers with the names of the customers they will chauffeur to their lodgings.

That's when the lump formed in my throat. Would we see "Martin" on one of those placards? It was so late that we were afraid the driver we had arranged would have given up waiting. We had no idea whom to contact if he wasn't there or how to get to our lodgings. Plus, our speed dial in Istanbul was empty.

Our eyes darted everywhere. Suddenly, there he was, our handsome young driver, Kubilay, who looked as happy to see us as we were to see him! He shook Tim's hand, grabbed the bags I was pulling, and led us into the fresh night air. We gasped and flexed our knees while he hoisted our luggage into the minivan. After closing the trunk, he approached us with a small golden box. Opening it, he said, "Please, have my mother's Turkish Delight. Welcome to my country."

We were touched. The chewy candy sweetened our mouths and attitudes, the first of a thousand kindnesses we would receive in the following weeks.

We raced through the night along a modern multilane highway. The lights of Istanbul twinkled on both sides of the Bosporus. Asia sat on the right and Europe on the left, with lighted bridges linking them. Finally, we roared off the highway onto a cobblestone street. The Blue Mosque loomed on a hill right above our heads, its six minarets ablaze with lights and a flock of seagulls circling it like an animated crown.

What a spectacular introduction to the city and the start of our European adventure!

Chapter 6
Turkey

The van's tires rumbled over Istanbul's cobblestones, but Kubilay parked on a silent street. The Blue Mosque squatted like a sultan above the rooftops behind us, a hatband of seagulls circling it. Two men chatted quietly in front of the convenience store across the way. We never did figure out who the customers were at 2:00 a.m. or what they wanted to buy, but the store was always open.

Kubilay excused himself and disappeared around the corner as Tim and I kneaded the travel kinks out of our bodies and inspected our street. It was lined with low stucco buildings and absolutely silent at that hour. In a moment, a young man in a waiter's outfit came bounding around the corner. He smiled in greeting and unlocked the narrow door of the small apartment building for us. Four pairs of shoes—two large, two small—were neatly arranged on a Turkish carpet outside the downstairs apartment door. A baby carriage was tucked underneath the stairs. The boy lugged our big rolling duffel bags up two stories of the narrow, circular concrete stairs without making a sound. Kubilay followed with the rest of our gear, and Tim and I stifled our panting as we trudged up the steep steps.

The boy ran back to his job down the street. Kubilay gave us a quick appliance tour and explained the three locks: one from the apartment to the tiny entry hall, one leading to the concrete stairway, and another to our private terrace. He left his card, looked over his shoulder, and called out, "If you need anything, calling me please, at that number."

Then he vanished.

We were alone in our first apartment in Europe—all three hundred square feet of it. It consisted of a tiny bedroom, Barbie-size kitchen, bathroom, and a minuscule living room now overcrowded with luggage. All the appliances, furniture, and windows were brand new; there was even a dishwasher! The place was a marvel of efficiency. With our new lifestyle, our general approach to accommodations is that the less time we plan to spend in an apartment, the less important the layout and comfort of it becomes. For a stay of a month or more, we are willing to cough up a bit more dough for a larger place, but for a stay like this, for just a week, anything quiet and clean with a reasonably comfortable bed will do.

We used an iPhone flashlight app to negotiate the tricky lock on the door leading outside. The huge terrace featured ugly plastic chairs, a clothesline, and ample evidence of seagull occupation, but it was decorated with views of the Blue Mosque on one side and the Sea of Marmara on the other. Who cared about furniture?

As we stepped out, we gasped in unison at the vista before us, turned to look in all directions, and then indulged in our personal version of that silent dance football players perform when they've reached the end zone. Tim had outdone himself. I loved seeing his triumphant smile.

"Oh God," I moaned. "Look at that, honey." A full moon lit up the sky behind the mosque, outlining the six magnificent minarets.

"Look at the ships," Tim whispered. The running lights of mega tankers, their towering loads pushing them low in the water, blazed as they made their stately progress to the sea. Lacy electric necklaces lit up the graceful bridges, which spanned the Bosporus. "And there is Asia," he continued, pointing at the twinkling lights on the other side.

We shared a long embrace and a kiss. "Tim," I said, "this is worth all of the hassle, the stress, the anxiety. It's just exactly what we hoped for. Thank you!"

Exhaustion pulled us back into the apartment. We flung ourselves into bed without unpacking. Three hours later, we jerked to attention, alarmed as the muezzins' voices collided from speakers in the street near us, calling everyone to morning prayers. One voice came from a distance, then another closer, followed by many more, until we were surrounded by the sound. The Muslim *Ṣalāt*, calls to prayer, were electrifying, irresistible, and beautiful. We lay back and listened. The voices had a nasal quality, and although each was singing a different tune, they created a harmonious sound in a minor key so foreign to our ears. It was thrilling, exotic, and oddly comforting. Soon their five-times-a-day performance would seem normal as their voices blared from the minarets on the mosques. Eventually, we hardly noticed them.

We dozed for a while and rose to start the day-one routine we had established in Buenos Aires. Tim hurried down to the little market on the corner (it seems it was never closed) to get coffee and breakfast basics and to reconnoiter their wares while I inspected our new digs. The views were even more stunning in the daytime. In one direction, the sea sparkled beyond ancient red-tiled rooftops. In the other, the sinuous golden onion-shaped top of the Blue Mosque gleamed in the sun. The apartment was immaculate and the Internet worked perfectly, fulfilling two of our major requirements.

Only the bathroom presented a challenge. I had been too tired to notice the night before, but it was one of those curtain-less jobs, not uncommon in Europe, in which the entire room is the shower. The bather must remove everything from the countertop, secure the toilet paper in a safe location, and throw his or her garments out the bathroom door into the living room. After someone enjoys a shower, the entire room, especially the floor, had to be dried with a large squeegee provided by management. The idea was that the naked, shivering bather would shove the water into a drain in the middle of the floor. Not fun. Every morning, we indulged in subtle jockeying about who would be first in. The last one out would dance with the squeegee.

Soon we were strolling up the tree-lined street toward the Blue Mosque. Small shops opened in the bright morning light, scarf-covered mothers herded their children to school, and outdoor cafés filled with Turkish men drinking tea, smoking, and chatting. The low brick buildings reminded us of the East Village in New York, but with a colorful twist. Jewel-toned textiles were everywhere. Rugs, coats, jackets, sunshades, and furniture were bathed in vibrant shades of red, ochre, blue, and green. We sniffed the rich aromas of coffee, baking pastry, and meats searing over charcoal. Some of the savory whiffs came from the apartments, but more from the small restaurants and cafés. Boys with brass trays full of steaming pots, richly decorated tea glasses, and plates heaped with pastries darted through the streets, delivering breakfast to the shopkeepers. It was a busy scene, and everyone seemed to be in a great mood. People laughed and chatted as if they had all day to entertain each other. As it turned out, it was true.

Most of the Turkish people we met would drop everything to engage in lively conversations with us about anything from the weather to the sad state of American politics. We Americans may associate Turkey with its ancient sites, turquoise beaches, textiles, spices, minarets, and palaces, but its true treasure is the people. They are sweet, clever, accommodating, and hilarious. Someone cracked us up at least once a day, even when we didn't understand each other very well. Language is no problem when everyone tries hard to communicate.

We entered the magnificent open space that links the Blue Mosque to the Hagia Sophia, the monumental Orthodox patriarchal church, now a museum, and finally ends at Topkapi Palace, the primary residence of Ottoman sultans for four hundred years. All three structures sit upon a huge elevated flat plaza, which gives them the commanding position great monuments deserve. "Oh God, Tim, you've told me for so long that I would love this place, but I had no idea how magnificent it is," I said as I spun around, trying to take it all in.

"So glad you like it," he beamed. Presenting a magnificent city to someone you love is one of life's great pleasures, the best gift imaginable. "And I'm not surprised at all!"

When we reached the Blue Mosque entrance, silent women wrapped a floor-length piece of fabric around my waist and closed it with Velcro tabs. Every non-Muslim woman in the mosque wore a blue skirt. I heard each person who stepped inside involuntarily make a sound—a gasp, a sigh, a small "wow." It was impossible not to be impressed with the dome that soared hundreds of feet into the sky, covered in millions of mosaic tiles. Stained-glass windows cast an otherworldly light over the enormous space, and a golden altar gleamed on one side. Smaller domes surrounded the larger one, and people at prayer knelt where we were not allowed to walk. The space was carpeted in Chinese red with a blue floral design, and huge lighted candelabra had been brought down to human level. The colors and light were ravishing. I was in utter awe.

"So, what do you think?" Tim whispered with grin. He knew I was too moved to speak…a miracle in itself.

I said nothing. I couldn't.

After such a moving experience, naturally we were starved. We chose a small, attractive restaurant we had noticed that morning on our way to the mosque. We were seated quickly, and comfortable chairs, colorful crisp linens, and beautiful pottery set the stage for one of the best meals I can remember. Turkish food, like most Mediterranean fare, is heavy on olive oil, lamb, fish, nuts, and yogurt. All of those ingredients appeared on our table, artfully prepared and graciously served. I loved the first course of hot yogurt soup with dried mint and lemon, but the star of the meal was the dessert: walnut-stuffed figs poached in clove syrup! The waiter, the owner, and his wife, the chef, entertained us with wonderful tales and snappy patter. Fortified and happy, we set off for more discoveries.

When we arrived at the famous Topkapi Palace that afternoon, we ran into a long, slow-moving ticket line. That put us off immediately. Call us impatient, but waiting is agony for us, and the microscopic inspection of every site does not interest us too much. We are really not very good tourists. While we appreciate the history of the places we visit and study before we are on the ground to see them, we just aren't the kind who must read every plaque and pore over each item or painting in a museum. We'd rather appreciate the monument or museum as a whole, then dip into the things that are of interest to us. At our age, we also have to take into consideration our stamina. That and the fact that, whether we like it or not, our energy and our time on the planet are finite. While we discussed our options, an enterprising guide, who twinkled with practiced enthusiasm, told us that he would help us skip the line and see the highlights of the palace in one hour. Just our style.

Tim and the man negotiated a price that wasn't too outrageous. "How many people will be on the tour?" he asked.

"Eight."

Tim looked around. No one there but us. "Where are they?"

"Stand right under that tree, and I'll go get them," the fellow replied.

We watched as he walked along the queue of tourists shuffling slowly along. Within five minutes, he recruited another six people, scooted into a side door of the ticket booth where he procured eight passes, and led us on our way. Evidently there were other people who favored an overview like us! Impressed by his efficiency, we were even more delighted with his tour. He was well informed, articulate, and entertaining. We saw the highlights, drank in the stunning views of Istanbul and the Golden Horn, marveled at the crown jewels, and then we were back "home" enjoying a cocktail in our plastic terrace chairs before sunset.

* * *

We loved every minute of Istanbul. In contrast to our experience in Buenos Aires, we were having the time of our lives and feeling very grateful that our home-free adventure was all we had hoped for. Well, we loved almost every minute, except one cold, spluttery day when we decided to find the ancient Spice Market. We inspected our map and knew it wasn't too far to walk, so even though it was late afternoon, we decided to make the trek. After a few blocks, though, we realized we had gone astray. The street wasn't even on our map, so we asked a shopkeeper lounging in his doorway to set us straight. He pointed in the opposite direction, and we followed his instructions. This happened several more times. The last person we asked assured us that we were just moments away from our goal. Instead, we became more confused with each encounter.

The splutter grew thicker. Just when the skies opened, we realized we had walked much too far to scurry home for cover. There was no possibility of catching one of the taxis whizzing by, loaded up as they were with bedraggled people escaping the monsoon. Meanwhile, since the bus system was a mystery to us, there was no hope there. In moments, we were soaked up to our knees and as lost as we have ever been.

After forty-five minutes walking in our search for the bazaar, we were parched, wet, exhausted, and very irritated. We ducked into a little restaurant for shelter and ordered drinks. The place reeked of steaminess and wet clothes and hair. When the rain finally let up, we paid the waitress and asked for directions to the Blue Mosque, our landmark for our way home. She was a little salty since we hadn't ordered food, and brusquely pointed over our shoulders. "Right there," she said.

We stepped outside, annoyed. "I know she's lying," I said angrily. "We couldn't possibly be that close to home. We've walked miles!"

Tim clutched our damp map, turning it this way and that, trying to make sense of it. "Of course not," he mumbled. "That would mean we've been sloshing around in a circle."

But when we reached the corner, we looked up to see those damned seagulls flying in their endless circle around the golden spire! The waitress hadn't let us down. We staggered down the street, laughing like lunatics at our grumpiness. (Some guy waiting for customers in his shop door said, not unkindly, "Have you been dranking?" To this day when one of us has a laughing fit the other asks, "Have you been dranking?") Five minutes later, we stood in our apartment, wringing out our jeans. We still haven't figured out how we managed it.

We finally found the Spice Market the next day. For this foodie, it felt like Mecca. Just outside the market under a colorful tent is an enormous plant nursery. The scent of fresh herbs and edible flowers sweetened the air, and then we turned the corner into the vast hall of the market itself. The combined fragrances—saffron, curry, mustard, vanilla, and dates—swirled up into the vast arched ceiling as hundreds of people filled the wide corridors, their chatter and the vendors' calls rising and falling like a tide. Ground spices were displayed in great piles in each merchant's stall, and as we browsed it was difficult to be content with only photos to take away.

Had we succumbed to our desires and taken some along, our clothes would have been forever permeated with spicy reminders of that afternoon.

We also found the Grand Bazaar, where four thousand stalls house an abundance of fabulous clothes, jewelry, food, textiles, and treasures. That market is even more elaborate and exotic, its ceilings and walls completely covered in exquisite tiles, enormous flags hanging from its train-station-size ceilings. The colors, textures, and intensity of the crowd were breathtaking. So abundant were the wares that we again walked away empty-handed. Two Librans are hopeless and helpless when presented with that many decisions.

Istanbul's wondrous delights were capped by the Hagia Sophia, rising at the other end of the mall from the Blue Mosque. It presents the perfect synthesis of the Ottoman and Byzantine empires under one enormous dome. An Eastern Orthodox cathedral built in AD 537, it was briefly a Roman Catholic cathedral from 1204–1261 and became a mosque in 1453 after the Turks conquered Constantinople. In 1935 it became a museum. It would be impossible to describe the profound effect of the colossal building. We gaped, openmouthed, at its marble walls and magnificent dome, with forty windows below it letting the sunshine stream into the huge expanse. It has withstood time and earthquakes and has been fascinating art historians, architects, and engineers through the centuries.

Grandeur always makes us hungry, so we went to look for lunch. Walking down from the mesa of architectural treasures, we found ourselves in Akbiyik Caddesi, the tourist street, which runs through the middle of the old section of town, anchored by the Four Seasons Hotel at the more refined end. The hotel was very discreetly marked and guarded by gentlemen who did not invite a casual inspection by peasants like ourselves. At the other end stood the neighborhood where real people like the Martins spend their nights in Istanbul. Sidewalk cafés of every description jammed the intervening blocks, filled by day with German, American, Asian, Scandinavian, and other tourists of all ages. Later in the evening, raucous young people enjoyed beer from enormous self-serve canisters, laughing and puffing away on colorful hookahs, water pipes, which are provided at every table. Usually, Tim and I are satisfied with being mature, and we consider ourselves fortunate to have negotiated life's pitfalls and come out whole at the end. In Istanbul, however, we wished we could plop down, order a beer tube, and grab a hookah while laughing and swapping stories with twenty-five-year-olds. I'm sure we would have enjoyed it for at least ten minutes or so.

Instead, we settled in for lunch in a typical spot, an indoor/outdoor bistro with bright umbrellas and small tables. They all served kebabs, rice, eggplant/tomato purée, pillowy pita, and honey-laden fruit and pastry desserts. We were fascinated to see people puffing away on flavored tobacco filtered through the water in the container!

Several courses later we ambled down toward the water. Small shops line the streets in the old section of Istanbul, and their owners hang out in front, offering their wares with the most ingenious come-ons they can muster. One rug guy said to me, "Oh, come on, just give me your money," while a man on a street where we walked every day finally said, "Good morning, I've been waiting for you!" They're persistent and good-natured, which helps them sell a lot of gorgeous rugs to the tourists. Since we are permanently on the road, we do not collect anything except photos and memories, but we certainly enjoyed fondling the merchandise and having great fun with the enterprising shopkeepers. Even people who don't own stores find ways to relieve tourists of their money, especially around the big attractions. I saw one fellow sitting on a stool selling a stack of satin hats. He was dressed in full sultan regalia, looking completely authentic, except for the cell phone stuck to his ear. Moments like that were exactly what made us want to be home free! In that instant the fellow with the hats became indelibly part of our lives, a person we will remember forever. It's those little impressions that add up to a world full of magic.

✳ ✳ ✳

Every day as we left our house, we passed a small tour office. We began a nodding acquaintance with Remzi, the slender, balding owner who seemed to be there all the time, chatting with people who stopped in to have a glass of tea with him. Remzi spoke good English and knew everything about having a good time in Turkey. His assistant was a big, smiling bearded fellow who wore the same T-shirt every day. One afternoon as we perused photos of Turkey's Turquoise Coast in his window display, Remzi invited us in for tea. An hour later, we knew the names of his grandchildren, in what part of Chicago his brother lived, and his thoughts on the coming U.S. presidential election. One other thing: we booked a very expensive daylong boat tour along the Bosporus. The boat tour proved pleasant enough, but not nearly as entertaining as Remzi himself, and our burgeoning friendship with him made the expense worthwhile. We still correspond, and hope to return to buy a four-day sailboat tour of that Turquoise Coast. "Just give me a call and it will all be arranged perfectly," he said the day we left. I believed him.

We swung into our time-to-move hustle on our last day in Istanbul. We still wanted to see several sights in the city, and we'd begun staging our belongings for an early flight the next day to Izmir, in the heart of Turkey. Tim left the apartment and walked out onto the terrace, where he watched an enormous cruise ship plow its way toward the ocean. I'm always the last one to be ready and I hate making anyone wait, so I quickly grabbed my purse and pulled the apartment door closed behind me. "All set," I said. "Where shall we have lunch?"

"Let's go back to that terrific place where we had that yogurt soup," he replied. "I'll be right with you." He stepped into the hallway and grasped the knob of the apartment door. "Looks like you've already locked it," he said. "Let me have the keys, please. I need to get my other glasses."

"I don't have the keys." I was slightly alarmed.

His brow wrinkled. "How did you lock the door without the key?"

"I just pulled it shut and it must have locked itself," I said defensively.

"Oh brother." Turning slowly, he gripped the handle of the door that opened to the stairway. It was locked, too. We hadn't left the apartment all day. "Why in the world did you pull it shut? I had just stepped outside. I wasn't ready to go yet," he said rather sharply.

I shot back, "Well, excuse me, mister, but when you went outside and had your bag with you, I assumed you were ready to leave, and that you had the keys with you as always."

We walked away from the doors in chilly silence to review our options. We stood on a third-floor terrace at noon with little shelter, about half an inch of water in a plastic bottle, and no way to get into our apartment or leave the building. We sat down in the plastic chairs, which we'd pushed into the sliver of shade offered by the building. "Look," I said. "I have my iPhone and it's still connected to Wi-Fi, so I can send the owner an email and ask him to help us."

"Good idea." Now calm, he looked slightly apologetic for having snarled at me.

I sent the email and we waited. And waited. No reply. We considered yelling down to the store to get help, but we knew we couldn't explain ourselves to the Turkish-speaking fellow who was on duty. Besides, it would be embarrassing to shout our stupidity from the rooftops, so we waited some more. After sitting in silence for about fifteen minutes, inching our chairs ever closer to the wall to escape the hot sun, Tim said, "Hey, you have Skype on your phone. Try calling him."

The owner answered immediately. I explained our problem and he said he'd send Kubilay and a locksmith as soon as possible. We offered to pay for the mistake, but he said he wouldn't hear of it. He told us it had happened before, which eased our humiliation. Somewhat.

We shared the few sips of water as the sliver of shade disappeared completely. I tried to remember if I'd slapped on sunscreen after I finished swabbing down the bathroom floor. Then we heard voices in the stairwell. The locksmith opened both doors. He and Kubilay, who resisted teasing us too much, were gone in minutes. Relieved, we walked back into the apartment to get Tim's glasses and guzzle water.

I was rinsing out my glass when I heard Tim curse in the other room. "What is it?" I asked.

He looked at me sheepishly. "I want to apologize. I feel like such a jerk. Look what I found in my bag." The apartment keys dangled from his finger.

We collapsed in laughter. "I will never tell a soul," I told him. And I kept my promise. Until now.

The next morning, while I was busy saying farewell to our local pals, Tim called to me from the famous balcony. He pointed to Kubilay, who was waiting in the car, and I scurried back to leave. Within moments, we headed for the airport for our trip to Kusadasi, a resort town on the Aegean Sea. It sat just a few miles from Ephesus, home of the Temple of Artemis, one of the Seven Wonders of the

Ancient World. Tim, who remembers everything, announced to me during a discussion the night before that Ephesus was originally situated on the water, but through the ages, it "moved" inland as the adjoining river slowly silted up the harbor.

Thus began our second week in Turkey, which we spent on the road, a departure from our normal plan. There were several antiquities Tim wanted me to see, and we found hotels more practical than rental apartments for short stays of only a couple days. The magnificent Temple of Apollo at Didim sat on our agenda, too, followed a few days of playing by the Aegean in Marmaris. We thought that would send us to our next stop, Paris, tanned and rested.

After our short flight to Izmir, we set out for Kusadasi.

"Tim, look at this," I exclaimed, just as he dodged a cart pulled by a pony and swerved expertly to avoid a tourist-packed bus heading straight for us. "The countryside reminds me of Central California!" I was fiddling with Victoria, our GPS companion who had made the trip with us and was busily downloading data so she could make her Turkish debut. We were in love with Victoria, since she never said "recalculating," but simply changed course when we made an error, instructing us calmly about how to repair the damage and reach our destination.

Family farms dotted the low rolling hills, and the beige dried grass and scrubby trees felt familiar. A low mountain range ran along the right side of the valley and another on the left, with a verdant bowl of fertile land cradled between them. Soon, we turned toward the foothills and began to climb. The delight and heart-lifting thrill of cresting a hill, then suddenly encountering the sea—any sea—makes me catch my breath every time I see it stretching toward the horizon. Even after decades of living near the Pacific in California, the surprise still staggers me.

I exclaimed in pleasure at the sights, but poor Tim didn't dare glance while he had a steering wheel in his hands. I tried hard to stifle my ecstatic comments because it wasn't fair that he had to miss them, but sometimes, I couldn't help myself. He's very gracious about it most of the time, but I know he must get tired of being the chauffeur. The fact is that Tim is a better driver than I am, especially since a vision problem affects my distance judgment. I'm the better navigator because I know how to coax Victoria into doing her job. So with the three of us doing our jobs, we conquered all kinds of traffic woes without a scratch.

We pulled over so he could look down on Kusadasi, which commands a curvaceous turquoise bay. The coastal road is crammed with condominiums, hotels, and restaurants, and dotted with hulking cruise ships snuggled up to its docks. Rug merchants, kitschy tourist shops, convenience stores, and marinas full of gorgeous, expensive yachts punctuate the town. As we crawled along the road, I craned to see the hotel while Victoria urged us to drive straight ahead. Tim stayed busy trying to avoid killing tourists, who flip-flopped their way back from the beach while he also contended with cars, buses, and bicycles that crammed the street.

"Watch out for the kid on the bike!" I cried.

Tim scowled at my backseat driving. "Please do NOT do that," he retorted. "You scare me to death when you do that! I saw him."

I bit my tongue.

Of course, fifty feet later, while stuck behind a barricade, having trouble breaking back into the traffic, he groused, "Why didn't you say something about the right lane closing ahead?"

I sighed. Constant travel requires partners to hang on tight to their civility, and I was not about to risk one of us finding the closest airport for an unplanned departure!

Near the very end of that long, congested avenue, we found our target, the Caravanserail Hotel, a big, square, turreted affair built in 1618 by an Ottoman sultan to serve passing pashas and their entourages. Completely different from the modern buildings on the boulevard, it leads the way into the old town's thriving bazaar.

Tim had stayed at the hotel many years before. He took great pleasure in watching my enthusiastic reaction to the vast courtyard, where dinner tables were being set by people in Turkish national dress. Two men carefully removed individual yellowed leaves from the small trees, little tables and chairs sat on wide verandas on the second floor, and blooming bougainvillea vines tumbled down the ancient walls. Perfection. Gorgeous Turkish carpets were draped over the walls from the balconies, adding luxurious softness and jewel-like colors to the picture. A room in this sultan's palace was ours to enjoy, well, at least for three days!

As we checked in, Ali, the owner, introduced himself. Tim replied, "I thought I recognized you! I stayed here ten years ago during the big rainstorm."

Ali gave Tim a long look and said, "Ah, yes, I remember you, too. It was the worst night of my life! I'm delighted that you returned after such an experience."

Later, when we were settled on our veranda overlooking the courtyard, Tim brought me a glass of the wine we'd bought along the way. "So, tell me about the big storm when you were last here," I said.

He chuckled. "Well, Ali had draped the courtyard with canvas awnings to keep it cool during the day, and that night the place was filled with tourists from the cruise ships. Several hundred people were enjoying a big nightclub show and banquet. We were having a great time when it began to rain, slowly at first and then hard—the kind of sudden deluge like that one in Istanbul. Because everyone was watching the belly dancers and jugglers, no one noticed that the awnings were bulging with water. BLAM!" He hit the table for emphasis. "The first one broke, followed instantly by the rest.

The place was flooded—legs of lamb on skewers and the guys who had been shaving off portions of them, musical instruments, tables, cutlery, waiters, and guests all gussied up for an evening out were soaked and floating in three feet of water."

By now, he was laughing. "I didn't get caught because I had noticed what was happening seconds before all hell broke loose, and I beat it for the stairs. Ali came upstairs hours later and brought sandwiches for all the guests, because nobody got dinner that night. I remember commiserating with him the next morning and he said, 'Well, no one was hurt and I needed to replace those chairs anyway.' I think his attitude pretty much sums up the Turkish personality, don't you? Maybe it has to do with their being such an ancient civilization. They have learned not to sweat the small stuff and just get on with it. Kinda like us, huh?"

I laughed. It was true. We were learning not to sweat the small stuff.

That night we dined by candlelight in the courtyard, a mysterious, romantic space where spice traders once stopped. They secured their animals there, too, to protect them from harm. Our room, up a flight of stone stairs lined with enormous pots of bright geraniums, was small but decorated with mosaic tile and high ceilings capped with elaborate molding. We tried to imagine how many thousands of tenants the space had housed in five hundred years and wished we could hear their stories. A DoubleTree Inn this was not! And we were so grateful for it.

* * *

In Kusadasi, colossal ships dock daily and disgorge tourists who are herded into buses and ferried a few miles inland to Ephesus. They tromp around the ancient ruins, furiously snap photos of each other declaiming in the ancient theater or perched triumphantly, and strike poses on long-empty sarcophagi. The next day, we did exactly the same things—minus the tour bus and umbrella-wielding guide—and we tried to tread a bit more lightly on such hallowed spaces.

Ephesus, an ancient Greek city, had a population of over 250,000 in the first century BC, during the Roman period. It was one of the largest cities in the Mediterranean world. It is a glorious World Heritage Site, but, we found it difficult to become emotionally engaged because thousands of elbows and shoulders poked at us, and too many bodies blocked the views of the ancient ruins. Even so, we felt privileged to stand where the Ephesians received St. Paul's letter, and to sit on the stone seats of the theater where twenty-four thousand people saw plays and performances two millennia ago in what is believed to be the largest outdoor theater in the ancient world.

Next, we visited the colossal Library of Celsus, a two-story architectural miracle. The library once held twelve thousand scrolls and was built to face the east, so that the reading rooms could make the optimal use of the morning light. We jockeyed our way past throngs of tourists to inspect wonderfully reconstructed shops and homes along the streets. The archaeologists provided informative plaques about the buildings' former inhabitants, which we found fascinating. Cleopatra's sister lived in one and was dispatched by an assassin at that very spot.

We didn't stay long because black, threatening clouds moved in quickly. Lord knows we'd learned about Turkey's wild weather in Istanbul and through Tim's previous experiences here. We fled to our sultan's sanctuary for cool drinks on the veranda. The rain hadn't followed us home, so as we sat chatting in the afternoon sun as two Australian gents walked up the wide stone staircase, following porters who were horsing their bags. Soon, we were swapping stories and drinks, and making plans to share a table for the next evening's gala tourist event at the hotel.

Our amusing cocktail hour evolved into a jolly evening of dinner and lively conversation. Hugh, an attorney, and Mike, who spent his career in the Australian foreign service, were partners in an antiques business in Melbourne. They spent part of each year combing the globe for inventory.

The next night, we relished dinner and a deliciously touristy performance featuring belly dancers, tumblers, imitation whirling dervishes, and showgirls. That was topped off by a long chat on our carpet-strewn terrace, while a massive moon hung low, lighting up the balustrades of the noble old hotel. Mike's stories of living in India and other exotic locales during his career held us in rapt attention. He told us about being in Berlin when the Wall came down. He witnessed family members weeping and embracing after decades of living blocks away from one another but never being allowed to cross the barrier. His eyes grew moist when he spoke of the experience. All of us were affected by his story, and we discovered that none of us ever expected the Wall to come down in our lifetimes. It was amazing to hear his firsthand experience, and we were delighted to have some good conversation. His tale of renting a boat to be in the middle of the Ganges at dawn when the faithful come by the thousands to bathe in the holy river touched my heart. Mike said it had been a spiritual awakening for him.

Later, as our pillow talk drifted to the subject of Mike's stories, Tim said, "Gee whiz, I just don't get what's so thrilling about getting up before dawn, hiring some leaky boat from a guy you don't know anything about, and then watching a bunch of starving people splash around in a river."

My husband is a lovely man, but perhaps his soul could use a little work.

★ ★ ★

After a morning of cruising the tourist shops ("Del Boy, the Famous Genuine Fake Watch Store" won the Martins' Most Hilarious award with extra credit for honesty), I parked myself at a little table on the wide stone veranda outside our room. I was determined to stay at my computer until I completed a story about our transatlantic cruise for my blog. I'd reached my favorite part—the food, of course—when I heard a familiar click. After a brief pause, I heard another click, and then a low chuckle. I glanced over the second-floor railing, draped in a gorgeous silk Turkish carpet we had been admiring all afternoon. Ali, the hotel owner, and another man sat under the broad-leafed trees, playing backgammon so fast that I could hardly see their hands move.

Let me explain: I love backgammon. So after a brief struggle with my work ethic (which I won), I marched down the broad stone steps to the table. I explained that I was an enthusiastic backgammon player and asked if I could watch the match. They politely agreed and beckoned for me to sit with them. The next forty-five minutes were outrageously entertaining. Both men were experts, and it was evident they had played hundreds of games together during their long friendship. They passed the smallest pair of dice I had ever seen back and forth at blinding speed, making savvy, dangerous moves I never would have tried. Or even considered. We didn't chat at all, but I think they loved having a tall blond enthusiastic American lady as an audience, because they played more and more aggressively. They seldom spoke between themselves but smiled when one or the other made a particularly delicious or sometimes a bad move. They laughed aloud when a stroke of luck changed the game entirely.

Finally, my guilty conscience propelled me to traipse back

upstairs to my task. A few minutes later, I was surprised to see the owner walking across the terrace toward me. I saw a board under his arm. *Oh, my God*, I thought, alarmed. *He wants me to play backgammon with him and I will be humiliated.*

I have played the game for decades and have had the good fortune of winning often. However, he played on an entirely different level. He held out the board. "This is a gift from the hotel. Such a devoted player deserves a proper board."

I was speechless. I told him that it was one of the nicest surprises and certainly the most charming gift I could imagine. Although we travel light, the backgammon board from the Caravanserail Hotel earned its place in our luggage...no matter what! His unexpected thoughtfulness reinforced our love of the Turkish people and appreciation of their generosity to visitors.

Every day as we came and went through the main courtyard, we noticed a store tucked under the building. Unlike its competitors in the bazaar, where goods were piled high and presided over by assertive salesmen who noisily competed for tourists' attention, Tayfun Kaya's store was discreet and refined. The rugs that gave the hotel such a luxurious feel belonged to him. They were available, along with expensive, tasteful jewelry. We chatted with him several times and found him to be sophisticated, sincere, and an excellent English speaker.

One day as we passed by, he was demonstrating how silkworms create their sought-after product to a group of tourists. The larvae were bobbing in a water trough that was about waist high, and a contraption above it moved back and forth as the operator pushed a lever with his foot, pulling the silk from the larvae and winding it onto a spindle. It was fascinating to see the basic task that precedes the weaving process of the gorgeous silk rugs we saw in the more upscale rug stores. After his presentation, we talked with Tayfun about returning to Kusadasi for a longer stay. We mentioned that the rental opportunities we saw online in Kusadasi seemed to be overpriced, and we didn't know the neighborhoods or realities of living there for a time. "Come with me, my friends," he boomed. "Step into my office and let's see what we can do."

First, he showed us photos of his family, two drop-dead-gorgeous teenage girls and a wife who looked like a New York model.

Next, he tapped away on his computer and found a Turkish website presenting excellent apartments and condominiums at half the price of the same sites on English-language sites. He offered to help us find one when we return. We were delighted to learn about that, and it means that one day, we will take him up on his kind offer. Turkish people were moving up fast on our favorite people list.

The next day, as we were leaving the hotel, he walked with us toward the lobby. "Gosh, Tayfun, I feel guilty about taking so much of your time," I said. "I wish we could buy a rug from you, but you know we don't even own a floor to put it on."

He stopped in mid-stride and laughed. "Are you kidding? I wouldn't sell you one of these rugs. They're strictly for the tourists."

We giggled at his joke halfway to Didim, site of the Temple of Apollo, the fourth largest ancient Greek sanctuary and the spot where the Oracle of Apollo dispensed her wisdom. The ruins sit incongruously in the middle of a modern neighborhood and are surprisingly unsought by tourists, perhaps because they're off the beaten track. The bases of the one hundred twenty-two carved columns and soaring entryway were ours to enjoy in peace on that beautiful spring afternoon. Unlike Ephesus, there were no other tourists at the site.

The ancient Greeks situated their temple on top of an impressive hill so their enemies would see the evidence of the Greeks' mastery over their part of the world. I touched the intricate designs and imagined the person who chiseled them into the stone, never dreaming that his work would be intimately admired thousands of years later. We sat on the very spot where the oracle predicted the future. What a thrill! Our willingness to get off the tourist track rewarded us with a personal connection with history.

I wish the goddess's prophetic powers could have saved us from our next hotel, but it was not meant to be. Historical beauty and lofty thoughts were not enough to compensate for the terrible night we spent in Didim. It seems we failed to read the fine print about both the town and the hotel, a lesson that will remain with us always.

What we thought would be a couple of nights in a glamorous oceanfront resort turned out to be a one-night stand in a sleazy, ill-furnished joint in a town comprising hundreds of substandard, concrete condominium complexes with the charm of military bunkers. The sole purpose? For freezing Europeans to thaw themselves on a budget. Our "all-inclusive" hotel turned out not to include incidentals like towels, sheets, or air conditioning. Every amenity, even basics, carried an extra charge. Cash, if you please. All of this was listed behind a tiny toggle on their website, which unfortunately we missed in our research. To make matters worse, the management was fond of piping loud Euro-trash music—the last straw for a woman who wears two pairs of earplugs and an eye mask to bed. By the time we were ready to leave, the young man whom we summoned with each discovery looked ready to do us bodily harm. Needless to say, the feeling was mutual.

We scurried away a day early. Even the grandeur of Apollo couldn't compel us to endure another night of torture.

Besides, we were anxious to get to Marmaris, a magical place Tim had touted since we first rekindled our romantic flame.

"Honey, Marmaris is the perfect place for us to relax for a few days before we move on to Paris. I'm telling you, that bay is something. Two mountain ranges come together at the Aegean and it's spectacular..." Tim raved at every mention of the place.

"I'm crazy about the hotel," he gushed. "It's magnificent—a beautiful setting where the trees come down to the water, lovely rooms, great food and service, and *cheap*! That's a good thing because we know Paris is going to cost like hell. We'll have a wonderful time! We can read and swim and be pampered. It's quiet and peaceful. The Israelis used to come here, so you know everything will be first class. The food is fantastic. You're gonna *love* it."

Even though I had heard it all before—Tim couldn't help but repeat himself, he was so excited about this place—I responded with enthusiasm each time and pretended it was the first time he'd told me about it. After all, it did sound great—especially after our last accommodations.

The building and setting were as advertised. Gorgeous. A snappy uniformed bellman took our luggage, the desk clerks were efficient and helpful, and the enormous lobby and bar impressively designed and populated with inviting furniture groupings. This was going to be great!

Mr. Uniform drove us down a tree-lined cobblestone path in a golf cart, and we admired cute four-plexes with balconies and attractive façades. When we entered our room, we looked right past our little balcony to the sea and mountains beyond the bay. Perfection. Tim was elated with his excellent choice.

As we settled on our balcony, gleefully making photos of our unobstructed view, I heard a boom, then a boom-boom, then a chukka-chukka-boom. The sound settled into a solid boom-chukka-boom-chukka-boom-boom-boom. The Euro-trash music had followed us! It became our constant companion for four very long days.

It seems that in Tim's absence, the Israelis had been replaced with the Russians, for whom it was a quick, cheap three-hour flight from Moscow. Over-muscled KGB types with shaved heads and tattooed biceps dragged their spouses and gaggles of children south for a week at the beach. Everyone wore resort clothes right out of a nineties disco movie; it was a sea of double-knit polyester and enormous sunglasses. They occupied every inch of public space, sprawling in the lobby, by the pool on every available surface, and encouraging their children to exercise their bodies and vocal cords as much as possible. Since food and booze were part of the all-inclusive package, imbibing began early and continued into the small hours, always accompanied by the much-appreciated boom-chukka-boom-boom soundtrack.

I'm not sure that the small print would have saved us in this instance. However, the car did. We fled the scene for most of the day, dined elsewhere, and used our rattling air conditioner at night to tune out the boom-chukka-chukka-boom. We did catch some sun, great views, and a delightful seafood dinner—for an extra charge, of course. It was served on a floating pier at sunset, far from the rhythm section. But in this case, the extra charges were worth every penny.

That last evening provided a fitting farewell to Turkey. During dinner, we raised our glasses to the new friends we had made and the archaeological wonders we had seen. Turkey had been such a rich experience for us and I remember thinking that if the rest of our journeys could be that much fun and that interesting, rainstorms and locked doors notwithstanding, I would never doubt our decision to live home free.

However, to this day, the boom-chukka-chukka-boom sound makes me smile. After all, embracing and conquering challenges were what we had longed for!

Chapter 7
Paris

The woman across the way reached through her polished French doors to trim the bright red geraniums in her wrought-iron window box. Below the box, a froth of blue and white blossoms drifted down three stories to the pavement. Her stylish stone town house looked like something in *Architectural Digest*. The owner was equally picture-perfect. A string of pearls set off her pale beige cashmere sweater set, which matched the color of her perfectly coifed hair.

I hated her.

Her sin? She lived in Paris full time, while I would be here for just one month.

As I watched her, the elevator across the hall in our three-story building opened and I let Tim into the apartment. He was grinning and chuckling. "What's so funny?" I asked.

"Well, I've seen just about everything now, and I need to go clothes shopping."

"What are you talking about?" Tim's thought process is a little hard to follow because his brain works so much faster than most people's. I chalk it up to being part of his charm...most of the time.

"I went down to the corner just to get the lay of the land, and there, sitting on a bench in the sun, was a great big black guy wearing a long gold caftan and matching fez."

"So? I've seen lots of African men in outfits like that," I replied.

"I bet none of them were reading something so conservative as the *Wall Street Journal*. It just struck me as so Parisian!"

As the bizarreness of this juxtaposition—such a flashily dressed man reading such a buttoned-up newspaper—dawned on me, we dissolved into laughter. When we recovered, he repeated, "I've gotta go shopping. I'm much too tame for this burg. Anything goes in Paris."

Later, we found a man's pastel floral scarf. When Tim wore that scarf thrown casually around his neck, his beret from a previous visit, and his Viva La Resistance T-shirt, he looked hilariously French.

✷ ✷ ✷

When we had arrived in Paris the day before, and Andie, the apartment owner, opened the door to greet us, we knew right away that we were going to be happy. She was an ebullient, pretty, pint-size Brooklynite who owned an English language school and had lived in Paris for thirty-five years. Generous, amusing, and energetic, she took wonderful care of us. We could tell instantly that she was destined to become our very good friend.

Our one-bedroom apartment was small but very clean and well decorated. It possessed an excellent Internet connection (hurrah!) and big windows that splashed the main room and open kitchen with light. Across the street, next to the elegant cashmere lady's gorgeous establishment, stood a classic French three-story house with a jarringly modern twist. Andie told us that some big-name avant-garde architect had persuaded the owners to make a statement by slapping a glass box around the whole structure. Strange, but wonderful. We puzzled over the designer's intention every day, and nosily watched the occupants' coming and goings inside from the safety of our apartment across the street. A movie-star good-looking French family with big cars inhabited the apartment, which they kept surprisingly messy. Once more, we found ourselves viewing other people's lives, just as we had in Buenos Aires.

We lived in the fifteenth arrondissement, a homey neighborhood that offered just what we wanted: bistros, cheese, wine and meat shops, newsagents and flower stalls, tiny shoe stores and clothing boutiques, subway stops nearby, a twice-a-week farmers' market six blocks long, and the chance to live with local people rather than tourists who tend to stay in the fancier sections of town. We could hardly sleep because we were so thrilled with our luck to have found such a place!

Paris is divided into twenty arrondissements, with the first arrondissement in the center, and the rest spiraling outward in a clockwise direction. We were in the second geographical circle, from the center, several subway stops away from the action. Our neighbors treated us kindly, even though we were linguistically challenged.

Many people in France speak English, but since some are reluctant to use it, we learned to say, "*Pardonnez-moi, Je ne parle pas français*" (Pardon me, I don't speak French). An apology for our ignorance, accompanied by a sincere smile, would usually disarm the other person. In turn, he or she would smile sympathetically at our ignorance and then make a true effort to communicate either in English or the old standby, international charade language. I'd be willing to bet that what they thought we should say is, "Pardon me, I can't speak French, because I come from a linguistically challenged country where we only learn our own language." It made me even more grateful to the people who did try to help us.

We shared the building with just one other tenant, Mme. Fanny Acquart Gensollen, a ceramicist whose kiln sat in the basement next to the laundry room. The hallway leading to it had one of those timer lights Europeans favor in hallways and public bathrooms to save energy. It reminded us of the same diabolical setup in our Buenos Aires hallway. You could turn on a light when you stepped out of the elevator in the basement, but if you didn't reach the laundry room in time to flip the light switch, you were plunged into total darkness, stumbling around dropping dirty socks and underwear all while trying not to fall into the large hole in the floor next to the kiln. It was a challenge.

The automatic light situation was not our only flashback to Argentina, since Buenos Aires truly is the Paris of South America. The cities resemble one another so much that, for several days after we arrived, we kept thinking we had somehow wound up back in the Southern Hemisphere. I turned a corner and looked down a beautiful leafy street lined with gorgeous French town houses and stopped short, horrified. "Oh God," I said to Tim. "Look at this street…for a second I thought I was back in Buenos Aires."

"Happens to me all the time. I keep waiting for everyone to answer every question with a 'No!'" he joked.

But after a few days of people treating us courteously, the feeling dissipated. We knew we were in the true Paris.

✷ ✷ ✷

After Andie departed that first morning with promises to keep in touch, we started our regular move-in routine with a stroll down the avenue a block away. We read menus, which are always posted outside, and were delighted to discover so many culinary choices close to us. We salivated as we peered into windows stacked with exquisite chocolates and pastries, gorgeous as gems in a jewelry store. We spotted a branch of Carrefour, the international super-market chain that seems to have locations everywhere, and found several good drugstores. We also located the Metro station. We were in business.

"Ah!" we sighed in unison when we found a small cineplex just a few blocks from home. It thrilled us to pass a shop that sold duck in every form imaginable, and goose liver pâté, fresh, canned, and jarred with every nuance you could dream up. It stood right next to a world-class cheese store, and beside that a patisserie that pumped out celestial bread aromas all day. Life was going to be wonderful, even though we knew we would need to walk forty miles a day just to stay even on the scales.

For our first dining experience, we chose an utterly French corner bistro. It featured dark mahogany walls, a bar top traditionally wrapped in zinc metal, waiters in long aprons, and tables filled with people lingering in quiet conversation over two-hour lunches. The place was to become one of our favorites, in part because I received the distinct pleasure of witnessing Tim, an adamant avoider of anything liver, convert. It was like watching a person fall in love. Of course, this wasn't your generic grocery store chopped liver. This was the real deal: handmade, homemade, authentic French goose liver pâté—smooth, creamy, irresistibly complex, and buttery, accompanied by perfectly prepared pieces of crunchy toast. Impossible to resist. Tim would need a twelve-step program if he ever hoped to rid himself of his new addiction. Sure enough, several days later, as we were heading home after a satisfying day of ogling art, he said, while crunching off the top of the hot baguette we had just bought, "Honey, are you sure we have enough pâté at home for the cocktail hour, or should we stop at the duck store?"

That week, keeping to our moving-in plan wasn't easy, but we knew it would make life simpler if we followed our own rules. We wanted badly to dash over to the Champs-Élysées or stroll the Luxembourg Gardens that second morning, but we knew that unpacking and stocking our kitchen properly would allow us more leisure later to enjoy the city.

On our second day, we passed our African friend, and I could see firsthand what Tim had been referring to our first day. He strolled down the street in a bright red outfit, clutching the latest *WSJ* and looking quite regal and elegant. I struggled to maintain my decorum because he might have misunderstood my giggles—I certainly wasn't laughing at him but rather at the drab, sorry-looking paper in his hand. It didn't stand a chance against his beautiful silk pants and flowing robe, topped with a matching fez, whose extra inches made him look about seven feet tall.

That day, we bought a nifty waterproof two-wheel rolling cart to drag our groceries to our apartment, just like the one we left behind in Argentina. We now buy one everywhere we go, and we have left a trail of them in apartments from Florence to Mexico. They are necessary in big cities, if you don't mind looking like someone's grandmother. (Trust me, after you've lugged thirty pounds of groceries in plastic bags up a cobblestone street a couple of times, you won't care if you look like a *burro*.) Which brings me to a curious realization: the longer we live home free in foreign places, the less it concerns us to look foolish or naive in front of other people. Our egos—whatever they originally were—have shrunk.

I think that older people can find it more difficult to be out of their depth, especially when people around them know exactly what to do while they flounder around, trying to figure it out. As members of the older (or I prefer the word "mature") crowd, we believe there is some expectation that we know what we're doing all the time. This is simply not the case. For instance, that afternoon in Paris, we suffered through a terrible time buying our first Metro (subway) tickets. The dispensing machine didn't like our credit card, and it even spat our euros back at us when we tried to use cash instead. The people behind us grew impatient in that singularly French way—small sighs and foot tapping, edging just a little too close behind the offender, to tell them subtly to hurry up! Finally, an attendant called us over to his cage and sold us the tickets himself. Rather than risk being embarrassed again, we decided to always seek out a booth to top up our passes. Of course, since attendants weren't always present, we finally bit the bullet and tried again, risking foot tapping and sighing—and our corresponding frustration. Eventually we got the hang of it and enjoyed the satisfaction of feeling empowered and independent.

That said, now that we've been on the road for a while, we have learned to stand our ground and ignore muttering and dirty looks from others. We just soldier on until we have completed our task and don't mind looking as if we don't know what we're doing… because, well, we don't! We eventually learn the system, and it gives us an enormous sense of accomplishment and confidence to master it, like learning a new skill.

Our first market visit took well over an hour as we pored over the culinary riches available to us. Most French markets are treasure troves for deprived Americans. The cheese cases artfully display offerings of five or six kinds of veiny blues, goat cheese rolled in everything from herbs to ashes, and those stinky cheeses (the true cheese lover's religious experience) that smell so awful and are like heaven on the tongue. It took us a long while to contemplate walnut, rapeseed, olive, and nut oils, vinegars wrought from fruits, wines, and mysterious origins that we couldn't read, plus condiments from exotic international locales. When Tim spied the huge section devoted to all forms of prepared liver and duck, he grew misty-eyed. We discovered cans of duck cassoulet (beans and duck in a rich sauce that would take days to prepare from scratch); once we tried it, our pantry was never without it. The pickle and olive section held us in rapture for quite a few minutes, and even the grocery store bread section gave us more thrills.

The fresh vegetable department featured peaches just perfectly ripe, glistening fresh candy-sweet berries, tiny potatoes with translucent skin, and haricot vert as thin as toothpicks. We were so delighted with the fruits and vegetables that we forgot our lesson about observing others first and began greedily scooping delicacies into small plastic bags.

When we arrived at the checkout stand wearing big grins at all of our discoveries, the clerk looked at the produce quizzically. Uh-oh. While smiling at us, she spoke to the bag boy, who grabbed the produce and trotted off while she continued ringing up the rest of our purchases.

Only later did we learn that, in France, the shopper is supposed to place fresh produce in a plastic bag and then wait his or her turn at the weighing machine, where she/he pushes the button with the picture of the item. A sticker with the price spits out, and the shopper slaps it on the bag. We were so busy stuffing our bags with produce that we had missed that whole procedure! But neither the checker nor other customers groused at us. Being forgiven politely for our first *faux pas* in France gave us yet another reason to fall in love with the country.

✳ ✳ ✳

We hurried back to our apartment, put away our bounty, and finished unpacking. We deserved a reward. So we left, popped up out of the Metro near Notre Dame, and began to search for one of our favorite places, Au Bougnat, an old bistro in one of the little streets that surround the great church. We had dined there on a past trip years ago. Although considered a tourist establishment by some, we found the food to be consistently delicious and the service very pleasant.

Tim took the lead and we started walking along the river. People hurried past and we tried to match the pedestrians' rhythm. Being cautious and aware didn't save us from several pokes and a couple of near collisions, but we forged ahead for a while. When we looked around, we discovered we'd been going in the wrong direction. "Rats," Tim muttered as he turned left and headed down another street.

"Darling," I called sweetly, "I think it's the other way."

After a series of other wrong turns and near-collisions, I finally blurted out, "Could we just sit down over there for a minute?" I pointed to an empty bench.

Tim continued to dodge the oncoming foot traffic before acquiescing. "OK, I could use a break anyway."

We sat down and I took several deep breaths.

Tim sensed my frustration trying to keep up with the hustle and gently said, "People in cities all over the world are in a hurry, sweetie. They're not on vacation and they're not here to entertain us."

"Yeah, but why are we getting so frustrated and upset? Are we the intolerant ones?"

"No, we're simply the ones with the big learning curve, and you're the one who says that the view from there can be pretty ugly," Tim replied. "We just need to toughen up, babe. I'm worse than you are when it comes to accepting the fact that new cultures require new levels of patience."

I looked at him and nodded, thinking how right he was. If we were going to be true citizens of the world, then we needed to leave our expectations at home in that 10 × 15 storage unit and learn to be much more adaptable! I vowed on the spot to try to remember that every day.

Reassured, I kissed him gently on the cheek. "Thank you. You're absolutely right. Lead on, master, even if you don't know how to get there."

Once we found the restaurant, we were not disappointed. Tim's warm leeks, topped with a soft-boiled egg and shallot dressing, looked as beautiful as they tasted. I enjoyed the best piece of perfectly tender and mildly flavorful calf liver I have ever tasted. We splurged on caramelized fried bananas with rich vanilla ice cream on the side and then waddled several blocks to the eternal, majestic Notre Dame Cathedral, which dominates the island in the middle of the Seine.

I have seen Notre Dame many times, during different seasons and times of day, but still it lifts my heart with joy. How can such an architectural gem be so powerful and yet so delicately rendered? The rose windows soaring at the north and south sides provide a visceral effect. I can conjure them up whenever I like and marvel at their beauty. I am continually enchanted by the rose garden on the other side of the church, too, and the flying buttresses that soar there.

As we admired the view, I offered to take a young Asian couple's picture with the church in the background. They reciprocated. The photo became extremely important to us in the months to come. Who knew that it would become an illustration for my story in an international newspaper? It was a good example of the power of saying "yes."

Saying "no" to constant activity is important, too, because we need time to recharge every now and then. The Russian invasion of Marmaris, the trip to Paris, and the challenge of getting settled had started to take its toll on us by the time we finished our pilgrimage to Notre Dame. Being home free doesn't mean that we operate in a constant holiday frame of mind. We require a chance to cocoon just as we did at home.

So that night, we locked our door, put on our "loosies," and while Tim tackled our entertainment and communication systems, I surveyed our dinner options. The cassoulet in the can was irresistible, and I found some gorgeous salad makings in the fridge begging for a garlicky little vinaigrette. Tim had nabbed a hot baguette on the way home from the Metro, we had some gorgeous pâté, so we were all set.

This gave us a good opportunity to call home. We manage to speak with our daughters and friends often and have learned to compensate for the nine-hour time difference between Europe and California. They're having coffee while I'm toasting them on Facebook or Skype with my first lovely Côtes du Rhône of the day. That day we fired up Skype on our computer and indulged in a long chat with Amandah, Tim's daughter in Florida. We got to see four-year-old Sean paddling around in the pool! We miss our family deeply, and longing for them is the only part of our experience that makes us sad. It's dreadful to miss many family events, and we know that whole dramas come and go in our absence. Sometimes we do hunger for their hugs and kisses, parties, and the connection that living near loved ones and friends full time can provide. We miss seeing first-hand family history in the making, but thanks to modern technology, perhaps we are creating a new brand of intimate communication. When we do get to be with them, our time together is much more intense and lovely, so perhaps it's just a different way to stay close.

After we'd caught up on the latest, Tim fiddled with the electronics some more and suddenly exclaimed, "Eureka!"

"What is it?" I asked.

"Oh, man, I've finally got it. See this doohickey?" (He's a master of technological terms.) "Well, this end goes into my computer and this part plugs right here in the TV. Voila, m'dear, we shall have *When Harry Met Sally* this very night!"

Call us old-school, but we had discovered the wonders of an HDMI cable. God only knows how we survived without one before. We now carry around a little portable "theater" that combines our computers, HDMI cable, and tiny portable speakers. They fit right in our luggage and work aboard ship, in apartments, and everywhere else that we want to relax and be at "home."

"Well, put your feet up and allow me to serve you dinner right there on the sofa, you technological wizard," I laughed.

It was wonderful to slurp duck cassoulet, washed down with a lovely French Bordeaux, and snivel over Meg and Billy in this romantic classic as a light drizzle made the streets of Paris glisten outside.

Speaking of rain, we almost always planned our outings around the weather. Since we were having a rainy day, in fact a wet week, we decided to combine a grocery shopping trip with a visit to the cineplex we spotted the first day. We took our little cart along so we could shop on the way home, and the pretty girl at the counter kindly stashed it away for us. At the theater, we stepped into a crimson screening room with velvet chairs. When the lights went down, I whispered to Tim, "Hey, look—there's a toilette sign right over there at the front of the screening room!" The French understand the human need for a toilet several times a day, and they place them where they're really needed—like inside a movie theater. Instead of an irresistible bodily urge dragging you away from the screen (inevitably causing you to miss the most exciting part where the bomb goes off or where the couple finally kisses), you can step quietly to the back of the room, use the facilities, placed right by the door, and even wash your hands before the fuse is lit or their lips even touch. We went to the cinema at least once a week in Paris and saw several movies released in Europe before they made it to the United States. It was fun to tease our movie buff friends with reviews of things that hadn't yet opened in California.

Our spur-of-the-moment inclinations also determined our daily life, and we embraced all side trips and distractions enthusiastically. On a typical day, a short trip to the Apple store would lead to a stroll along the Rue Royale, where we gawked at the Vuittons, Diors, St. Laurents, and the rest of the big names. We ended that tour in a store we could actually afford: the Gap.

I found a wraparound dress with an ecru, navy, and black pattern that instantly made me look ten pounds lighter, and a desperately chic navy sweater to toss around my shoulders a la Catherine Deneuve. Tim's narrow wale mustard-colored corduroy shorts were so French that I expected him to burst out in fluent *français*.

Now, you may ask how we could make purchases when we move from destination to destination all the time. Here's a great packing truth: we can travel light because it is possible to find something to wear any place we go! We just have to be willing to part with something old when we buy something new. Our rule is that we must be madly in love with the item. Only people with consistent closets get to have ten sweaters and seven pairs of jeans.

By the end of week one, we were so in love with the city, we had already decided to return for three months the following year. Andie and Georges's place was so popular that they were already booked, so we began immediately to search for something nearby. Knowing that we would return also made our sense of urgency to see absolutely everything fall to an all-time low, so we wandered the city without a plan, indulging ourselves every day as we pleased. If it rained, we sometimes stayed in all day writing and reading, or taking a little stroll just to get a breath of fresh, damp Paris air. It was an extravagant life, and we loved every minute.

✳ ✳ ✳

We have come to cherish the European pace of life, especially on Sunday, when most people really do stop everything. They play with their children, stroll in the park, go out to lunch, play games, and ride their bikes. Traffic is light and most stores are closed tight, so people have a chance to recharge.

One Sunday, we wandered to Luxembourg Gardens, which

surrounds the exquisite palace Marie de Medici built in 1611. She modeled it after the Pitti Palace in Florence, where she grew up as a member of the powerful family that, in the previous century, began financing the Italian Renaissance. Luxembourg Gardens is one of the busiest parks in Paris because it's centrally located, easy for walkers, and offers many activities for all ages. Parisians use it for a Sunday stroll, a picnic, and to rent toy sailboats for their children to race one another in the grand Fontaine de l'Observatoire in front of the palace. Or the kids race go-karts up and down on a track under giant trees. Men play bocce on several courts, and people lounge with a picnic or a book on the vast lawns. Lovers smooch on benches, guarded by hundreds of impressive statues scattered throughout sixty acres of formal gardens. It was just delightful.

In Paris, everything is an excuse to eat, so we found lunch in a little café and enjoyed our meal while watching the action. A band began to form at the pavilion nearby. The members drifted into the park wearing their black suits with lots of gold braid, carrying their instruments, double kissing and chatting with one another as they set up music stands and chairs. Before long, the big Salvation Army Band had assembled, and they treated us to an hour-long concert. They played everything from rock to classical, capping off a Sunday afternoon as charming as any I can remember. This is what Sunday is supposed to be like.

We felt very much a part of the scene that day, but our lack of language deterred us from making conversation with those around us. A sense of isolation is one of the challenges of a nomadic life. No matter how much we thrive on one another's company, we are both quite social and do need the company of other people. Soon after we hit the road, we realized that both the new people we did manage to meet and also the people we had left at home had important obligations and interests, and we couldn't expect them to change their plans just because we showed up or rearrange their schedules just because we happened to call or Skype spontaneously. It's one of the prices we pay for our freedom.

But, I will readily admit, I needed a little girl talk, just to make me feel normal. Trouble is, one has to have to have a girlfriend if one wants to dish the dirt! And I had yet to find one, especially a French *amie*, so we set about looking for friends in Paris.

We began by attending a gathering of travelers and locals, conducted weekly by Jim Haynes, an American writer who has been opening his apartment to strangers for thirty years. I had read about it in the *New York Times* and made a reservation via email long before we left home. It is a nifty arrangement. For thirty euros, he serves a mediocre dinner and some box wine, but the big draw is the opportunity to meet new people. Jim wears a red apron as he perches on a bar stool at the end of the buffet, collecting money and chatting up newcomers while the place fills up with people who look like deer in the headlights at first. Within five minutes the conversation is so loud and animated that a person could use earplugs! Everyone has a story to tell. We had fun, even though a hundred bodies were jammed into a space for twenty. We chatted with a lot of Americans and others passing though Paris, but as we walked toward the Metro, Tim said, "Well, that was okay, but I really didn't meet anyone I wanted to pal around with, did you?"

"No," I sighed. "I just wish Andie would call us. She's so darling and animated, and I just know we'd have fun with them. I thought we all connected with each other that first day. I'm dying to meet Georges, too. D'you think we should phone her?"

"Not yet, sweetie," he said. "Let's give it a few more days. We don't want to intrude. Remember, they have lives, and we're just passing through." I sighed and agreed with him.

To our delight, when we got home I found an email waiting

from Andie. She invited us for cocktails the next evening. We were overjoyed. At last, we had potential new friends in Paris! The next night, giddily clutching a bottle of wine and a little bouquet, we rang their bell at precisely 6:00 p.m., anxious and excited like kids on a first date.

Their charming apartment was spacious and inviting, full of light, art, and colorful mementos brought home from their travels around the world. At one time, their apartment connected with our tiny one-bedroom in the adjacent building, so we were literally next-wall neighbors. Andie was as warm and fascinating as she had been the first morning, and Georges, her handsome and thoroughly, authentically, emphatically French husband, made us feel welcome immediately. Those two had experienced some enviable athletic challenges, something almost foreign to us. They were much more athletic than we. They climbed Mount Kilimanjaro on their honeymoon, while we took a leisurely two weeks strolling the streets of San Miguel de Allende. They bike, hike, ride motorcycles, and run marathons, all of which we two couch potatoes found wildly exotic and impressive.

Our first "date" grew quickly into a relaxed, pleasurable friendship. As the weeks went on, we shared memorable meals, talked, walked, and laughed together. They gave us insights into living in France that we could never have gained without their guidance. Our topics were all things French: history, politics, architecture, language, and especially food, something in which sane people indulge when they are in Paris. I even picked up some tidbits of gossip. It didn't matter that I didn't personally know the subjects of the rumors. It still satisfied me to hear about the follies of others. It's a funny thing, but somehow knowing more about the real lives of the people around me made me feel rooted and connected, not like a tourist or spectator but more like a participant in the life of the city that was my temporary home.

One evening, over an outrageously delicious dinner at Le Dirigeable, a great restaurant right in our neighborhood, we discussed the national French personality and the people's extraordinary relationship with food. That prompted Georges to give us examples of the numerous everyday French expressions that originated in the culinary world. We thought they were hilarious, and he wrote them down for me:

"*Il y a du pain sur la planche*": "There is bread on the breadboard." Or, to put it another way, we have our work cut out for us.

"*On a mange notre pain blanc*": "We ate our white bread." Or, we did the easy stuff first.

"*Ce n'est pas d'la tarte*": "It is not a pie." Another translation: it's a tough go. Just the opposite of our saying, "A piece of cake!"

"*Ça va mettre du beurre dans les épinards*": "This will put butter in the spinach." Or, this will help make ends meet.

"*Il pédale dans la choucroute*": "He is pedaling in the sauerkraut." How might you feel if you were stuck pedaling in sauerkraut? At a total loss, right? That's what it means.

"*Il s'est fait rouler dans la farine*": "He got rolled in the flour." Which is to say, he's been had.

"*Ça ne mange pas de pain*": "It doesn't eat any bread." Or, it's not a big deal.

If it wasn't obvious already, the French take food and wine seriously. If they aren't eating or drinking it, then they are talking about it.

Our friendship was a "*mange de pain*," a big deal, at least for us. Our relationship with France was brightened by Andie and Georges' generous willingness to welcome us into their world. We are forever grateful to them for this, and we continue to be close friends to this day. We think of Paris as one of our homes now, and seeing them for several months every year is a highlight of our home-free life.

The next afternoon, I rooted around in my miniature closet in the bedroom when Tim asked, "Hey, whatcha doing in there?"

I peeked around the corner to see him typing away at his computer. "Looking for something to wear tomorrow. I'm beside myself!"

"Sweetie, anything you wear will be just fine. Remember, Julia will not actually be there." He smiled indulgently.

Saturday was my big day! I had decided to watch a demonstration class at Le Cordon Bleu, the seat of all that's holy in the culinary world, a shrine to America's beloved Julia Child, and the apex of my personal food journey.

Did I mention that I love food? I'd wanted to walk these hallowed halls since a friend gave me the original *Mastering the Art of French Cooking* in 1965. After nearly half a century, it was finally happening. The school was located in our neighborhood. My sweet husband, recognizing its importance to me, helped me find it the day before, just to be sure I had the right place and wouldn't be a second late for my big moment.

I set the alarm, even though it wasn't necessary. I was like a six-year-old at Christmas, and I could hardly wait to bound out of bed and race down the street.

The next day, as I rounded the corner to this famed culinary institution, young people in chef's togs marched into the building, clutching their leather knife rolls. More than a *soupçon* of envy washed over me at their chosen paths. Although my list of regrets is pretty short, I think that if I could have a do-over, I would find a way to make my living in the kitchen. Being a food professional is just about the most gratifying occupation I can think of! (The closest I came was when I briefly owned a gourmet cheese company that did very well. It was one of the most rewarding experiences of my professional life. You can't imagine how much I loved playing with those big ovens, that enormous Hobart mixer, and having all the refrigerator space in the world.)

Soon, I sat in the small stadium theater with a big mirror over the work counter, so those of us watching wouldn't miss a thing. Assistants scurried to ready the *mise en place* for the chef, who entered to enthusiastic applause. He was informative and entertaining, particularly when he mimed a duck being force-fed to enlarge its liver. He shook his head in disbelief that California has outlawed such practices, thus depriving Californians from enjoying real pâté! No comment from this Californian who lives with a pâté addict.

Chef prepared an entire meal from appetizer to dessert; after each production, we were treated to tastes. It felt like receiving communion in a culinary cathedral. Of course, I stopped at the tiny school store to purchase the best (and most expensive) apron I've ever owned. It wraps all the way around and has lots of pockets and a slot for my instant-read thermometer. I feel terribly grand and professional wearing it. My waiter's wine opener, which travels wherever I go, sports the Cordon Bleu label and gives me a little charge every time I use it. I'm charged up several times a week— every time I open a bottle of wine! I floated home on a cloud of well-being. I had communed with the spirit of my favorite chef, learned some new world-class cooking techniques, and when I got to the apartment, my sweet, indulgent mate was appropriately impressed with my tales. My brand-new apron got a workout that very night.

✳ ✳ ✳

Just before we left California, I had seen an article in the *Wall Street Journal* about a California couple who traded houses with people all over the world for at least six months a year. The article said that they would be in Paris the same time as we planned to be, so I sent Jim Gray an email suggesting that we have lunch with him and his wife, Carol. We met at L'Ami Vin.T in our neighborhood and shared another of Tim's new favorite French foods, marinated beef cheeks served family style in a tureen.

"So, Jim," I said, munching the pâté and crunchy bread my hus- band, the pâté addict, had ordered as his entree, "I'll bet there was great reaction to your piece! You wrote it so well."

"I was surprised," he said. "There was a huge response, and it was so popular that they asked me to do a follow-up. I'm working on it now. You know, it's amazing how interested people are in house trading. It sure works for us.

"As a matter of fact," he continued, "your blog is really fun. After you emailed us, we started reading it. We were fascinated with your concept and your writing is very good, too. If you like, I'll put you in touch with them. They're wonderful people to work with and I'll bet they'll be interested in your story."

I took a healthy sip of Bordeaux and smiled weakly. "Thanks so much. How nice of you to say that!"

The conversation burbled along, but my neurotic brain started ticking away. I was thinking, *Me? Writing for the* Wall Street Journal? *You must be kidding.* Sure, my ego quivered a little with pleasure at the thought. Who wouldn't want a feather like that in her cap? I'd always enjoyed writing and was secretly ambitious, but never brave enough to believe that anyone would be too interested in what I had to say. After all, I had always been the muse, not the creator, the woman behind the scenes who made life smooth for Guy Deel, a well-known artist, for twenty years. There was even a running joke about it. I, like other artists' wives I knew, called myself "the wife of." It had been my job and my pleasure to handle all the details of our life, while he concentrated on the business of art. He worked very hard and he was so talented that his efforts looked easy to the viewer! In my role, I made all the reservations, managed the money, remodeled the houses, planned the trips, gave the parties, and kept the calendar. I also provided encouragement, inspiration, and applause from the sidelines, and was happy to be window dressing at banquets and exhibitions where Guy's talent was celebrated.

When Guy passed away and I eventually married Tim, the lyricist/writer, I thought I would continue in muse mode, offering the kind of domestic atmosphere that would enhance his worthy efforts as a budding novelist. It never entered my mind that I might take on the role of creator while my mate became the temporary muse!

Granted, I had written two sample chapters about our proposed home-free life while we were in San Miguel de Allende the first time, hatching our home-free plan, but I didn't take them seriously. Tim was already booked to attend the Southern California Writers Conference in San Diego on our way back to California, and since I was going along, he suggested that I try writing a chapter and an outline and run it past a couple of agents at the conference. The idea made me extremely uncomfortable because I wasn't the front man—I was the woman behind the curtain. But to please him, I slogged through a couple of chapters. Besides, it gave me something to do while he worked on his novel for submission. We did have fun reading our daily output to one another over cocktails.

Always enthusiastic, he had even persuaded me to have calling cards made while we were in Mexico, so I'd have something to hand out at the conference.

"I don't need a card," I complained. "I'm just going along for the ride. Besides, what on earth would I call myself, 'Chief Cook and Bottle Washer'?"

After a second's pause he said, "No, you will be a travel writer."

"What? Are you completely nuts?"

"Listen to me." He gave me his best devilish smile. "You travel, don't you?"

"Yes."

"You can write, can't you?" His devilish smile was growing wider.

"I believe so."

"Well, there you have it—you're a travel writer!" We both laughed at his logic, and I reluctantly agreed to have the ridiculous things printed. I was embarrassed every time I handed one over at the conference. The agents found our notion exciting and treated me kindly, but at the time, they didn't seem to find my halfhearted efforts at two chapters appealing enough to consider taking me on. Thankfully, Tim's work was well received and he came away encouraged. I was just relieved when the whole thing was over so we could get home and put our new plan into action.

I ruminated on that writer's conference episode as I worked up the courage to say, "So Jim, how would I go about submitting this?"

I half-expected him to laugh or brush me off. Who was this wannabe of a writer sitting next to him?! But instead, he replied, "Hmmm…well, I'd suggest that you write a 1,200-word article and send it to him in the body of an email. They don't like attachments."

That's it? He made it sound as easy as creating the blog posts I was writing for my friends and family. Summoning up the courage to write an article and then suffering rejection was not what I had in mind for my golden years. But ignoring my inner chicken voice and embracing my burgeoning desire to create something, I said with bravado, "Thanks so much. I'll look forward to hearing from you about what they say!"

We parted, standing in the warm June sunshine outside the restaurant, hugs all around, promising to stay in touch. By the time we returned to the apartment, I managed to sublimate the whole conversation and returned emotionally to my former status as cheerleader, not quarterback.

The next day Jim emailed me to say that his *Journal* contact would be happy to consider a piece from me.

Oops. Too late to turn back now. The muse had opened her curtain and was on her way to becoming a writer.

My assistant in the PR company I owned years ago once told me that she could always tell when I was facing a writing project because that's when I chose to balance the checkbook, clean off my desk, pass projects on to others, and sharpen all my pencils. Anything to avoid starting the press kit, press release, bio, whatever task it was. A blank page to a writer is like a blank canvas to a painter—full of possibilities and dread that it won't all work out right. A milder version of that aversion had plagued me since I started the blog, but this was different. This was the *Wall Street Journal*. An editor there was willing to take a look at my story. It made me weak with ambivalence. I wasn't the one who was supposed to be doing this. It was Tim's thing. So, instead of getting down to it, I ran away and found other things to do.

As always, Paris beckoned, and we answered. We lunched at Le Timbre, named aptly the postage stamp, because it seats only twenty-four in its elegantly simple space. Chris Wright, an English chef, serves up dishes in the classic French style, and it's fun to watch him and his assistant dance around each other in the impossibly small kitchen. It reminded me of the women swirling around in Lidia's Mexican kitchen. Tim swooned over the fried pâté de *foie gras*, while I sighed with pleasure over my delicate fried pig's trotters followed by quail on a bed of potato/apple purée, drizzled with a touch of citrus sauce.

Later that afternoon, we strolled past the gorgeous Hôtel de Ville, Paris's city hall since 1357. "What are all those people in lawn chairs doing?" Tim asked.

I followed his gaze. Hundreds of people were lounging on chaises, while others sat at tables shaded by bright orange umbrellas. "I don't have any idea. It's three o'clock on a Wednesday afternoon. What on earth could be going on?" Then I noticed they faced in the direction of the river, pointing, laughing, commenting to one another, and, of course, drinking wine. Then I saw why. "Oh, Tim, look at the size of that giant TV screen! They're watching the French Open!"

Sure enough, in typical French fashion, these people chose an afternoon of tennis over their jobs and were enjoying themselves completely. People in business attire had set up chairs, and served each other refreshments. No one looked furtive or concerned about taking time off in the middle of a weekday.

"After several weeks here, I'm beginning to get an idea of why these people seem so happy," Tim said. "I think it's true what we've been told forever: for the most part, the French work to live, not the other way around, and the work they do seems to be appreciated. Have you noticed how courteous they are? The cabbies, waiters, even those guys in the green suits who sweep up the joint seem satisfied with their jobs. They're courteous to the public, and I don't see anybody treating working stiffs like second-class citizens." He snapped photos as we walked.

"You know, I think you're right," I said. "People are busy here, but they take Sunday off, and they quit working at five-ish, and have long lunches and dinners. I don't think they're in their offices at dawn, either. And consider all the gorgeous parks…people really use them. Remember seeing families yesterday afternoon having picnics by the Seine, sipping their wine, having a good old time watching the boats and playing with their kids? By the way, I really, really want to do that before we leave."

As we walked I thought more about the French attitude about money and work. Everyone in the country is allowed eight weeks of vacation every year by law, although companies can alter that plan. I once discussed having some custom shoes made for my extra-large feet, and the shoemaker informed me it would have to be "Next year, because I do not work in July and August." Can you imagine an American who charges $250 for a pair of sandals saying that?

We observed in many instances that French culture does not necessarily breed motivated entrepreneurs. It *does*, however, breed great appreciators for wine, art, food, music, and beauty. And if the French workers don't like an edict or a contract, they'll shut down Paris with a strike to make their opinions known. It's a French attitude of personal responsibility that I do admire.

We crossed the street to walk along the river. We had just enough time to stop into the Musée d'Orsay, home of the world's largest collection of impressionist art. Built on the eve of the 1900 World's Fair as a railroad station, the museum is a work of art itself. In fact, it, and Montparnasse, a traditional mecca for artistic types and the home of Luxembourg Gardens, were the inspirations for Martin Scorsese's magical film *Hugo*, about a little orphan boy who lives in the space behind the massive clock and keeps it on time to avoid being taken away to an orphanage. The station was closed in 1939 and reopened in 1986 as the museum. Its grand spaces and unparalleled natural light in the Beaux-Arts building make it my favorite place to savor the paintings I love best. The high ceilings in the main part of the building create intimacy in the adjoining galleries and enhance personal interaction with the art housed in those rooms. We luxuriated in the breathtaking collection and surroundings.

As we walked along a passageway at the highest point of the museum, where the railroad clock tower offers a stunning view of the Seine, my eyes welled with tears. It happens sometimes, out of the blue, when I least expect it. When I return to places my late husband, Guy, and I enjoyed together, or see spectacular sights that I know he would have appreciated, I am reminded of how much Alzheimer's took from him. This sentiment does not diminish my passionate love for Tim at all. In many ways, having had a happy marriage makes it easier for a person to love profoundly, without reservation.

Tim took my hand. "Oh, honey, I'm so sorry. Just remember what a wonderful life he had, and how fortunate he was to have had a great career that he loved. And best of all, the lucky devil got to be married to you for twenty years!" He understands and appreciates the fact that Guy was very dear to me, and often we point out things to each other that he would have enjoyed. Tim's sensitivity is just one more trait that I cherish in him.

He smiled and pecked me on the cheek. The man always knows just how to make me feel better.

We made the trek to Montmartre, the artists' neighborhood high in the hills above Paris. Toulouse-Lautrec and his contemporaries hung out there. Picasso, Salvador Dalí, Van Gogh, and many more colorful characters lived and worked in the area. We climbed the impossibly steep stairs up to Sacré-Coeur, where thousands of tourists jockeyed for what must be Paris's most memorable view, the city's skyline spread out for miles below the church. Of course, once we reached the summit, we realized that there is an efficient, cheap funicular that whisks tourists who have bothered to look at their Rick Steves guidebooks right to the top. As we looked longingly at the cool, crisp tourists bundling in and out of it, we told ourselves that our pounding hearts, sweaty bodies, and aching knees would benefit from such excellent exercise.

However, the climb had offered no such benefit to my already frizzed hair. When I got home and took a look, I knew I could no longer postpone some professional assistance.

Andie to the rescue. I explained my plight: on a ship for two weeks, then two weeks in Turkey, and now halfway through a month in Paris. I needed help. I could no longer disguise the silver roots with clever combing, and the sides resembled either George Washington's "do" or Barbara Bush's, who, one could argue, somewhat resemble each other. Think about it.

"No problem," she said. "There's a local place that does a nice job and they're reasonable, but since you're in Paris and you need the works, I think you should spring for Dessange International. It's pricey, but you'll be a happy woman. It's so luxurious you'll need a special visa to go in the place! Want me to phone them for you tomorrow?"

I meekly nodded.

Several days later, Tim accompanied me along the Champs-Élysées to Avenue Franklin Delano Roosevelt. Going to Dessange International was not a challenge I wished to accept on my own. A discreet gold sign (note the operative word "gold," as in gilded, glittering, and expensive) announced we had arrived at the gorgeous neoclassical building on a swanky street. We walked up the wide stairs and entered a white marble lobby, mirrored, pristine, and crowned with a large sparkling crystal chandelier. A gorgeous young brunette with a dynamic haircut and a beautiful smile greeted us in French, to which I mumbled my standard, humiliating reply. She signaled for me to wait a moment.

I had thought I looked pretty cool when I left the apartment. In fact, I'd worked to plan a nice outfit and took special care with jewelry and makeup to make sure I could hold my own against the impossibly stylish French. As soon as I walked into the salon, however, I immediately felt like a bag lady, pitifully out of place in the intimidatingly chic surroundings. Tim told me later that when the woman from the coat check closet came toward me to offer a white smock, I glanced over my shoulder at him with a panicked look, as if she were approaching with an opened straitjacket.

Luckily, my alarm turned to delight when Roberto, the impeccably suited Italian manager, appeared. His English and style were equally impressive. He was so good at his job of welcoming customers that in moments, my bag lady fears had vanished and I believed I belonged there after all.

Roberto touched my elbow and steered me to the main salon, where customers and technicians were swathed in dazzling white kimonos, and more crystal chandeliers cast a flattering light. Gucci and Chanel handbags sat neatly next to the other clients' enviable footwear, and the click of scissors and soft chatter rose slightly above soothing classical music. No funky rock 'n' roll, pop, or hip-hop would bother the patrons in this temple of beauty, the way it does in the United States.

After seating me, Roberto and I chatted pleasantly while Karen (Kah-reeen), a tall blond, completed her ministrations to the elegant woman in her chair. Kah-reeen stepped over to us. She and Roberto talked over my case in rapid French, inspecting my poor ragged "do." They refrained from "tut-tutting," thank God, but I could tell they pitied me.

Roberto then explained in English that I would be returning to Kah-reeen after my color had been administered, and he escorted me down a wide-curving, white-carpeted staircase with a polished brass rail to the hair processing parlor in the basement. Patrons sat in separate cubicles, each facing its own tiny garden outside the large window. Their Guccis and Chanels at their sides, their feet in Christian Louboutin and Jimmy Choo, the strands of hair where color had been applied were wrapped not in the kitchen foil regular salons use, but in gorgeous, iridescent, sparkling cellophane. They looked like Christmas gift baskets waiting to be delivered.

Roberto summoned Raul, who pranced to my cubicle, shook his head, and did "tut tut" as he fingered my faded, over-bleached,

gray-rooted locks. He and Roberto engaged in an animated conversation about my dire situation. Finally, with a gentle pat on my
shoulder and dazzling smile, Roberto assured me that I was in good
hands and that Raul would transform me into a goddess.

Raul returned with a silver tray laden with pots and paint-
brushes. Soon, I looked like the rest of the women, my head trans-
formed into a porcupine with lustrous quills of hair. I watched the
French customers sip champagne, consume their tiny lunches (no
wonder they all weighed eighty-nine pounds), leaf through slick
French fashion magazines, and receive manicures administered
by young women who crouched on milking stools trying not to
look uncomfortable. Not wanting to make a spectacle of myself
by asking someone else to do it, I slipped into the marble and
gilt bathroom and took a picture of myself in my plastic helmet. I
thought that my friends who were reading the blog needed to see
this, and as usual, I was just plain tickled by the whole thing. I'm
sometimes my own best audience.

When I returned, a white-clad girl invited me to the shampoo
area. This began another heavenly experience. The warm chair mas-
saged my body as if I were in a spa, a world removed from the beauty
salons I was accustomed to where the shampooer would be distract-
edly rubbing my head (always more on one side than the other) while
she carried on an animated conversation with the shampooer doing
an equally inattentive job with the customer at the next bowl. While
all this pleasant chitchat took place, my neck would be slowly stiffen-
ing as it rested in the hard porcelain divot of the shampoo sink. The
Dessange shampoo lasted forever, and I was so comfortable that I
would still be there if they'd let me stay. When I awoke from my
happy coma, the girl wrapped my head in a warm towel and folded
it as neatly as a surgeon. If I'd had a Gucci bag and some Christian
Louboutin shoes, I could almost have passed for one of "them."

Roberto appeared on cue, and I drifted up that curving stair-way to meet Kah-reeen once more. She created the elegant, perfect haircut of my dreams. When she finished, we double-kissed and I floated to the pay station. The bill was staggering, but in my current state of euphoria, I would have gladly signed over half my assets. Roberto provided me with discreet little envelopes into which I could tuck a little extra for the shampoo girl, the colorist, and my fantastic new friend Kah-reeen.

Tim greeted me in the lobby, where the coat attendant traded my crisp white linen smock for my practical, dull black coat. Roberto saw us out the door, and I was once again a bag lady. But I was an American bag lady with the most gorgeous hair in Paris!

★ ★ ★

During our month in Paris, we never made it to the Eiffel Tower, or to Giverny, Monet's lovely home not far from the city. We also didn't get to picnic by the Seine, because the weather didn't cooperate. Instead, we ate lunch at home many days, loading up our little table with goodies scrounged from the local market and leftovers in our pantry and fridge. While June in many places signals the beginning of summer weather, in Europe it can mean cool temperatures and daily rain, which can ruin a picnic and certainly give hair the frizzies (a horror I never want to put poor Roberto, Raul, or Kah-reeen through again). Or it can turn hot and dry, making a sprint to the Metro an extremely uncomfortable enterprise. Wise visitors prepare for just about anything and use that old layering trick to their advantage, something we have since learned by heart. We also walked hundreds of miles through our beloved city with no particular place in mind, even dawdling an afternoon away at the Montparnasse Cemetery where the poets, writers, and composers rest together in harmony under the trees. So we commiserated near the graves of such French cultural greats as Baudelaire, Sartre, and Beckett.

On one of our final days, we enjoyed scrambled eggs, creamy and golden, along with a leftover baguette, some *crème fraîche*, a little caviar, honey in the comb, smoked salmon, and a salad of maiche, parsley, arugula, and red lettuce topped with walnut oil and mild vinegar. When we are in places where "ordinary" food is all that's available, I sometimes daydream about the contents of our French refrigerator and pantry. I had a glass of the last night's fruity sauvignon blanc, and Tim enjoyed a great German non-alcohol beer. He also chose some soft jazzy Madeleine Peyroux tunes for our background music, and we watched the dignified geranium lady go about her business while the movie-star mom from across the street climbed into her big BMW and roared away. We felt completely at home and comfortable in our surroundings because we had actually managed to set up a life as we lived home free! Life had a rhythm; we had friends and a social life. We were on the right track.

So now that our time in Paris was running out, we were despondent at the thought of leaving. Although we had tried hard to control ourselves, the volume of our possessions had increased significantly. All that saved us from sinking into a serious blue funk was the knowledge we would return the next year for three months.

* * *

That afternoon I knuckled down and began to think about what I could possibly write that would be worthy of a publication like the *Wall Street Journal*. All of my writer's neurosis came roaring into my head, but as I began to consider some kind of framework for it, I began to see that people would have some interest in our home-free life, and even benefit from the story of mature people striking out to do something daring and different from what's expected of them.

Almost everyone we had met along the way thus far had been intrigued about what we were doing, and my little blog audience was growing a bit every day. They all had so many questions about how we had managed to let our belongings go, about the details of insurance, visas, housing, transportation, and even more important, how we felt about striking out in the world without a base. The idea of being in a position to share a new approach to retirement with so many others helped me to overcome my terror and get on with it! I convinced myself that it was just a query, and a rejection would not be the end of my world, after all. Then I could retreat to the place where I felt more comfortable and happily assume my role as "the wife of" again.

✴ ✴ ✴

We stayed up late our last night, fiddling with last-minute details, phoning the children and grandchildren since we couldn't predict the quality of our Internet access for the next few days. We also snipped at each other, a predictable attack of nerves and free-floating anxiety that repeats itself every time we're in moving mode. It's nothing serious, just our own worries surfacing. We both think of things like, *I wonder if the next place is going to be as nice as this one? Should I have bought another pair of those pants? They really fit well and I'll never find any more the right length. Did Robin sound cross with me on the phone, or was it just my imagination? How bad will the traffic be after we pick up the car at Charles de Gaulle?*

The next morning, we received a surprising tap at the door at 8:00 a.m. Couldn't be the driver who was to take us to the airport where we would rent the car; we didn't expect him for another thirty minutes. Nor could it be Andie and Georges, who always slept until nine. Yet, there they stood in running clothes, their hair askew, coffee cups in their hands. They had come to see us off! We were touched that they would come and made promises to see each other again soon, exchanged double-kisses, and joined together to drag our belongings through the little lobby. "*Au revoir!*" the geranium lady called as she waved her garden snippers. I waved back, delighted that she had acknowledged us at last!

I glanced to the end of the street. There was our African friend looking regal in the costume I always liked best, a purple number with gold stripes. I wondered if he was really playing the market as he read his *WSJ.*

Andie and Georges blew kisses as the cab drove us away. A bag of our dirty linens, bound for the laundry, sagged beside them on the cul-de-sac's sidewalk, the remnants of our extraordinary month in Paris. We could hardly wait to return.

Chapter 8
Italy

We picked up our leased Peugeot at Charles de Gaulle Airport and headed south through Paris traffic. No one spoke except Victoria, the GPS, who enunciated directions in her refined British accent. She was unflappable, even when wrong, which was rare for most people, and especially for us. So far, she had managed to guide us through Mexico and Turkey, and would serve us well on the drive through France and for two months in Italy and on to England, Ireland, and Portugal. We were grateful for her company.

Victoria led us through the French countryside to Vézelay, in the Burgundy region, an ancient village famous for its tenth-century abbey. The landscape was so beautiful that it looked almost unreal. Graceful spires anchored charming villages, and cows grazed on tidy green pastures next to leafy vineyards. I gave myself a sore throat from all the "Ooohs and "Ahhs." As always, poor Tim saw very little scenery, but thank God he did see—and dodge—all the crazy drivers, wandering livestock, and rattling horse-drawn carts filled with branches. We were elated by our good fortune—to be so free, healthy, and surrounded by natural beauty we could thoroughly enjoy.

When we arrived in Vézelay, the Hôtel de la Poste et du Lion d'Or looked as perfect as we imagined. It featured a mansard roof, French blue shutters, an old stone façade, and window boxes brimming with red geraniums beneath four large chimneys. We walked into the lobby to find more delights: luxurious carpets, antique furniture, paintings, and miles of shiny brass. "Vee are so 'appy to see you!" the pretty girl behind the desk chirped. "Your room vil be en the floor four. We do not 'ave an elevator, but there vill be one next year after zuh remodel."

Our elation faded a bit. We had no interest in "next year," since this year it was hot, the stairs were steep, we were tired, and we had brought far too much luggage to drag to the attic. We tried to negotiate with her for another room, but it didn't work.

We had a problem. "Okay, here's what we can do," I said as we approached the car. "We'll just reorganize right here. We don't need much for one night, and if we try to drag all that stuff up those stairs, paramedics could be involved."

"Do you really want to root around in suitcases in the parking lot, looking like hillbillies? Underwear and socks flying around?" Tim asked.

"Oh, get a grip, darling!" I teased. "I have no shame and we'll never see any of these people again."

Thus began our parking lot humiliation. We reorganized toiletries and undies, and shoved them into smaller bags. Other tourists were amused by the spectacle, but we barely noticed them. We dragged our odd assortment of luggage into the lobby, panting from the effort. A young man scowled at us as he lurked behind the desk. He did not offer to help but gestured to the girl instead. Apparently, the girl was not only the receptionist, but also the porter! She grabbed two of our bags and trotted up the stairs, encouraging us to follow. She remained perky all the way to our fourth-floor room. We were embarrassingly breathless.

After settling in, we walked up the picturesque little cobblestone street to join the other visitors in the medieval church. For three hundred years, worshippers have gathered here to start their pilgrimage to the shrine of Santiago de Compostela in Spain, one of the most important of all medieval pilgrimage centers. In 1190 Richard the Lion-Hearted and Philip II Augustus met there to leave for the Third Crusade, when European leaders tried to recover the Holy Land. Inside, nuns and priests were chanting, their harmonious voices floating up to the high stone arches. Within the building's flickering candlelight, we could feel the presence of the millions of devout visitors who had celebrated their faith in this serene place. We were both utterly transfixed by the mystery and sanctity of the church.

All that beauty made us hungry, of course, so before meandering back to the little hotel, we stopped first for a break at a busy outdoor café. Tim needed a little downtime after his first European driving adventure of the year. Later, in the hotel dining room, the scowling chap from the front desk greeted us. Now, he manned the bar and acted as maitre d'. His attitude had not improved. Another young man, whom we had seen parking cars earlier, appeared with our menus.

Confused, we felt a *Fawlty Towers* theme emerging. The maid we had seen pushing her cleaning trolley earlier in the hallway bussed the tables. By now, we fully expected John Cleese to silly-walk across the room as Basil Fawlty and punch Manuel, the surly waiter. Instead, it was the pretty girl who had checked us in and carried our bags. She now served my escargot with puff pastry and a creamy little sauce, as well as Tim's sublime *foie gras*. Our steaks were perfect, the vegetables well prepared, and the wine excellent.

We mowed right through our meal, which was surprisingly as beautiful and delicious as any we had in Paris. "Boy, this was a fabulous meal," Tim said. "But the way this hotel operates, I wouldn't be surprised if the chef is also the head gardener or the electrician!"

Apparently, everyone had several jobs in this little country hotel. They certainly had a long, hot summer ahead of them.

The next morning, after an excellent breakfast, served by the same odd cast of characters, we dragged our hobo luggage to the Peugeot and instructed Victoria to take us away to the sea.

But first we had to climb the Alps, our gateway between France and Italy. If the Romans could push over the top in brutal winter weather to conquer ancient Gaul, we could go the other way in much warmer temperatures. Well, slightly warmer. We paused for several stop-and-gawk breaks, gasping at their majesty while digging through the car for jackets. As we drove on, there seemed to be ten thousand tunnels, along with plenty of rain. This was not an ideal situation for claustrophobic Tim. I turned to him and joked, "Hey, look at that. The French installed blue neon lights in the tunnels at regular distances. See…the idea is that if you stay a blue light length away from the car ahead, maybe you won't cause a huge pile up and be asphyxiated in a ten-mile tunnel."

He laughed. "Thanks for the great imagery, dear. What a comfort you are to me!"

The Italians do not hold to such strict safety rules. When we reached their side of the mountains, no blue lights appeared for those risk-taking macho guys. It was every man for himself, and some were in such a hurry that they actually passed each other inside the tunnels. I closed my eyes often and tried to control my impulse to scream. This was our introduction to the Italian way. They drive just as they speak—fast.

We were happy and relieved (and warmer!) when our spry little car delivered us safely through the mountains to Santa Margherita Ligure, a lovely Italian beach town about twenty miles southeast of Genoa, near Portofino. The sea sparkled below a comfortable balcony in our adorable room, and a little town glittered on the other side of the bay. Down below, rows and rows of precisely placed chaise lounges and umbrellas filled the beach. Uniformed servers tended sun worshippers, bringing drinks and towels on command. It was exactly what I'd always imagined an Italian beach resort would be. Thankfully, my darling Tim had stretched our budget so we could enjoy it in luxury. "Playing rich," my mother would have called it.

By now, we'd grown accustomed to planning these mini-vacations between long stays, in the same spirit and for the same reason as a weekend getaway in the United States: to relax and recuperate. Even home-free people need a break from shopping, cooking, and doing the laundry, regardless of where they might be.

We spent one more vacation night in Livorno at an enormous, recently refurbished hotel, a complete departure from the places in which we'd stayed. It featured what seemed like miles of marble hallways, and gorgeous rooms with high ceilings and lavish bathrooms, but its most unusual feature was a glass infinity swimming pool on top of the building. What a rare treat: to swim while looking out across the Mediterranean. Our sunset dinner on the rooftop terrace offered the perfect conclusion for our little holiday.

As you probably know by now, Tim and I don't quarrel much. However, the next day, Florence's hysterical traffic brought out the worst in both of us. Roundabouts and lights control the traffic flow, and sometimes, they offer four or more possible routes at each exit of a traffic circle. Being in the wrong lane can prove disastrous, because most of the streets are one-way; there is no such thing as driving around the block to start over. In a more modern city, one would make three right turns, come back to the original street, and turn in the opposite direction. That would do it. Not so in ancient cities because the streets wind in and around one another until the tourist is hopelessly, helplessly LOST. Florence is so crowded that on many streets, cars are parked with wheels halfway onto the sidewalks, leaving barely enough room for a very small vehicle to drive down the middle. Sometimes, our side mirror clicked with a parked car as we crept by. Nerve-racking, to say the least.

This idiosyncrasy is not peculiar to Florence, or to Italy. Many European cities were founded a thousand or more years ago, and most were developed from the ring pattern, in which the church or cathedral was at its center and all roads radiated from that central circle expanding outward, in all directions, like the rays of the sun leaving their source. That was the intent, anyway. It looks simple on a map, but when driving at eye level in those cities it's nearly impossible to detect any plan at all.

Under these adverse conditions, my job was to program Victoria, look at her map, and keep an eye out for the correct turning lane to alert Tim. His job was to execute whatever upcoming, death-defying maneuver was needed to deliver us to our destination without killing anybody. Both of us were so nervous that naturally our conversations got snappy.

"Hey!" he shouted that first day as I hemmed over which way to go. "Do we go down through that little tunnel or NOT?"

I scrambled to read the GPS map, which the bright sun had obliterated. "Hang on, the sun has washed out the map. I can't tell."

"An answer this week would be fine," he responded flatly.

"Hold your horses, bub. She doesn't show a tunnel at all, but I think that instead of taking that little off ramp, you'd better just get in there with them," I replied in an equally unfriendly tone.

Of course, he ignored me and took the off ramp. For his efforts, we had to double back, drive half a mile through heavy traffic, double back again, and get across three fast-moving, crowded lanes circling a big monument to some big-deal general. All of this allowed him to again push his way into that tunnel road. And all of which did nothing for our souring moods.

"Oh great," he moaned, once he settled into the lane. "It's petering out here and I don't know what to do now."

"Make a legal U-turn as soon as possible and proceed to Via

Nazionale," Victoria said calmly. I glared at her. Making a U-turn
in Florence holds the same likelihood as me becoming the editor
of the *New York Times*. We finally ignored Victoria's high-brow
yammering, pulled over, and dragged out a paper map. Between
the map and a re-booted Victoria, we finally made it through
the center of the city and drove toward the hill where we would
be living.

Once we were on course, I dared to glance at the city. Sun-baked
red tile topped all the stucco buildings in their faded pink, ochre,
and tan. Along the wide boulevards, venerable trees canopied massive bronze generals eternally riding their steeds and classical marble
Roman deities intertwining with sculptured angels. We passed shops
offering fine jewelry and silk scarves, and almost every block boasted
an enticing gelato shop. At little sidewalk cafés, people downed cups
of espresso and munched on their afternoon pastries.

A loud car horn blast interrupted my tourist observations…and
was the last straw for the agitated Tim. After shouting an obscen-
ity and favoring the offender with the international hand signal of
displeasure, Tim's glare suddenly softened and he said, "Wow! Look
at this. There's the gas station Martha mentioned and that little deli
where we are supposed to turn. I think we've made it."

In retrospect, I have no idea how we managed to reach our new
home that day. As if getting through Florence wasn't beastly enough,
a hairpin turn confronted us at the bottom of our road every time we
returned from an outing. It was so sharp that, during our entire stay,
Tim managed to make it in one try only twice. The other hundred
or so times, he stopped, backed up, and started from another angle,
while keeping a sharp eye for oncoming vehicles and scooters from
both directions. Or should I say, onrushing. Before making the next
turn, a blind corner, Tim hit the horn to prevent someone from
screaming down the impossibly narrow street and killing everyone

involved. Italians, like the Irish, drive as if they are certain of a happy afterlife (and I'm sure many of them are).

When we arrived, there to greet us were ecstatic dogs, our host Francesco and hostess Martha, the gardener, the maid, and a neighbor who was passing by. All of them helped us drag our suitcases up a steep hill to our gate. Suddenly, it felt like we had walked into a scene from *Under the Tuscan Sun.*

Likewise, the apartment was HUGE by our standards. We were accustomed by then to living in apartments that were five hundred square feet or less. This place was at least a thousand square feet! Every room offered postcard views of vineyards, villas, churches, orchards, and neat rows of Italian cypress bordering verdant fields. In the center of the valley, Florence's Duomo gleamed. On the terrace we had an outdoor fireplace, a deep sink, and a serving countertop for entertaining. Our arrangement also included use of the pool on the next level up, so we could splash around and take in the view at the same time. *Perfezione!*

Francesco, who is an attorney in Florence, invited us to a dinner party the next night downstairs at his and Martha's apartment. When he left us, we rounded up cool drinks and nibbles that Martha had thoughtfully provided as a welcome gift. "Now, this is terrific!" Tim exclaimed. "We have two whole months here, so we can really settle in and enjoy ourselves. We can write in the morning and then get out for a while in the afternoon and see some things. I'll bet I can make some headway on my book while we're here, and you'll have plenty of time to finish the *Wall Street Journal* article and get it submitted. Then, later in the day, we can come home, have a swim, prepare a simple dinner, and dine on the terrace."

He's a very organized person, thank God. Somebody needs to figure it all out. I admired his enthusiasm.

"Simple is the operative word here," I replied. "After a month in Paris and four days on the road, I could skip some dinners altogether."

But in the meantime, I took a big sip of Chianti and reached for some fresh-herbed goat cheese slathered on homemade bread, topped off with some sun-dried tomatoes.

Martha, our hostess, was the half-sister of a dear friend back in Los Angeles. They shared the same father, but Martha was 100 percent Italian in every possible way. This beautiful, dynamic woman wore her silver hair in an appealing, messy bun and dressed in floaty, soft outfits perfectly suited to the climate. Through the years, when Martha had come to visit her half-brother in California, who was a composer and a very dear friend of Guy's and mine, we grew to know each other very well. Tim and I had stayed at Martha's country house, the castle Porciano in the Casentino Valley about an hour outside of Florence (yes, I did just say she lives in a castle) the previous year, but this time we wanted a Florence experience, so she gave us a discounted rate for the apartment while its regular tenants were away. Our situation seemed ideal, and we settled back in our terrace chairs to watch the pink evening sky fade while the twinkling lights of the city came alive.

The next day, Martha drove us to Esselunga, a major supermarket. In typical Italian fashion, she used landmarks to help us remember the route. "See that clump of cypress at the end of the median?" She veered suddenly to avoid a Vespa carrying an Italian family of four. "That's where you go around the circle so you can turn left up that street. And look," she continued, merrily waving one hand at a long terra-cotta building with a tile roof, as if that near-collision with the Vespa never existed. "At the end of this building, when you see that very large pine tree, you'll turn right."

Our heads were spinning trying to remember it all. Let me tell you: there are probably five thousand pine trees and six thousand cypress clumps in every neighborhood of Florence. Also, every building is some shade of terra-cotta with a tile roof. Martha did her best to teach us, but we proved poor students. For a long time, the true location of Esselunga remained as elusive as Bigfoot. We knew that each time we struck out for a shopping expedition, we would get lost at least once, sometimes more. As the Italians say, *così è la vita*, such is life!

✳ ✳ ✳

That night, we arrived at the dinner party, where twelve people of five nationalities were gathered on Martha and Francesco's terrace. Everyone was multilingual—except us. Did we just land in a *Bon Appétit* magazine photo spread? You know the kind: lots of glamorous, intelligent-looking people lounging around a colorful table, candlelight glowing…and, for added measure, authentic Tuscan food and good wine in abundance. The sophisticated Europeans were kind to us less fortunate mortals and translated so we could participate. The surrounding hillsides echoed with stories told in several languages and accompanied with laughter (which sounds the same, whether it's in Italian, French, English, or Croatian).

As the conversation rippled along, Tim mentioned how anxious we were to get into the wonderful city of Florence again. Imagine our surprise when the guests, and even Martha and Francesco, unanimously lamented its sad condition.

"What do you mean?" I asked. "We were here for a few days just eighteen months ago, and it was just as captivating as it has always been! The piazzas, the wonderful sculpture, the sophisticated stores, the unparalleled art and architecture…how can that have changed?"

"That's what we want to warn you about, so you won't be so disappointed," one of the guests, Alta Macadam, a travel writer who has edited over forty Blue Guide to Italy books, said. "Our city has taken some terrible economic hits, so Florence has suffered badly recently. There isn't enough funding to keep everything in good order. It's breaking our hearts."

Dejan Atanackovic, a Serbian who was teaching visual arts to New York University students in their study abroad program and also rented an apartment on the villa's grounds, concurred. "You know what Florence is like today? It's turned into a big Renaissance Disneyland, in my opinion, and a dirty one, at that. The average tourist spends four and a half hours to see a city that has the greatest art collection of any city of its size in the world. But the city doesn't have enough money to clean the streets and care for its homeless. It's shocking and sad." The others shook their heads in agreement.

"It's the cruise ships," his friend from Croatia commented. "The people come into the city on buses or on day trips from places like Venice or Rome, have a piece of pizza and some gelato, stand in line for hours to see the David, and then get back on their buses, leaving tons of trash but little cash behind them in their wake." We knew what he meant. We had privately thought about that the previous year when we saw the seemingly endless lines of "boat people" waiting to see Michelangelo's magnificent statue of David at the Accademia Gallery. It didn't look like our idea of fun. A woman at the far end of the table, who taught art history in Venice, tossed in a few remarks about the similarities of the tourist problems in that much-visited city.

As the dishes were cleared away and coffee was served, a deep discussion between Dejan and the Croatian about the nature of reality riveted everyone at the table. I must admit that my tired brain was having a little trouble following those brilliant remarks. It was a fascinating group.

Later that night, as we sat on our own (private!) terrace, wearing our jammies and eau du mosquito repellent, we replayed the evening. "Nights like this make me understand why we're leading this crazy life," Tim said. "I haven't heard such smart dinner conversation in a long time: a Serbian educator and a Croatian statistician discussing whether mathematical equations and probabilities can be used to prove or disprove whether just thinking of something means that it can occur? I couldn't believe how he tinkered with the wording of the question until he expressed it in a way that 'yes' could be the answer. It was a pretty good party trick."

I sipped my wine. "Yes, you're right. I kept looking around the table, overhearing bits and pieces of such interesting conversations. Did you get to speak with the boat builder who made a transatlantic voyage single-handedly in a sailboat? What a triumph! But hearing about Florence's decline was discouraging."

Tim poured the last drop of Chianti. "Well, I think we'd better go see for ourselves in the next day or so, after we get our pantry set up."

✳ ✳ ✳

The next morning, we adhered to our model routine, and went out to get groceries. We sat in the car on a tiny street outside the villa, waiting for the temperature to cool from what felt like 150 degrees while we prepared ourselves mentally for taking up the gauntlet and facing Italian traffic again. I tapped instructions into Victoria. After taking a few deep breaths to summon his courage, Tim started down the hill to Avenue Bolognese (which Victoria pronounced BOWL AGH KNEES). He negotiated hairpins and blind corners with the courage of Mario Andretti, the famous race car driver. Once again, Tim's skill at getting us where we needed to be made me gaze at him in wonder. He even remained semi-calm when scooter drivers whizzed within inches of our car and sped off into the traffic. (Not quiet, mind you, but calm.)

We reached the Esselunga Market in spite of Victoria, who seemed to be having a bad day, and despite our inability to find Martha's cypress tree or other landmarks. In other words, we ended up just following our instincts, something we could probably benefit from doing more often. Esselunga is like all large supermarkets, but with a decidedly Italian sensibility. In other words, it's confusing and crowded with people in a hurry who don't appreciate looky-loos who slow them down.

We quickly discovered that grocery shopping at Esselunga is a contact sport that requires skill and determination. Here's the drill for produce shopping in an Italian supermarket: a machine in the middle of the area dispenses flimsy plastic gloves and bags. The shopper snaps on a little plastic glove, grabs several plastic bags, and then makes his or her choices. Squeezing is not allowed. One must look, choose items, and plop them in the bag using a gloved hand only. Quickly, please.

For the first few visits, I kept my cart alongside me, which resulted in some pushing and shoving from other shoppers. At first, it annoyed me no end. I never thought of the Italians as being rude! Tim usually (and wisely) stayed on the sidelines in overcrowded situations for obvious reasons. Since I was the one fully engaged in field combat as he observed from a little distance, he could detect patterns I couldn't see. After a few excursions, he pointed out that the Italians parked their carts in the center of the department and just carried their little plastic bags around as they filled them. This way, they weren't bumping each other and shoving their carts into the tomato bins. Bingo. When I copied their method instead of bucking the system, things got easier. Adapting to our host country is an important part of being good travelers—not to mention a relief. I keep reminding myself of this all the time!

Back to the produce-buying process. After choosing fruits and vegetables, the shopper jumps into a haphazard line in front of the weighing station. The purchases are plunked on a scale and the buyer punches the picture button, which matches the item on the machine. If the product's picture is not featured on a button, he must type in its product number, which is displayed in microscopic letters on the price card in the bin. Not remembering that number means giving up your spot in line to the next person who, unlike the more passive, hands-off French people, has been nudging you to hurry up with her bag of peppers; marching back to the bin, avoiding the elbows of territorial shoppers and minding your feet so your toes are not squashed by a fast-moving cart; and then retrieving the number and starting all over. Finally, the machine spits out a sticky label, which is supposed to adhere to the bag, but usually grabs your glove, too.

I usually stuck to buying produce that had a picture, because I could never remember the numbers. Also, it seemed there was always some tiny elderly Italian widow in a floral dress breathing down my neck—or up my neck, owing to our height difference—as I made a fool of myself, caught in a sticky loop of label, glove, and plastic bag as I hurried to tag our purchases. At this point, my teammate, who watched the action from the bench, helpfully snorted with laughter. It took some time for me to see the humor in it.

After a few visits, we started to find our way with little difficulty. Once we had conquered the rules, we enjoyed the great bounty an Italian market offers, if not the sporting aspect of getting it. We feasted for an entire summer on sweet white peaches shaped like little sultans' hats, melons always at the peak of perfection, abundant fresh fish, and perfect Italian tomatoes that tasted as if a neighbor had grown them. Tuscan bread, made without salt, is the basis for the Tuscan bread salad Martha later taught me to make. We also indulged in cured Italian ham, olives, and other antipasto treats, the best in the world.

The food was to die for, but the drivers were not. Every time we stepped into the car, Tim learned another way to save our lives. For our entire stay, it seemed we were the target *del giorno* for every Tuscan driver. Tailgaters and hostile motorcyclists charged us daily, seemingly without reason. We thought Tim was driving really well and courteously, so we couldn't figure it out. When we asked Martha why we were trouble magnets, she looked at us with pity and informed us that the blue F on the back of our car told other drivers all they needed to know. F, as in France. Once Martha explained that the Italians she knew were not fond of the French, rather than being oddly displeased with the two of us, we stopped taking it personally and just accepted the abuse.

Unfortunately for us, many Italians had sunk into a collective bad mood even before we arrived. Locals told us that the country was sweating through its hottest summer in two hundred years. Day after day, the temperature soared above 100 degrees and barely cooled off at night.

The heat was so intense that we ran errands and played tourist only in the morning. Then we retreated to the apartment, where we could move little and stay in range of the several fans we ran all the time. One day, as we hunkered down waiting for evening so we could open the shutters, Tim said, "I feel like a mole living in a renaissance convection oven!" He was right. There was no rain. Not a breath of air moved, except when we batted at mosquitos.

* * *

That said, we did enjoy one haven on those hot afternoons: the sparkling pool. It sat at a higher elevation than our apartment, giving us an even more spectacular view of Florence. On days when the heat was slightly less beastly, we took drinks, snacks, and our books and computers and whiled away our afternoons under the trees. We read and chatted and wrote as cicadas provided the perfect summer soundtrack, then we dipped in the pool to stay cool.

Each day, the celebrated Tuscan light would change the hills and the city into a glowing golden work of art. It was easy to see why the celebrated Italian painters had given the world the priceless gift of such wondrous skies in their work. That golden light had also drawn our friend, Judy Butcher, to Florence to take art classes at one of the institutes. We'd kept in touch since we met her in Mexico, and she was a senior member of our growing international community of friends. After all, we were forever indebted to her for telling us ahead of time about the Schengen Agreement. Judy had sublet an apartment near the Arno River in the heart of Florence from a woman she had met in Alaska on a bus of all places.

We made a dinner date at her apartment and met her in the square of Santo Spirito Church. By then, Tim and I had learned how to park at the train depot, Santa Maria Novella. In fact, the depot's main attraction was its big underground parking lot, which was easy to negotiate and kept the car relatively cool. But by the time we slogged from there through Florence, across the Arno bridge, we were panting and damp. We were very happy to find Judy waiting to take us around the corner into her small building.

As we laughed and celebrated our reunion, she called for the old-fashioned cage elevator to take us upstairs. When it came, Tim the claustrophobe balked at entering. As we pushed him inside, he said, "Well, I certainly hope this thing isn't what it looks like—it's shaped like a coffin!" It was—with the "foot" end just wide enough for a small child. We let Tim take it all by himself.

Judy had really been lucky on that bus ride because her friend, an artist, had completely refurbished a fabulous space that looked right into a gorgeous, flower-laden courtyard surrounded by colorful antique tile roofs. It was tastefully decorated, completely outfitted with the latest in appliances and furniture, and it was air conditioned. If I hadn't been so attached to Tim, I would have asked to become Judy's new roommate!

We had several great meals together in Florence during her stay, and she came up to the villa several more times to swim. One afternoon, as we sat in our wet bathing suits sipping cool drinks, trying to concentrate on the view instead of the temperature, she admitted that her enthusiasm about Florence had weakened during her visit this time, just as ours had. We valued her opinion since she was an intrepid traveler and a flexible person who knows how to adapt to circumstances on the road. When she said, "You know, Florence is hard to love in its current condition. I can't wait to get away from this heat and dirt and congestion. In fact, I'm thinking of leaving early and going on to Germany," we felt a little less like complaining American babies.

Determined to be flexible, we continued to find ways to beat the heat. One morning, as I sipped my coffee, trying to enjoy the majestic view of Florence, the garden hose next to my feet jerked so violently that I jumped up and sent my cup flying. Tim stood at the far corner of the terrace, ready to begin what would become our daily watering ritual. He had yanked the hose to make it long enough to hold over his head, and he stood there, chuckling and smiling, pleased with this new idea. I giggled and joined him in our private wet T-shirt contest.

"When we're finished watering, let's get out of here and go into the city," he said. "At least we'll find an air-conditioned restaurant, and maybe we'll take in some sights."

He sprayed me with more water, which I relished. I had long since given up glamour. In that heat, hair wilted and makeup melted, no matter what.

When we had dried off, we headed for the Tourist Office across the street from "our" parking lot at the depot, found a decent city map, and slogged to the Duomo, sticking close to the buildings and ducking into stores whenever we needed a breath of cool air. Lunch in an air-conditioned restaurant restored us, but by 2:00 p.m., with the temperature still rising, we realized that visiting a museum was out of the question. We could think of nothing but the pool. But the fact that we had made it that far made the whole adventure feel like a victory to us.

✶ ✶ ✶

The highlight of our summer in Florence was a ten-day visit from my daughter Robin. We'd been anticipating her arrival for months, and I hardly slept the night before she landed. We had stuffed the house with wine and food and put flowers in the small apartment above ours, where we decided she would stay. It offered two major attributes: instant access to the pool and those two magical words: AIR CONDITIONING. We left an hour early to fetch her at the airport to allow for our inept driving and Victoria's general confusion in the tangle of Florentine streets, but Victoria was having a good day. We arrived in a hurry.

How glorious to see our sweet, beautiful, bubbly Robin after such a long time! We all talked at once as we gathered her belongings and set out for home. But our harrowing route back quickly silenced us. In Florence, since there are so many one-lane and one-way streets, routes to and from a place are often completely different. The way Victoria chose to take us home was probably the shortest, but it involved climbing a narrow, steep hill that culminated in a turn so sharp, the car door drew to within a hair's breadth of meeting a rock wall. We couldn't turn back, because the hill was too steep. We couldn't move forward without scraping the corner of a building. A high rock wall gave no quarter on the opposite side. Tim made his way around it one inch at a time. It was so terrifying that we couldn't speak. When I glanced in the backseat, our poor jet-lagged daughter had pulled her sweater over her head. I thought I heard her praying softly.

We made it, but on future excursions in that direction, we carefully studied the route to avoid the turn from hell. When we told Francesco and Martha about that scary moment, they shook their heads. They knew the spot well. I think they were impressed with Tim's fortitude and driving skill, because even they as natives said that they, too, would go miles out of their way to avoid that infamous, dreaded bottleneck.

Robin's sunny disposition and offbeat sense of humor brought a fresh perspective to our doggedly hot days, and we loved showing her the magnificent gifts Florence preserves for the world. Even its decrepit state couldn't mask its beauty.

Martha and Francesco also invited us to bring Robin to Porciano. An hour-long, winding drive away through the countryside, the Casentino Valley boasts several castles and many picturesque towns along the way. Martha's parents, in collaboration with the Italian government, restored the castle's tower in the sixties, making a modern miracle out of a ruin.

As we rounded a corner to begin the final climb to the castle, Robin cried out in delight, "Oh, this is unbelievable. I've seen your pictures, but I didn't dream of its being this gorgeous. Didn't you tell me that Dante stayed here?"

"That's what they say, and as they excavated for the restoration, they found evidence that humans were living here long before the castle was built in about the year 1000," I said. "When Tim and I stayed here, I was alone for a few minutes in the castle. Everyone had gone out. In the profound silence I swear I could hear people rustling around. It was a little spooky, but they seem harmless enough. Martha claims that it's not haunted, but she also has told me that she has never stayed all night by herself. When she comes up here alone, she uses one of those small apartments on the castle grounds where the town folks used to live."

When we arrived, the elegant Francesco was stretched out on a lounge chair under a tree, reading in the garden. He greeted us with double kisses and his lovely chuckle, and took us inside. Porciano's fairy-tale exterior includes Juliet windows and several small balconies. It is wildly romantic, dressed in lavish climbing greenery that turns deep dramatic red and gold in the autumn. Positioned on a hill, the tower faces directly across the valley toward its sister castle, where Dante wrote a portion of the *Inferno*. Perhaps Dante, too, was home free and just mooched from castle to castle.

A small museum and conference area now occupy the first three floors. The family's living quarters begin on the fourth floor and are surprisingly homey, with comfortable overstuffed chairs and sofas in lively prints, a long refectory table with twelve chairs, and cushioned window seats in each graceful window. The kitchen is small but efficient, with a little step-out balcony and bird's-eye view of luscious farms and grazing land surrounded by rolling Tuscan hills. Several more stories house beautifully decorated bedrooms and lead the way to an enormous terrace at the very top, the perfect venue for cocktails. The Spechts, Martha's family, installed a small elevator, but it's only big enough for two people. When it's time to repair or reupholster furniture, the workmen must do it within the castle. There's no way to get the furniture down!

After the castle tour, Martha took us farther up the hill to the start of the Arno, the 150-mile river that runs through Florence before flowing into the Tyrrhenian Sea near Pisa. Here, it was a country stream no more than six feet across. I found it hard to believe that a brook could become such a mighty waterway. It pooled into a green swimming hole not far from the castle, shaded by ancient trees, and then tumbled over a small dam on its way to Florence. We watched children splash and play on the banks and wished we could jump in with them. It was lovely to see people having fun in such a peaceful spot. A country fix was just what we needed after the bedlam of the city, and we were glad to give Robin a different view of Tuscany, one that she would never have seen from a tour bus.

We took everyone to lunch in Stia, the picturesque Tuscan village at the foot of the hill, and chose a favorite restaurant from our first visit. "Robin, you are about to have one of the best meals you have ever had," I told her excitedly on the way down the hill.

The tiny place was beautifully decorated in soft greens and pale pinks with crisp linens and sparkling cutlery. It was so elegantly turned out that it could have fit perfectly into a big-city neighborhood, yet here it was, in a tiny country town. Everything was pristine and understated—except the food, which was over-the-top haute cuisine. The owner's mother, the chef, outdid herself with two kinds of homemade ravioli, one with meat sauce and one with cream sauce, both delicious. Her risotto with beet sauce was outrageously good, and I found the dessert of caramelized fruit in a flaky crust with homemade ice cream practically a religious experience! We ordered everything they offered; each of the fifteen dishes we sampled was memorable. Robin, who was sitting across from me, rolled her eyes throughout the meal, a family signal that means "This is just about the best thing I've ever put in my mouth!" I was thrilled to watch her have such a good time. She was her usual entertaining self, and even the owner and his mother joined in our fun.

After lunch, we strolled to the town church, where Martha introduced us to the chubby little priest. He was very happy to have visitors and proudly showed us the highlights of his little church. We chatted with him for a moment. When he left, Martha said, "There are people in this village who would like to kill that man."

"Why on earth would that be?" I asked.

"Because he rings the church bells every hour on the hour, seven days a week. He's got the bells electronically programmed and they are loud."

"Well, that's one of those things I guess you could get used to if you lived here."

She laughed. "Not if you own the hotel next door. Nobody ever stays in that place more than one night. The owner is practically going broke, and nobody can get the priest to quit ringing those damned bells. I think they're having another town meeting tonight, though I doubt it will do them much good. He's a very stubborn guy." Martha raised both hands heavenward, palms up in the classic Italian "what're you going to do?" gesture of surrender we'd seen many times since we'd been there.

Before Robin left, we made several very short visits into the city center to show her the highlights: the Ponte Vecchio Bridge, museums, monuments, and major churches. We drove her to Siena and took a train to Venice, but in the punishing heat, our trips were brief. Instead, we spent a lot of time at the pool. Robin was kind enough not to complain, even though her vacation turned out differently than we had hoped because of the heat. Even so, it was wonderful having her with us because we were able to focus on one another without the distractions of children and social obligations. We had the luxury of playing cards, having long, leisurely chats, and catching up on the little things we miss when we are gone so long. And best of all, we laughed constantly because Robin is one of the funniest people I know. She's been amusing me all her life with her wacky sense of humor and fertile imagination. We were so grateful that she came to be with us and got to experience a slice of our new life.

After we saw her off for the long trip home, Tim and I were quiet and a little sad. We worked on our projects in the afternoon while we tried to stay cool and distract ourselves from boredom. It was just too hot to think about going into the city and although we tried driving out of town for a change of scenery, it was just as hot there, too, so we would scurry home to our fans to wait for sundown. Tim sat at one end of the dining room table with a fan blasting at him, making headway on his detective novel. I sat at the other end, fiddling with my article for the *Wall Street Journal*. For over a month, I had been trying to work up the courage to send it to the newspaper.

The idea of moving from my homey little blog to submitting my work to the *Wall Street Journal* terrified me every time I thought about it. Tim was the writer in the family. I was just a dilettante, a dabbler!

Poor Tim had listened to me read it so often that I'm sure he wanted to bash me over the head with my computer. Instead, he politely said, "Honey, I think you should probably just bite the bullet and send it now. It's fine."

I appreciated his encouragement, but I was still terrified of embarrassing myself and being told "Thanks, lady, but no thanks." Finally, I was so tired of it myself that my finger hit the "send" button before my brain could stop it.

I expected the article to languish in cyberspace for a while and maybe, just maybe, one day someone there would bother to send me a kind rejection note.

Instead, to my utter surprise, I received a response within a few hours: the *Wall Street Journal* had accepted my story idea! We were thrilled, of course, and had no idea just how much our lives would change with that news, or that the next month would be our last bit of lollygagging for a long, long time. We hadn't a clue that our roles were about to change. But that night the Chianti flowed and we rejoiced once more at the power of saying "yes"!

The next day over breakfast, as we felt the temperature climbing yet again, I said, "You know, honey, I realize that we have paid for several more weeks here, but I'm not so sure I can put up with this for much longer. Maybe we should pull a Buenos Aires and just bite the bullet and get out of here. What do you think?"

Tim thought about it. "It's been on my mind, too. And I've even looked around at some possibilities, but we still have those opera tickets in Verona. I would really love for us to see *Aida* and *Turandot* in that fantastic Roman arena. I think we should wait it out for the next few days, go to the operas, and then make a decision, okay?"

He made the right call. We fought truck traffic all the way to Verona, but it was worth the effort. The pedestrian-friendly city was a joy. It was cooler than Florence, pleasant enough to enjoy an evening stroll, and we loved its pretty buildings and immaculate, tree-lined streets. The relaxed, welcoming people matched the slow, easy pace perfectly. Verona is romantic, its reputation assured by a certain famous play of Shakespeare's. We even managed to negotiate our way through the hordes of tourists to see the balcony where Juliet never stood.

At lunchtime, we stopped in one of a long line of restaurants that face the arena on one side of the square. The food was excellent. We started with a crisp cool salad, welcome in that climate. That was followed by a sublime pizza, a delicate, perfectly made crust with just the right amount of cheese and excellent Italian sausage. Our efficient waiter's eyes had a twinkle of humor that even his dour expression that invited little conversation couldn't hide. We joked with him, saying that we'd return for dinner that night if he'd save a front-row table for us. Sure enough, when we returned for dinner before the opera, he spotted us and escorted us to a table for two in a prime people-watching position. We were surprised that he remembered us.

Again, the food surprised and delighted us. The seafood risotto was creamy and full of luscious scallops, shrimp, and octopus. Tim enjoyed tender, flavorful pasta, and this time, the waiter treated us as if we were old friends. We were flattered and a little puzzled because he lavished so much attention on us.

The mystery was solved when he brought the check. He hesitated for a moment, then pointed at the silver skull ring Tim wears every day in homage to the Rolling Stones' Keith Richards. The waiter smiled and pushed back his sleeve to reveal a silver bracelet of linked skulls. We expressed our delight and inspected it carefully. His smile got bigger as he opened the neck of his shirt to show us a skull pendant on a leather thong. His smile grew even larger when he quickly opened and closed his shirt. Underneath was—you guessed it—a big, heavy-duty black skull on his T-shirt. People stared as all three of us laughed like lunatics! Who would believe that a skull ring would result in the best table in the house and royal treatment by a world-weary waiter? It proved once more that Italians, like people everywhere, respond to warmth and respect and that we all have more in common than it may seem at a glance!

After dinner, we approached the ancient arena. The stone facade glowed pink in the sunset, giving more definition to its graceful arches, and we entered through the same portal that has welcomed millions of visitors through the millennia.

No one should miss the opportunity to see grand opera in such a magnificent setting. We found our seats and looked out at the audience as the sun began to set behind one end of the oval. Four tall arches, the only remnants of that original tier, stood in relief against the sky. "Now watch this," he said with a note of pride, as if he were the director. Just then, thousands of tiny candles began to flicker, held by each person who entered the arena. The astonishing sight offered the perfect beginning to an unforgettable event.

A third of the oval arena was dedicated to the stage. The ancient colosseum was built in AD 30 to accommodate thirty thousand people. At one point, while two white horses pulled a chariot onto the stage, forty men dressed as Roman soldiers stood evenly spaced on the top tier, holding fiery torches aloft while the entire cast, three hundred strong, sang at top volume. For two evenings, we were completely immersed in lavish spectacles of light, costumes, staging, and music on a scale that I do not think I will see again. I've seen many big productions in New York, London, Hollywood, and Los Angeles, but the combination of stagecraft, setting, and musical presentation was like nothing I could have imagined. Tim, who is a true opera fan, had been to Verona before and enjoyed not only watching the show, but seeing me ecstatically appreciate such a rare treat.

The next day, we set off for Trieste, which we chose because it was featured so often in the Cold War novels we read in the sixties and seventies. Trieste made us think of spies skulking around in fedoras, handing off secrets and ratting each other out to the Commies. Its rich literary history also attracted us. While living in Trieste, James Joyce wrote most of the stories in *Dubliners*, turned Stephen Hero into *A Portrait of the Artist as a Young Man*, and began writing *Ulysses*. He and other writers like Italo Svevo and Umberto Saba regularly visited its literary cafés, making it the cultural and literary center of the so-called Austrian Riviera. The third largest Adriatic port, Trieste has a rich history that stretches all the way back to Roman times, which intrigued us. Neither of us had been there, which made it even more of an adventure.

The approach to the city was dramatic. While driving through a forest, we made a sharp turn. Suddenly, stretched out far below us, was the Adriatic—pancake flat and bright blue. Trieste curved around a deep bay, with impressive estates hugging the tops of the cliff. Designer houses lined terraces that marched down to the sea.

Tim booked a room at the Grand Hotel Duchi d'Aosta, which has hosted just about every visitor of note since 1873. It was wonderfully elegant and the old-world service impeccable. The hotel sits in the best location in town, directly on the square facing the Adriatic Sea. The neoclassical buildings that surround the square are huge. When illuminated at night, their elaborate exteriors look like wedding cakes. The city oozes a middle-European feeling different from any other place in Italy. After the collapse of the Austro-Hungarian Empire, it was annexed to Italy, but it still retains its unique Austrian look and atmosphere.

In the hotel, porters in navy uniforms with epaulets and shiny gold buttons made the rounds with dust mops, constantly polishing the dark wood floors. The brass fittings looked as if they've been prepared for the king's arrival. Floral wallpaper and velvet settees contributed to the sensation of an elegant bygone era. Our room was awash in inlaid furniture and gilded botanical prints.

The pedestrian-only city center features a short canal, a failed attempt to compete with Venice. We explored the wide plazas and narrow alleyways, enjoying cooler temperatures than we'd experienced for many weeks, but found ourselves looking around corners expecting shady characters with dark secrets to appear any second! We enjoyed the hotel and appreciated the beauty of the city because it was so different from other places we had seen in Europe, but there was a melancholy feeling about the area that made us slightly edgy. Its dark history during World War II—Jews were gassed to death there—had left a stain that, for us, even its physical beauty could not erase.

Florence was still a furnace when we returned. We tossed our bags in the apartment and hurried to the pool for relief. As we paddled around, Tim said, "Look, we have just a couple of weeks left here, and our only commitment is to see *La Bohème* at Puccini's home. I want you to see it, but the weather report says it will be 104 in Lucca that night. Can you imagine the cast in their wool coats and scarves, passing out on stage?"

"We'd probably faint, too," I replied. "Didn't you tell me that we had to walk quite a bit to get to the arena? I'm not sure that's the best plan, are you?"

"No, I don't think it is. I say let's give the tickets to Martha and let's get the hell out of Dodge. I've already looked into it and I think I've found just the place for us. It's not too far from Paris, so we won't have any trouble turning in the car and getting to London. The apartment looks great, it's in a cute little town…and it has three air conditioners."

I gave him a big smooch and ran into the house to start packing. He was right behind me. Now we were moles in our hot hole, running at warp speed to get out of the tunnel!

We were not surprised when we phoned Martha days later to let her know we had safely arrived at our next destination, and she told us that her daughter, who had taken the tickets, said that cast members and some in the audience had fainted from the extreme heat during the performance. We were very pleased that we had not been among those prostrate in the aisles, and felt terrible for those who had suffered so in the name of culture.

The next day, we were so excited to leave that even the crazy driv-. ers in the tunnels didn't bother us too much. The higher we climbed toward the Alps, the cooler the temperature became. Soon, it was in the eighties. We were so happy to have surfaced from the oppressing heat that, during two days on the road, we never had a cross word, even when we were lost, hungry, held up by traffic, or caught in a surprise rainstorm. We felt free as a couple of kids ditching school.

After we negotiated the last tunnel, we stopped for lunch in a large restaurant that drew us in because we were amused by the full-size papier-mâché cattle on the lawn. After a beef sandwich (what else?), we took a look at their children's museum, in which they presented displays showing how well the cattle were treated and how happy they were on the farm. We also saw pictures of rapturous children chomping away on roast beef sandwiches. How cute. "I can't figure out how they explain to the kiddies that Bossie has to be offed before she shows up on their dinner plate," Tim said after we left.

We drove into La Charité-sur-Loire, a medieval town complete with towers and cobblestones, our home for the next few days. "I've saved a little surprise for you. There's a blues festival going on in this town over the weekend! Supposedly some really good performers are going to be here, and I've already booked tickets for us." Tim looked at me, grinning. "Is that cool or what?"

"Well, it's quite a change from *Aida*, and it sounds like fun," I replied.

The American owners of our fifteenth-century building, Kelly and Byron Harker, had converted it into several apartments. Ours was at the very top, up a steep circular stone staircase. Its tiny private terrace paralleled a fabulous medieval church, site of the festival. Not only was the place spacious and beautiful, it was also cool.

At the festival, we had fun listening to an American art form interpreted by pickers and players from all over the world. Not the best blues we ever heard, but the setting was marvelous and everyone had a terrific time. The audiences tickled us because many of them were dressed up in their impressions of what an American blues-goer would look like. There were lots of T-shirts with silly sayings that used words like "dude" and featured Harley Davidson logos (an odd choice to us). The venue, in the annex of the stately old church, did NOT have air conditioning, so before long the entire audience and the performers were soaking wet. The German guy sitting in front of me was so hot that he dumped his water right over his head. I didn't even mind the splash-back. But eventually the heat got to the comfort-seeking Martins. We left after the first set and fled next door to our temporary home where three air conditioners were blasting away and we were still close enough to hear these guys sing the blues. It was blissful.

We explored the countryside, picnicked along the river, and even hopped the train to Paris for one more lunch with our pals Andie and Georges. We felt so cosmopolitan strolling up the little main street of town and boarding the train bound for Paris. The views of the French countryside were even more enticing when Tim was able to enjoy them, too. The pleasant two-hour ride brought us to the station at Bercy, where we easily caught the Métro to meet our friends. We strolled up the street beside Luxembourg Gardens and here they came, as planned. I also managed to spend a couple of hours at Dessange, which made me feel terribly *soigné* and continental, and ready for our next move to cool, rainy Britain. We repeated our little train ride down to La Charité and felt as if we were leading a golden life when we stepped back into our cool digs. Days like that, when everything worked out perfectly, we spent time with people we adored, and we were completely satisfied, made the times that were not so rewarding seem worth the trouble.

We had come full circle from Paris. Our experiences in Italy reinforced what we suspected: new friends and travel enliven our lives, and we can cope with almost anything as long as we keep laughing and stay flexible. We also came away from that experience with some new resolutions. We agreed that in the future when someone offered us a really great rental deal that we would not allow the benefits to render us deaf to the details. We now knew that Italy is HOT—and I mean way hotter than we ever could have imagined—in July and August, and renting a place with "traditional Italian air conditioning" (meaning none) was a mistake. Originally we had made that decision in deference to our budget. But in the future, this resolve would save us a lot of discomfort. We have declined several attractive offers because we looked clearly at the circumstances and knew we would be setting ourselves up for irritation or disappointment.

As we've discovered many times in this adventure, it's important to listen to that little inner voice we all have. You know, the one that pipes up during horror movies as you watch the hero step into a sinister room where the killer is lurking behind the curtain and you and the rest of the audience silently scream, "Don't go in that room!" I suppose these are lessons all of us have to learn more than once before we really get it. Luckily, unlike the poor guy in the movie walking into the killer's trap, we lived another day to do so.

Chapter 9
Britain

No, no, no—I'm NOT doing it. I don't care what she says, it isn't happening!" Tim shouted as he banged his hands on the steering wheel.

He stared at the hand-lettered sign in front of us and then glared in defiance at Victoria, the GPS, reached down, and turned off the ignition. "Not Advisable for Motorized Vehicles" the sign read. We could see through the rain-splattered windshield that after about six feet of pavement, the road turned into a black, muddy bog full of waterlogged potholes.

"Okay, okay, take it easy," I said, patting his left hand that rested on the gearshift knob. Yes, his LEFT hand. This was Tim's first day of driving on the left side of the road, shifting gears with his left hand, and learning to glance up at the rearview mirror, which was on exactly the WRONG side for everyone on earth except the British and the countries they conquered over the centuries.

That morning, we had picked up the car at Heathrow Airport in London. Our goal was to reach Bucklawren Farm, a B&B on the Cornish coast, before dark. And preferably in one piece. It was beginning to look as if we had made one of our famous miscalculations, because Tim was thrust into this new form of driving with no time for a practice run. I had driven in Ireland when I lived there for a couple of years in the nineties, and I didn't remember it being terribly difficult. Of course, I was younger (and therefore less daunted), had already been a passenger many times in the cars of experienced

Irish drivers, and had been aided by plenty of parking lot practice before I made my first solo excursion. So I had much more help before I actually took off.

Our drive started well on the M3, a major six-lane artery that runs east to west. After a few hours on that highway, Tim felt like he mastered the car's basics. British traffic was well regulated, the drivers competent and courteous, and Victoria, the GPS, was having a great day of accuracy, probably because she was on her own British turf. Seriously, she sounded much more relaxed than she had in Italy and France.

"You know, honey, I don't think this is going to be too big a problem for me," Tim had said. "The mirror is disconcerting [he never did get used to looking left when he glanced at the mirror], but overall, it's not so hard. I think I'm getting used to it."

Moments later, when we got off the highway and approached the first traffic circle, things changed dramatically. In Italy and France, we entered and exited the roundabouts from the right. Here, they were exactly opposite, with traffic moving in and out on the left. The trouble was that right-hand drivers automatically look to the left for traffic. In this case, everything is happening on the right, so with every maneuver the driver is required to ask his brain to switch its focus. It's terribly difficult. The gear shift is also on the driver's left, and as I mentioned, the rearview mirror is on his left, too, which is disconcerting when you instinctually reach or look the other way in the middle of a busy intersection and find it's not there.

It took all three of us—Victoria, Tim, and me—to get through the traffic circles. We worked out a routine whereby long before we reached a roundabout, I'd study the GPS map and say things like, "Okay, in three kilometers you'll enter the roundabout and take the exit at one o'clock. It's the third exit. One o'clock. Got it?" I tried very hard to speak with a calm, unhurried cadence.

"Yep," he would respond through clenched teeth, a death grip on the wheel.

Half the time, we picked the wrong entry lane. We circled again, struggling to stay in the lane that would release us from the circle at the right place. Every time we got it right and no one honked at us, we felt victorious.

The road to Bucklawren took us through quaint villages, where the owners of authentic cottages displayed their well-tended gardens, and through tiny farming hamlets, forests, and fields outlined with ancient gray stack-stone fences festooned with vines. It was very beautiful, very English, and very nerve-racking. The deeper into Cornwall we ventured, the narrower the roads became. Those low stone fences crept closer to us and grew taller until they were about three inches from the side of the car and impossible to see over. Every oncoming car looked as if it was going to hit us head-on. Tim instinctively dodged to the left and hit the curb more than once. Just to add a little excitement, the skies chipped in: a light drizzle became more insistent. We were soon listening to the grinding of an improperly adjusted windshield wiper. Grrrriiiiinnnnchhhh, grrrriiiiinnnnnchhhhhhh, grrrriiiiinnnnchhhhh. Great for the nerves.

Suddenly, the road reduced to one lane, but cars were still coming our way! We saw small, muddy pullouts along the road. Each time we met another car, someone had to back up and wiggle into a space to let the other pass. Most of the people drove Range Rovers or some other four-wheel-drive beast that looked as big as the Space Shuttle. Backing up and squeezing into a space half as big as their car didn't seem to bother them at all, but it terrified us. By this point, Tim and I had given up conversation. Occasional gasps, groans, or long sighs were our only forms of communication.

Eventually, between the instructions emailed from the B&B

owner and Victoria, who finally got a grip on her homeland's strange road system, we crunched onto the farm's gravel parking lot. Hurray! The TripAdvisor listing made much of the fabulous views, but through the rain and fog, we could barely see the house, let alone anything like a vista! We ran from the car to the building and stood dripping in a little covered vestibule, sheltered from the weather. At that moment, the door opened and the owner, Jean Henly, a tiny woman wearing a welcoming smile and a crisp little apron with a strawberry theme, shooed us inside. "We've been waiting for you. This weather is dreadful. Please come in and we'll see to your things later. Come with me into the sitting room. Would you like tea or coffee? Are you hungry?"

We felt as if our mother were welcoming us home after a particularly bad day at school. She parked us in the parlor near a little electric fireplace and brought us coffee and homemade cookies—plus the bright news that the next day would be sunny.

A young English couple occupied the sofa in the living room. The girl, with the unlikely name of Fliss Mooncannon North, told us she had been coming to Bucklawren Farm since she was a child. Her beau, Sean Twomey, was a mechanic. When the rain slowed, we were so grateful when young Sean wouldn't hear of Tim's hauling our luggage up the steep stairs alone. That day, we needed all the help we could get.

The old house looked typically English: cabbage roses and figurines, painted teacups and small flower prints hung a little too high on the walls, a creaking staircase and linoleum on the bathroom floor. The quilts and towels were thin but very clean. It felt like a trip to Grandma's!

In addition, the farm next door had been converted to a small hotel and restaurant. How fortunate: we would have rather starved to death than attempt those roads at night.

After Jean handed us a flashlight, we found our way next door and joined a chipper group at the bar. We placed our dinner orders, relaxed over a drink, and then walked downstairs. We were surprised to find a warm, attractive dining room where they served us an impressive steak dinner. The day, for all its drama, ended pleasantly, for which we were grateful.

That night, as rain pounded our bedroom windows and we waited for sleep to engulf us, I turned to Tim and sighed. "I don't know, honey, but after a day like this, I sometimes wonder if we've lost our minds. I'm so tired and I know you are, too. Do you think we've taken on too much?"

Indeed, the dampness, cold, and uncertainties along the way had wrung us out. The whole day left us more than a little apprehensive about how we would fare with so many challenges ahead. We had no idea if the apartment in England would be a haven or a hovel (it's always a relief when the places we rent turn out to be what we'd hoped), and moving in always presented a new set of unpredictable hurdles that had to be addressed. We still had London, Ireland, Morocco, and a couple of nights in Barcelona ahead before we were able to collapse in our stateroom on the way home. And who knew what that ship would be like? Being tired didn't help our outlook. Plus, both of our birthdays were coming up, and we felt a little vulnerable. Although we are lucky to be completely healthy, we certainly are aware of our age and the lessening of resilience that comes with it. Our recovery time from stress and exertion was much slower than it had been a few years earlier.

"No, I really don't," Tim replied reassuringly. "I do think we shouldn't have tried to come this far in one day, and we'll have to remember not to make such an ambitious start in the future. But I'll bet you'll feel much better in the morning and be ready to see what's around here!"

Of course, Tim was right as always. Jean's weather prediction hit the mark, too: the new morning revealed acres of deep green cornfields. Beyond the stalks and tassels, the Cornwall coast sparkled in bright sunshine. The wind whipped up whitecaps and howled through the trees, just as it was supposed to do in this section of the world. Our spirits were further revived by a great night's sleep in our cozy room under a downy duvet, followed by a full English breakfast in the old-fashioned dining room. Cut-work linens and hand-painted Limoges serving dishes, silver toast racks and tasty sausage left no further doubt: we were in England! Our eagerness to see Cornwall replaced all worries.

As an enthusiastic English crimmie fan, a nut for P. D. James's, Ruth Rendell's, and Elizabeth George's deliciously complicated, colorful murder mysteries, I can tell you with authority that the Cornwall landscape factors into many books in that genre. Someone is always falling, being pushed, walking moodily along, or hearing a gunshot from the cliffs of the rugged Cornish coast. I came here with a reader's high expectations and perceptions of how it would feel. It proved to be everything I had anticipated and then some: wild, romantic, and even filled with suspense and intrigue—in our case, a splendid day dodging Range Rovers and tractors, which barreled along those narrow roads beneath immense rolled hay bales attached fore and aft. Despite feeling like a nervous wreck, Tim managed to pull off the driving chores without a scratch.

Until the next morning, that is. The fog and drizzle returned. After another of Jean's fortifying breakfasts, our young friend Sean and Tim dragged our belongings down to the front door. When they walked outside with the first load, they discovered that our left front tire was completely flat, apparently damaged by repeated collisions with the curbs on those narrow streets. Sean went to work. He was soon joined by Robert, Jean's husband. I peeked out to check on their progress and saw Tim doing his Tom Sawyer imitation. There he stood, sheltered by a tree, smoking a cigar as he watched the other two crouched on the gravel installing the little donut spare. I would like to think that he was ashamed of himself, but he didn't look at all remorseful to me. The scene amused me so much that I took a photo to record forever Tim's "special talent" for getting things done without getting his hands dirty.

We replaced the donut tire with a new full-size one in the next little town and headed off to Bath, another part of England that enjoys endless literary references. Think Jane Austen right up through Harry Potter. You get the idea. We spent two nights in a grand old hotel/spa and cabbed it to town, where we inspected the famous Roman thermal baths, gorged on Georgian architecture, and shopped for sweaters. The weather was turning cooler every day, and we were both tired and ready to get settled in our next home near London. We had traveled on the road like tourists for three weeks and badly needed some cocoon time to regroup.

Along the way, we stopped in a couple of Cotswold villages and paid a visit to Stonehenge. Sadly, the ancient astronomical observatory has lost much of its mystery and impact because its vulnerability to tourists forced the British government to cordon it off. Visitors can only view the massive stones from a distance these days. Furthermore, the enormous crowds who come to see them created a need for snack bars, toilets, and a visitor center. All of it seemed necessary and well done, but I felt very lucky to have visited Stonehenge many years before with my dad, when my parents were staying in London. In those days, we simply parked the car and walked through a field to the stones. No one else was at the site, and we stood silently for a long time with our umbrellas, wondering about the mysterious people who had moved the stones five to seven millennia ago and created the huge circle that aligns to summer solstice and other precise astronomical markers. I'm grateful that he and I were able to share that moment together.

As we drove toward London, Tim seemed much more relaxed behind the wheel, enough to occasionally glance at the passing sights. It was a big breakthrough. "You know, so far we're doing just fine, but I've been thinking about what you said last night, and maybe next year, we should reconsider the way we plan things," he said.

"What do you mean?"

"Well, it's occurred to me that when we take side trips at the beginning or end of our visit to a country, we are being tourists. We do love exploring, but we might want to do it in another way. See, we're not really tourists, because tourists get to go home. After a trip they unpack, rest, put away their stuff, and have a break. We don't. When we've been out running around, instead of getting a rest in familiar surroundings, we have to set up a new home and figure out the territory." He patted my knee. "It's hard work, and I think we can find an easier way to do this."

✳ ✳ ✳

I agreed. Tim whittles away on our plans constantly. His quest for repositioning cruises, flights, car rentals, and settling all the other necessary details never ends. (It's one reason why Internet quality matters greatly to us!) But his incessant attention to detail has proven vital for success in this type of living. As we thought where we'd like to be for the next year, we faced surprises we could not possibly predict, changes and opportunities that would radically alter our plans. Our life may be unusual, but it's certainly never dull.

We were relieved because the drive between Stonehenge and our apartment was remarkably easy. We had dreaded being caught in the tremendous traffic that surrounds the capitol, but we skirted London and easily found our new home near Hampton Court Palace. Tim connected with and settled into the rhythm of English drivers, so steering wheel banging and growling at other drivers occurred much less frequently. Hitting curbs was a thing of the past. Robin Hurblatt, the owner, greeted us in the sunny fourth-floor apartment. It would turn out to be one of our favorites. Right away, we were delighted with the place. It featured a spacious bedroom with ample storage, an equally comfortable main room, a fine kitchen separated by an ample island that gave me plenty of counter space, and excellent elevators, all in a clean and bright building. Forget Cornwall's well-tended gardens—this was my idea of an English paradise!

After Robin left, I said, "Oh, Tim, you've really done it this time! This place is just perfect, and I'm crazy about being so close to the Thames! Look at this little balcony. We can see everything that's going on at the river. We're going to have a really good time here! Can you believe we can walk just around the building to get to a big market? We're really in business this time!"

He smiled, pleased that his efforts were appreciated. "Hey, let's go have a look around. We can unpack later." We took off, anxious to see our new home-free neighborhood.

We walked a few yards to the towpath that runs along both sides of the Thames. Trees lined both sides, and lovely houses and an occasional pub appeared as we ambled along. Teams of rowers glided by as their coxswains shouted out instructions. Walkers, runners, families with baby buggies, and bicyclists shared the walkway. Sailboats and motorboats were on the move everywhere. Since the river is only one hundred feet wide in some places, it took their experience and skill to safely negotiate the water. People played Frisbee with their dogs in open spaces, and kids chased each other and played on park swings. Within a block of our house, there was a tiny dock with a dazzling white archway on which "Ferry" was emblazoned in nautical blue. People wanting a quick way across the river would ring the little school bell that hung from the post to summon the ferry man to take them over. He charged a pound for the trip.

We found a spot on a bench along the river not far from our apartment and sat drinking in the peaceful scene of river life. Tim said, "Now we're going to have an entirely new experience! I have a hunch we're going to be more relaxed here than we've been in quite a while. I think we'll enjoy being a part of this river life! I already feel as if we're part of the community just because everything moves so slowly and people really stop to have conversations."

"You're so right," I replied, taking his hand. "Every time we are in England, we're so wrapped up in London that we've missed this entirely different world. We're going to love it here. You made a terrific choice, honey. And by the way, I love you!" He squeezed my hand as we rose to leave that bench, which became "our bench" on many sparkling autumn afternoons that September.

We returned to sort out our new home. "Tell you what—I'll get us unpacked while you go next door and get the things we need to get started here," Tim said. "I'll bet you can just roll the cart across that little driveway that divides the buildings, and then I can help you get the stuff up here."

Off I went with my list to Tesco, a branch of the big grocery chain with stores all over Britain and Ireland. By now, four countries into our new life, we swung into our move-in routine without even thinking about it. I spent a happy hour buying what we needed. I'm fond of grocery shopping because I love food, and for the first time in four months, the labels were in English. The British are very courteous, and their non-combative shopping atmosphere was just what I needed! The offerings may not have been as exotic and plentiful as those in France and Italy, but it surely was easier to shop. I filled up a cart with the basic necessities, like wine and chocolate, and, oh yes, threw in some fruits, veggies, and meat, too. After the checkout, since I had so many things, I planned to quickly wheel the cart next door and bring it back when we'd finished unloading all the groceries. I merrily pushed the cart down a short sidewalk, past the little post office, and started across the driveway.

The cart stopped dead. One of the wheels had quit working. I pushed, shoved, and muttered things a woman my age is never supposed to say. Finally, I gave up, ran across the driveway, and called Tim on the intercom. We hoisted the bags to our building, and he manhandled the cart to the sidewalk. How strange. I'd never heard of a grocery cart getting a flat.

The next time I crossed the driveway to shop, I looked up and saw a big sign in yellow neon. It informed me that taking a cart off the premises would result in the wheels of the cart locking up. I glanced in the post office and realized that the attendants, whose counter was just inside the window, had doubtless enjoyed watching our little Yankee performance, wrestling with the stubborn thing! We've probably entertained a number of people as we stumble our way around the world, trying to figure out the local customs.

While I had been doing battle with the grocery cart, Tim had unpacked and begun sorting out the rest of the move-in details. He'd set up the Internet, so we were able to take advantage of the wonderful connection Robin had provided. The Internet allows us to indulge in conversations with our family and our pals on Skype and FaceTime. Email is a marvelous convenience, but there's nothing like hearing the voices and seeing the faces of people you love. It's amazing how important small details become when you're far away. Descriptions of birthday parties and first school dances, local news (good or bad), plans and disappointments, even weather reports, take on a whole new meaning after many months away.

A granddaughter showing off her puppy's new handshaking trick becomes a major event when viewed live on a computer screen.

We spent that first evening catching up with all four families, which reminded me of how different times were when my parents, who were truly travel pioneers, were abroad many years ago. After my dad retired in the 1970s, they sold their house, put their things in storage, and hit the road for seven years. They planned their journey without the Internet: finding places to live, arranging for transportation…all of it. In those days, we wrote letters and sent photos back and forth to stay in touch. We would set a time, weeks in advance, for phone calls from Morocco or Italy or Greece, and we'd eagerly take turns to have a short, expensive conversation with them. The connection was usually far from perfect. They were a hardy pair and made their final big journey abroad when they were both in their eighties. Tim and I call them our founders, and it would thrill them to know we've followed their trail around the world. They were particularly fond of Great Britain, so they lived very much in our thoughts while we stayed there.

We loved our little town, East Molesey, but we were also very excited about getting into London finally. Hampton Court Station was the end of the line for a little spur railroad that served the southeastern region of England. But the commuter railway was a new way of life for us. In the old movies I've heard James Stewart or Cary Grant or Ray Milland say something like, "Oops, must go, gotta catch the five-oh-two," and then put away the pocket watch he was holding, but it never really occurred to me that we might one day rely on them on a daily basis. We had a timetable and quickly learned to schedule our departure from home so we'd be at the depot five minutes before the cute little red commuter train appeared. It was usually full of people coming to see the famous palace which the station is named, where Henry VIII carried on with his six wives and countless lovers. As locals and tourists alike streamed out of the train, we'd zap our Oyster Card tickets on the electronic eye and find our favorite spot at the back of a car. We'd each have one of the gloriously cheeky English newspapers and a cup of coffee we'd bought at the station. It was fun pretending to be locals while we enjoyed a twenty-five-minute trip to Waterloo Station, a Grand Central in its own right. At first, that vast depot mystified us with its shops, bars, commuters, tourists, and bicyclists swirling through its enormous spaces, but over time, Waterloo became as familiar as our own little station. It's possible to go anywhere in London and make connections to all of Britain by train and the underground, to which we could connect without leaving the building. For Californians like us, who spent years trapped in wasteful commuter traffic, efficiently functioning public transportation remains a modern miracle.

Getting home was trickier. Either we made the train on time…or else. "Or else" meant waiting thirty minutes for the next train during the day, which wasn't too bad. At night, however, if we missed the next to last train at 10:30 p.m., we'd wait an hour for the last train, which put us home at 1:00 a.m. I have no idea what we would have done if we'd missed the last train, but I can tell you that a hike over Waterloo Bridge from Covent Garden in a chilly drizzle after being unable to find a taxi, trying to catch that last train from Waterloo station, is no fun.

After a session in hectic London shopping or sightseeing, it always made us happy to get home. We billed the apartment and tiny balcony as our "penthouse" because we sat atop a four-story building. From our vantage point, it was impossible not to check out the action at the river many times every day. We used the path often, strolling to the center of the village and being entertained all the way by stopping to chat with locals and river people who tied up and left their boats for shopping or to exercise their dogs. We saw fishermen park themselves in camping chairs, ringed with ice chests, tackle boxes, and backpacks, and they would proudly show us their catches and describe in detail their techniques. Sometimes their accents were so thick that we'd just smile and nod, never having understood a single word but enjoying the interaction. I've mentioned how much we enjoyed Sundays in Europe because people really do take the day off, and it's revealing to see what they do with their free time. The same goes for England. The English are outdoor people, and on Sundays, our tow path came alive with locals and Londoners enjoying a day of fun outside.

One time, we discovered the East Molesey Cricket Club, founded in 1871 and said to be the oldest in England. The scene could not have been more authentic. The players wore sparkling white pants, shirts, and V-necked sweaters. The stands filled with people in casual but great-looking garb. They personified the preppy look—khakis, subtle plaid shirts, Ralph Lauren belts, and cardigans draped just so over their shoulders, tied loosely at their collarbones. When the kids played, their moms and dads behaved exactly as the soccer moms and dads do in the United States. Everyone jumped into the act, urging William or Percy to smack the bowler's latest offering deeply down the pitch and quit staring at the sailboats on the river!

A little farther down the Thames, near the entrance where Henry VIII would have arrived from London to enjoy his country palace, we found a small dock for a local ferry line that ran between Hampton Court, Kingston, and Richmond-upon-Thames. One sunny day, we joined a little queue of passengers waiting for the boat, paid a nominal fee to the captain, and found ourselves a spot with a good view. As we drifted along, we viewed gorgeous estates with well-tended gardens and velvet lawns that led to private docks and boathouses, where spiffy yachts waited for a cocktail cruise with their owners. People got on and off at various stops, and we were even more fascinated with the lives of people who are on the river every day. To them, it's like the local Main Street, just with floating traffic instead.

Once more I was elated because we had made the choice to spend real time in other countries. These seemingly insignificant experiences, a chat with a fisherman, watching kids learn to play cricket, mastering the train from our little station, add up to an adventure, and a richness of experience, that I never dreamed would be possible in my later years.

When we arrived at Richmond-upon-Thames, we wandered up the tow path, looking at restaurants where people sat under the trees and enjoyed their midday meal. A café with wrought-iron tables and chairs shaded by weeping willows and leafy sycamores attracted us. It sat next to the path, offering front-row seats for a little sailboat regatta. Boys and girls rounded buoys in their tiny one-man sailboats expertly as I walked inside to get our lunch and Tim sat down at one of the tables.

When I returned with sandwiches and drinks, Tim was involved in a lively conversation with an attractive mature woman in a flowery summer dress who sat at the next table. We learned that the woman, Beatrice, had lived in Richmond all her life and walked to the river every day now for lunch by herself. "My husband, Harold, refuses to take me anywhere," she said in a well-bred English accent. "It's awful. I've retired recently and I thought he'd be taking me out, that we'd have fun together, take rides in the car, go dancing. I love to dance! But he just wants to play golf with his friends. It's a beautiful day, and I begged him to take me out to lunch, but he refused and has gone away with his mates. He won't return until teatime, so I'm on my own all day. He does this all the time. Even our children are furious with him for treating me this way. What do you think I should do?"

We glanced at each other and I recognized pity for her and a flash of anger at her husband's total lack of regard for her wishes wash over Tim's face. It made us sad to see someone so disappointed in her mate after all these years. We came up with all kinds of ideas: she should join a dancing group; get active in some clubs; head back to school and learn something she really wanted to know about; proceed with her own life until Harold came around.

Tim poured out ketchup for his French fries and asked, "Have there been any changes lately that would affect his behavior?"

"Well, the doctor has given him some new medicine to treat his prostate cancer."

"Then why don't you get in touch with the doctor and see if he could change the prescription to something that won't make him act this way?" Dr. Tim took a bite of his sandwich.

Beatrice and I looked at him quizzically. What's to say it was the medicine? "So, how long has he been treating you indifferently?" I asked, probing for more details.

"Well, let's see, I'd say forty-four years, for as long as we've been married. This is nothing new."

And there it was. Clearly, Beatrice had been so busy working for forty-four years that she failed to notice she was married to, well, a jerk. I volunteered Tim to go over to their house and punch him in the nose, then jump on the boat and sail away. We all laughed at the idea, and Beatrice thought that sounded like a winner. Tim? Not so much.

As our ferry left for Molesey, we waved to Beatrice. We still speak of her often. She did give us a small laugh, too, I'm embarrassed to say, because the notion of living with someone for forty-four years and not noticing what an uncaring person he was is almost absurd, the stuff of dark comedies. We wonder what she ever did about Harold's neglect, or if she just kept trying to ignore it. I certainly hope she branched out a little! Incidents like that always make me appreciate my darling Tim and his sweet nature even more than I already do.

* * *

Meeting people is the most interesting experience of our wandering life. An invitation to someone's home for a drink, dinner, or even coffee takes on added importance because being on the road, frequenting restaurants and public places all the time, makes us crave being inside a permanent home, just for a few hours. Speaking of homes, when people ask us what we miss most about not having a home, we say in unison, furniture. Of course we miss our family and friends most of all, but a comfortable chair molded to fit you perfectly over years of use comes in a close second! Think about it: who in their right mind would put really expensive furniture into a place they plan to rent out regularly to complete strangers? Most of our rentals have been very attractive, well situated, clean and fairly well provisioned, but not one has contained a decent sofa or a truly comfortable chair. For some reason, the beds have been uniformly acceptable, but the seating situation is usually abysmal.

Our deprivation has resulted in marginal behavior on several occasions: While we lived in East Molesey, old friends of ours, Margo and Rick Riccobono, who were living in London, invited us to Sunday lunch, to share a joint, which is what the British and Irish call a roast (now, now, no naughty thoughts, please), and spend the afternoon in their spacious town house. The instant the greetings and hugs ended, Tim and I bolted for the living room and rudely claimed the soft, cushiony leather chairs. As we sighed with pleasure, Margo and Rick looked at us as if we'd gone crazy. They sat in those chairs every day, so what was the big deal? When we explained that a soft seat with good back support was the thing we missed most being on the road, they kindly let us roll around in those big chairs all afternoon. They could have served cat food for lunch and we would have been happy, as long as we could spend another half hour loafing luxuriously. (Actually, they treated us to a fabulous meal, and even their dining room chairs were comfortable.)

We learned to restrain our new obsession with comfy furniture by visiting houses where we couldn't sample the furniture at all. We took a train to see Windsor Castle and particularly enjoyed the kitchens, which have functioned forever and still serve Betty and Phil (that would be Queen Elizabeth and Prince Philip, for those of you not in the inner circle) when they're home. Another morning, Tim drove us through traffic, fog, and rain to reach Highclere Castle, the magnificent estate where the BBC films its popular television series *Downton Abbey*. The castle, which sits in the middle of five thousand acres, is the most stately and beautiful home either of us had ever seen. We reveled in its understated opulence. In person, the home, with its priceless paintings and antiques, far exceeded its appearance on the series. As the sun began to appear later in the morning, and we toured the glorious gardens, Tim remarked, "I've really loved seeing this place. Too bad we didn't get to sample the furniture, but I'll bet you none of it is as comfortable as Rick's leather chairs!"

We also became adept at catching our little red train. When England gave us a beautiful day, we'd hop aboard and venture into London town. Old favorites like the Victoria and Albert Museum, or the Vic and Al, as it's called, the world's largest museum of decorative arts, claimed an afternoon. It remains Britain's granny closet, even after a smartening up with new display cases and fancy interactive features. I've visited the museum at least once in every decade since the 1960s, and it always seems filled with things of value the people in charge don't have another place for. Inlaid inkstands, lace bracelets made of human hair, and eighteenth-century Christmas cards sit alongside priceless furnishings, art, tapestries, and archaeological treasures. We could have spent weeks there. We stepped into Westminster Abbey to pay our respects to royals, poets, musicians, and clergy. We marveled once more in the British Museum at the Elgin Marbles, those huge chunks of Greece's Pantheon that the Brits took home for "safekeeping" in 1803 and refuse to give back to the Greeks. The museum, lovely and imposing, stands along a tree-lined street near a string of pubs that have revived exhausted tourists for two hundred years. The museum remains endlessly fascinating and daunting. We try to see one new portion each time we visit, while saving energy to call on our old favorites.

Portobello Road, famous for its Saturday outdoor market that stretches for many blocks, also gave us an entertaining afternoon. For once, this was a surprise I could offer Tim, since I had been there many times on other visits to London. Shops full of dusty castoffs stir up business next to stores selling high-priced antique jewelry, cart owners hawking plastic toys, and art galleries presenting high-priced paintings from known artists. The brick-and-mortar shops are fascinating, but the vendors under their tents also offer their own brand of excitement. Tim and I inspected silver pieces, old books, antique jewelry with arcane finds like champagne swizzlers gentlemen used to calm the bubbles that might annoy the lady he was serving, and trays of monocles, opera glasses, and hundreds of other curiosities. This browser's paradise tested our resolve to refrain from adding to our luggage burdens. Some of the boxes in our storage unit contain marvelous little goodies I have dragged home from Portobello in years past—a cut-glass bottle with a sterling stopper, a silver calling card case from 1848 with its owner's name engraved under the lid, a traveling wooden writing desk with its old glass ink bottles with brass lids. Unwrapping those treasures when we finally settle again will be like Christmas!

✳ ✳ ✳

The September weather and the leaves continued to turn. That meant spending several afternoons plying Oxford Street looking for sweaters and jackets. We had planned to shop for them in London anyway, since it made no sense to drag these heavy, bulky items along all summer. The big shopping streets led to some of the busiest pedestrian sidewalks we had ever seen, one of the few places where we became consciously aware that we were slowing down a little with age. London is full of people in a hurry. They give no quarter for those who hesitate. The other pedestrians weren't necessarily aiming for us, but they jostled us enough times to catch our attention. Our safest bet turned out to be walking single file, with Tim blazing the trail. When we needed to make decisions, we would stop at the side of buildings, not in the middle of the sidewalk. The Brits have thoughtfully provided signs on the pavement and lampposts, reminding tourists to look to the right before stepping off the curb (kerb, as they say).

Sometimes, we stayed in the city for dinner and a show. Seeing a play or a musical in London felt particularly comfortable. The theaters are smaller and more intimate than in many cities, creating a more personal experience. Covent Garden, the center of the theater district, is lively at all hours, full of tourists and theater patrons, and crowded with busy bars, restaurants, T-shirt and souvenir shops. We enjoyed two musicals and a play, after which we raced across the bridge to Waterloo to make that last little red train leaving on Platform 2. One play, *Chariots of Fire*, was entertaining because of its unique staging. It featured a short track on which a very physical cast ran. As we applauded at the end of the show, the cast began to applaud, too, and members of the audience came up to the stage. The Summer Olympics had concluded the week before, and medal-winning British athletes had been invited to the performance. We joined the excited audience in celebrating their excellence. The evening became particularly memorable for us. It was impossible not to be affected by the swelling of pride we felt around us. I always think of the British as being plucky. Being a child of World War II, I have faded memories of seeing news film at the movies of children picking through the rubble of bombed-out buildings, and of the lines of refugees boarding trains to be taken away from London to escape the horrible bombing raids. That spirit of nationalism erupts often in England. There's a "can do" endurance that is impressive and touching to me. Their appreciation of their countrymen's achievement and seeming devotion to sportsmanship has always spoken to me, so I had to hide my moist eyes and drippy nose from Tim, who might have teased me for being so sentimental about the British. He is, after all, practically 100 percent Irish!

Not every day was filled with tourist fun. Tim continued working on his novel while I was wrapping up my article for the *Wall Street Journal*. The *WSJ* had asked me to expand it to a two-thousand-word piece and had hinted that it would be the lead piece in the Next section, which addresses retirement issues. My muse, Tim, had also suggested that I begin working on a book proposal, so I was trying to do that, with mixed emotions of excitement and my ongoing terror of rejection. On many days, our writing work and household chores seemed just as mundane as they would have been in California, ending with a homemade meal like pot roast or chicken and an evening of TV or a downloaded movie. Again, we felt right at home in our home-free life, even if the sofa was slightly less than comfortable.

Our domestic horizons had also expanded to include a shopping area a few miles away, which boasted a more upscale supermarket, a big Boots pharmacy, and other stores we were happy to find. One day, as I was searching the drugstore for things I needed, Tim grew restless and said, "Look, I'll just go take a walk to see what's up the street. Take your time. I'll be back in a few." I muttered an agreement and continued my perusal of the merchandise.

About fifteen minutes later, he appeared at my side brandishing a large sack. "What in the world?" I asked.

"You're not gonna believe this." He pulled a gorgeous black overcoat out of the bag and put it on right there in the shampoo aisle. "Twenty pounds!" he said excitedly. It fit him perfectly, was the right length, and looked warm and fashionable.

"How on earth did you do that?"

"Salvation Army Store, m'dear, right up the road. There's one for you, too!"

I laughed and we hustled up the street. Sure enough, the Salvation Army Store carried a black double-breasted mid-calf gently worn coat just my size. Why not? That set us well for autumn in England and a chilly October in Ireland, our problem solved for around sixty dollars. We felt proud to have done our bit to save the planet, too, by buying used. When we returned to the apartment, we investigated the coats and discovered that mine, a name brand, retailed for around $400. We were even more puffed up with our brilliance.

Even though we try to keep our luggage to a minimum, wardrobe and grooming loom large in our nomadic adventure. They're important to us. We're not clothes horses, but we try to look presentable and appropriate. We have to remind ourselves that we're not seeing the same people all the time—except each other. We also have to remind ourselves to mix things up a bit. Sometimes, I step out of the bedroom, look Tim up and down, and say, "What time's the funeral today?" because we have once again fallen into the traveler's trap of wearing black all the time. Our thinking is that it always looks smart, doesn't show dirt, everything matches and—yes—it makes us look thinner!

By the time we arrived in England, after four months on the road, we knew that buying seasonal clothes in almost any city was easy, particularly since we are not tourists and have the time to shop as carefully and smartly as we would at home. Thus, finding a sweater, blouse, or jacket was never a big problem.

That said, we were (and still remain) on the perennial lookout for lightweight, multipurpose clothes that retain their good looks without the use of a dryer. In our experiences so far, those appliances are almost universally unavailable abroad, and the machines that claim to perform both washing and drying are plain useless. Thankfully, most rentals provided either a clothes drying rack or some other method of hanging out the laundry. But sometimes they didn't, and on laundry day, our apartments looked hilarious with underwear adorning lampshades and jeans splayed on towels over the dining room table. Since then, our braided nylon clothesline has become one of our most valued tools. We became shameless about wearing jeans far more often than we would have considered sanitary when we had unlimited use of laundry machines. We've discovered that as long as there's no evidence of last week's spaghetti dinner, we can still look presentable to those who don't know that our jeans could probably stand up on their own!

Shoes are another matter altogether, particularly for me. I left California without a pair of dressy shoes because my feet had grown from an 11 AA to 11½ AAA while we were in Buenos Aires. It was a shocking development for a woman my age. We couldn't find any dressy shoes before we left home, and neither Florence nor Paris offered any solutions. We searched the Internet and finally found Crispins, a shoe store in London that specialized in large ladies' shoes, and my sweet, sympathetic husband willingly went with me to shop there.

We boarded our little red train and negotiated Waterloo to the underground. After several subway changes, we stood within blocks of the store. The traditional Georgian street looked as if Henry Higgins was going to step out one of the elegant doors any minute. Distinguished boutiques, exclusive dressmakers, and chic designer shops lined both sides. It made me nervous because everything was so chic and expensive. Even though I had worn my nicest blazer, I still felt like a fraud. What was I doing in a neighborhood full of designer boutiques?

Finally, we found Crispins. When I told the saleswoman what I wanted, she snapped her fingers and said gleefully that she had just the thing. In moments, she reappeared and my Cinderella fantasies were realized. A pair of Stuart Weitzman 11½ AAA black suede wedge shoes, trimmed with elegant bows and a shiny black buckle, slipped on my feet like soft gloves. They were outrageously beautiful—and so expensive that both Prince Charming and I gasped. These treasures were not on sale. But, knowing a maiden in constant shoe distress when he sees one, my gallant man insisted I have them.

I have requested that when I leave this earth, I take those Stuart Weitzmans with me. (For the record, I'd also appreciate being dressed in Eileen Fisher for the occasion.)

The wedges were so special that they deserved their very own carry-on, so we looked a little like refugees when we bid England "cheerio!" and boarded our next flight a few days later on our way to our next home abroad. Tim had become so expert at left-hand driving that by the time we approached the massive traffic around Heathrow Airport, he didn't flinch at all. What a marvel he is! As we gathered our belongings, Victoria was the last to go into my carry-on. I'm not sure, but I thought I heard her whimper when I unplugged her from the British car. Maybe she had a hunch she was headed for the Republic of Ireland.

Chapter 10
Ireland

Dark clouds raced across the sky. Our black wool Salvation Army coats comforted us as we huddled in the car rental parking lot, waiting for the attendant to finish his inventory. As I looked up at the threatening sky, I realized I would need the overpriced Stuart Weitzman suede shoes in Dublin like a fish needs rain boots. No way would I risk water spots on those beauties, so they'd have to stay in storage for now. The fellow handed over the keys. As Tim maneuvered the second duffel into the micro trunk, I heard him grouse, "Crud! This is the smallest car yet. I'll bet sewing machines have bigger engines."

He slammed the trunk. The car was so light it nearly came off the ground!

But wouldn't you know, the tiny black Nissan became one of our favorites. It was small enough for Tim to negotiate narrow Irish lanes, and we could park it almost anywhere. We quickly discovered Tim's driving experience with the fast but orderly Brits had been good practice for driving on the opposite side of the road, but the Irish's quixotic habits required a new skill set. They were zippy and unpredictable, which required Tim to be extremely nimble. At least the Irish didn't seem to be as given to tailgating as the Italians or the French!

I hadn't been in Ireland for well over twenty years. My late husband Guy and I lived in Dublin for two years while he worked in visual development for a U.S. film company, and during that time, I fell in love with the country. Tim had heard so many stories about my great experiences that he agreed to go. His Irish heritage added to his enthusiasm for a visit, and I was excited about showing him a country I had come to love.

As Tim and I set out for Galway, about 125 miles away on the west coast, I was amazed to see the superhighway and the super traffic. Things had definitely changed since the Irish ascendancy in the mid-nineties. When I lived there in the early part of that decade, the road to Galway was two lanes wide. Traffic lights operated in the hamlets near their village greens, giving travelers a chance to pause and see a town's pubs, church, shops, and tidy cottages. The trip from Dublin to Galway took half a day then; we covered it in less than three hours this time, even though hard rain and wind challenged our little black car to stay on the road. The landscape was as lush as ever, punctuated by the ruins of twelfth-century churches and tumbled-down monasteries, the moody remnants of Oliver Cromwell's rampage in the mid-seventeenth century when he brutally decimated much of the country and certainly its churches and monasteries in the name of the Church of England. Although the road was efficient, I missed seeing the country towns since we sped and splashed directly across the middle of the island on the big highway.

When we arrived in Galway, we settled into a modern, chic apartment hotel in the city center, which lacked charm but offered incredible views of the city and the sea, across the port. It was a good location for seeing the city and the surrounding area. Later that evening, when we were seated for dinner in a nearby pub, Tim leaned across the table and said, *sotto voce*, "I can't believe it. What you've told me all these years is true. Everyone is speaking as if the KGB has bugs in all the saltshakers."

He had a point. Despite being full of diners, the buzz in the low-ceilinged, dark-paneled restaurant was even quieter than those famously refined tiny French bistros where everything, including the clink of cutlery, was muted. The Irish seemed conspiratorial to me, I had told Tim before we arrived, and their closely held conversation in pubs and restaurants had always fascinated me. The Irish are a superstitious lot, and native friends have confessed that a true Irishman is convinced that the fairies are always listening. Not all fairies are sweet like Tinker Bell, they tell me. They do have a vengeful side, especially toward those who brag about their good fortune. Of course, the cause could be something far less fanciful, such as leftover paranoia from the days when the IRA was a fact of everyday life.

Yet another typical Irish dining peculiarity arrived with our dinner, which made me smile. Fluffy mashed potatoes accompanied our beautifully grilled fresh fish—right next to a big pile of crisp, oven-baked spuds. Double starch is standard fare in almost every restaurant in Ireland and Britain. For example, in many pubs, lasagna is served with mashed potatoes right alongside the pasta dish! I have no idea what the origins of this culinary oddity might be, but it certainly isn't a slenderizing combo.

We gave Tim a break from driving the next day by taking a bus tour along the Burren, one of the largest rock landscapes in Europe. We continued onto the Cliffs of Moher, Ireland's most-visited, dramatic sight. The cliffs rise seven hundred feet above the crashing Atlantic waves. The wind and its chilly rain blasted us so furiously that we could hardly stagger up to the viewing point. Things only went downhill from there. The tour guide droned on, sharing too much information. At each stop, we waited in the car park for people too selfish to return to the bus on time. Those moments, along with the dull lunch spot into which we were herded, reminded us of all the reasons why we don't take tours as a rule. But our reward consisted of views we will never forget, and Tim was able to enjoy the scenery for once. That evening, chilled and tired, we were very happy to return to Galway. We spent a pleasant evening in a convivial pub, eating two kinds of potatoes among diners who whispered their secrets to each other.

The cold winds and icy rain of the Cliffs of Moher did not help a nasty little cold that had started to overtake me when we arrived in Ireland. It increased in intensity as we worked our way down the Irish coast. Tim booked a room at The Lodge, a charming B&B near the center of Kenmare, in County Kerry. The owner, Rosemary Quinn, an attractive young woman whose family lived in a large wing of the lovingly maintained old building, greeted us and showed us to our comfortable room. I snuffled and coughed, feeling miserable. "You'll be needing a little help with that cold. Have a seat and I'll be back in a minute with just the thing," she said.

I felt so rotten that I obeyed and watched while Tim unpacked our essentials. Soon, Rosemary returned with a small silver tray. I knew immediately what she had in mind: a pot of hot water, a plate with a slice of clove-studded lemon, and a flowered china bowl holding dainty silver tongs and sugar cubes sat on the tray. The business end of this graceful presentation contained a man-size tumbler with a big slug of Jameson Irish Whiskey! She quickly combined two sugar cubes, the lemon slice with cloves, and the whiskey, and poured in hot water to the brim. "This will fix you right up," she said. "You've lived in Ireland, so surely you're familiar with good old-fashioned hot whiskey! *Sláinte.*" She handed me the potion.

I certainly remembered that Ireland's wild, wet weather made frequent stops for a hot whiskey a necessary part of any walking expedition. A pub was never hard to find. I'm not so sure about the concoction's actual curative powers, but once the Jameson's hit its target, I didn't really care that I was sick. The Irish cure for cold weather and sniffles is much more fun than NyQuil.

Now, where were we on the other side of my personal fog? Oh yes, Kenmare. This picturesque village sits close to the Ring of Kerry and the Ring of Beara, roads that trace the edges of massive peninsulas that protrude into the Atlantic, two of Ireland's many natural wonders. Kenmare is also known for its gourmet food and live Irish music, but because I felt a little peaked, we limited our touring to a short driving trip to the Gap of Dunloe, a narrow pass between craggy peaks featuring five lakes and stunning scenery. Our drive through the gap and a plowman's lunch in the local pub sapped my energy for the day, and Nurse Tim made sure to tuck away his patient after several doses of Rosemary's magic brew that night.

The next morning, we headed to Kinsale, a seaside town once the hub of Ireland's fancy food movement. We chose a large modern hotel outside of the village, which offered spectacular views of emerald fields and dazzling lakes. People held wedding receptions and company banquets in hotels like these, so while it seemed short on warmth, it was long on dependable services. It was just what two bedraggled travelers needed: a big free parking lot, a huge bathroom, plenty of heat, great beds with fluffy duvets, a built-in clothesline in the shower, and a helpful staff. Sometimes, one must forsake charm for laundry facilities and easy parking!

Meanwhile, my *Wall Street Journal* article was due to appear very soon, in the third week of October. I thought I had wrapped the project before we left England, but when I fired up my Mac, I found a request for additional photos. They wanted a shot of us with our suitcases. "Wow! This is going to be tricky," I said, staring at the screen. "I mean, we don't know a soul here. How will we take a picture of the two of us?"

"Hang on a minute. I'll be right back." Tim disappeared.

Ten minutes later he returned, smiling. "I asked the desk clerk if

I could hire someone to help us, and of course she agreed. Come on, let's go scout some locations."

We went looking for likely spots, clicking and checking them with our iPhone cameras. When we chose some options, we scampered upstairs to smarten ourselves up for our photo session.

As we entered the room, I almost ran into Tim. He stopped dead in front of me and turned around, looking grim. "Hey, wait a minute, I just realized something. I'll have to shave my goatee!" he said, pulling a sad face. Tim was very fond of the impressive pelt he grew in England. Not my favorite look, mind you, but I didn't want to spoil his fun. "What do you mean, honey? It surely wouldn't make any difference to anyone that you'd grown a beard. You look very handsome," I said dutifully.

"Think about it. In the other pictures we've sent the paper, I'm clean-shaven. I doubt they'd want you to have two different versions of me in your pictures—one bearded, one not," he replied, looking a little glum. Before I could say anything, though, off he went to make the ultimate manly sacrifice for my budding career! He appeared a few minutes later with a face that matched his Parisian mug. I can't say I wasn't secretly pleased to see his great-looking face reemerge.

The patient clerk shot a series of pictures: inside, outside, single, and double, all for a mere twenty euros. I received the photos I needed, plus a clean-shaven husband. Lucky me.

★ ★ ★

Photo session complete, we looked around the little tourist village and enjoyed a pleasant lunch by the harbor. Then we headed back up the middle of the country toward Dublin. We were tired, damp, and ready to settle in after a week on the road. As we drove along, Tim said, "You know, we said we'd talk about the way we organize

our travels after we got to Ireland, and I think we've learned what
we need to know. I mean, look at us. You're still half sick, and I'm
awfully tired of driving and then dragging our entire luggage into a
new place every couple of nights."

"I'm afraid I have to agree with you," I said while gazing at the
ruin of an Irish castle perched on a high point in the middle of a
farmer's field. "I think that planning a driving trip when we arrive
in a country sounded like a great plan, but in every case—Italy,
England, and now here—we have arrived at our final destination
exhausted and hauling a pile of dirty laundry! I hate saying this, but
I think we've got to start considering our ages and give ourselves as
many breaks as we can."

As we continued the conversation, we agreed that in the future,
we'd head directly to our headquarters in whatever country we were
visiting, establish our "home," and then make short trips. By doing
so, we would only haul a few days' worth of clothes and other needs,
and then come "home" to our roost, just as regular tourists do. Or
residents when they take short holidays. Our new method would
cost more because we'd be paying rent on a headquarters, plus hotel
rooms on our mini excursions, but we decided that it would be worth
economizing in other areas, like skipping a few lunches and dinners
out, to alleviate stress and the danger of burning ourselves out. We
had been blazing a home-free trail for almost eighteen months and
were beginning to distill our experience into routines and planning
capabilities that would make our future adventures far easier.

We also began to realize we might now carry important knowledge and experiences to share with others. Almost everyone we had
met along the way was fascinated with our lifestyle, and the *Wall
Street Journal* assignment confirmed that we were on to something.

As we approached Dublin, I recognized no landmarks from
twenty years before. The freeways, interchanges, and slip roads

(on- and off-ramps) could just as easily have been in Los Angeles or Buenos Aires. Our trusty GPS, Victoria, prattled on, giving her wild interpretation of Irish lingo (for instance, Victoria would have pronounced our apartment manager's name, Siobhan, as "sigh-o-bahn," but the Irish say "Shiv-on," which sounds like "chiffon"). We enjoyed her phonetic antics as she led us to our new apartment in Bray, a beach community a quick twenty-minute train ride south of the city. The town looked dilapidated, as many beach towns do off-season, but when we turned and drove up a hill, we began to see impressive homes and estates. When we reached a splendid pair of black iron gates accented in gold, Victoria told us to stop.

As the gates swung wide, we took our first look at Old Connaught House, the massive two-story Georgian mansion that would be our home for a month. (Yes, we were staying in a true mansion.) Tim discovered the place on VRBO.com, the site we use, along with HomeAway.com, for all of our rentals. I had suggested that we stay in one of the quiet beach communities so we wouldn't have to fight Dublin traffic every day. The massive gray stone structure sat in the center of lavish lawns girdled by imposing stone walls. Tall paned windows shone in the afternoon sun. Behind the building, crops and horse pastures ran all the way down to the Irish Sea. What a thrill! We jumped out of the car, anxious to open the door (the property manager had already provided us with a key) and see what marvels awaited us inside.

It didn't take long. Imperial red carpet stretched across the lobby, which had once been the mansion's reception hall, with gorgeous paintings on its walls and a grand staircase with a polished banister sweeping down, all befitting the era. Plunket, the Lord Chief Justice of Ireland, built Old Connaught House in the late eighteenth century. Many of the trees on the property were over three hundred years old. Millions of moviegoers saw the house as well, in Daniel Day Lewis's Oscar-winning film *My Left Foot*.

Old Connaught had been divided into ten apartments. The ones on the ends of the building had been combined to form larger units with views on three sides, two bathrooms, formal dining rooms, and larger kitchens. The middle units like ours were two bedrooms. All of them shared the entrance and lobby, with hallways leading to various units. They had each been sold as condominiums, so some, like ours, were vacation rentals, while others were occupied by their owners year-round.

Our pleasure increased when we saw the modern elevator in the corner. It meant one thing above all others: Tim wouldn't have to lug our heavy black duffels up all those carpeted stairs! The elevator opened almost at our apartment door on the second floor. Once inside our new home, we found a nice big entry hall, a large bedroom with a comfortable king-size bed, a smaller bedroom just right for luggage, and a generous combination living room-dining room-kitchen. Every room featured the twelve-foot-high ceilings and tall, elegant windows reflective of that era. The main rooms faced lush fields and provided views of the Irish Sea. We had to tear ourselves away from the windows to begin the sorting procedure, figure out how to operate another cranky washing machine, and decorate the apartment with socks and underwear before setting off to buy items to stock up the kitchen.

When we drove down to the sea to reconnoiter, we saw clear evidence the place was packed all summer. Even on a chilly October day, the boardwalk filled up with walkers, dogs and their owners, baby buggies, and kids. Pubs, ice cream stores, small hotels, and touristy shops lined the road, facing the water. Many were already closed for the season, giving the beach a moody, melancholy feeling.

At the end of the beach we found the Harbour Bar, named The

Best Bar in the World in 2010 by *The Lonely Planet Guide*. We needed to fortify ourselves before confronting a new grocery market experience. I celebrated my improved health with a perfectly drawn pint of Guinness stout.

It was easy to see why the Harbour Bar won such an honor. We felt as though we were sailing on a wonderful old boat on a very quiet afternoon. The ceiling, floors, and walls gleamed with the patina of the pub's one-hundred-forty-year history. Nautical antiques and prints decorated every surface, and a peat fire glowed in the tile-framed hearth, its singular aroma distinctly Irish. Yes, we were really here. We sat down in worn but comfortable leather chairs near the fire. Soon, we struck up a conversation with Mike, a slight man with fine features and astute blue eyes who sat at the next table. He wore a flat tweed cap like the one Tim donned daily since he bought it at Cliffs of Moher's tourist store on our tour of the west coast. "I pick up the shopping for the wife every day and stop in here to have a pint with Joseph," he said, gesturing at the barkeep.

Our exchange drifted into politics, a conversational detour that happened often in Europe. It amazed us to realize how much Europeans knew about our government's policies, as well as the way they followed American headline news. International media gives global coverage as a matter of course. The weather in Dubai, a riot in Brazil, or a strike in Paris are all mentioned in print and on TV, and we realize the paucity of that kind of information in our own country's media vividly when we've been out in the world for a while. "So, how do ya tink it'll go? I hear the Romney fella is gettin' on purty well, but I tink Obama is the right man." His view echoed the opinion of many Europeans to whom we'd talked about the subject. We discussed the coming election for a while, as well as the Irish economy. "Ah, it's such a sad state of affairs that I prefer to just keep quiet about it all together," said Mike. He pinched his thumb and forefinger together and mimicked a zipper closing his lips. His gesture was so completely Irish that all three of us exploded in laughter.

As we dragged ourselves away from the warmth and comfort of the Harbour Bar, Tim spotted a well-used dartboard in the corner. He paused, picked up a handful of darts, and sank one into the bull's-eye on his third go. His expertise tickled me. "I didn't know you could do that!"

He laughed. "I didn't spend years in the music business hanging around bars in Santa Monica for nothing, you know." He opened the door for me. The unlimited talents of my brilliant renaissance man never cease to amaze me.

Over the next few days, the weather improved greatly. The winds calmed down and the pelting rains slowed to a drizzle. It gave me the opportunity to show Tim some of the places I remembered vividly from the years I lived there. One old favorite was Powerscourt, a grand Palladian sixty-eight-room house built in the 1700s in the Wicklow Mountains, twenty minutes south of Dublin. Its acres of woodland walks and gardens, exquisite any time of year, looked especially stunning in the colors of autumn. When I last saw the mansion, it had not been restored from a devastating fire in 1974 that left only a shell. I was delighted to find that the building now houses Irish design shops, restaurants, and a visitor center. As well as a Ritz-Carlton Hotel, of all things, new to the property.

As we wandered through those gardens, it gave me great pleasure to see them in better repair than before. My gardener's heart sang at the way the historic garden was cherished and properly tended. We stood at the top of the graceful stone staircase, absorbing the superb views of a two-and-a-half-century-old garden. We looked down the colorful terraced formal flower beds, across the man-made lake with its majestic fountain and abundant water lilies, and onto the Wicklow hills scored with dozens of small fields outlined with ancient handmade rock walls. "Well, just think, honey, we could be here looking at this glorious scene, or we could be at the Park Cinema in Paso Robles watching Bruce Willis blow something up. Tough call, huh?"

I laughed and said, "Ladies and gentlemen, I present my husband, the king of understatement! Tough call...not!"

On another lovely day, we drove farther into the Wicklow Mountains and Wicklow National Park to see Glendalough—in Irish, "the valley of the two lakes." I had visited many times, but it thrilled me to see it again.

When one lives in an attractive destination like Ireland, it can stimulate a procession of visitors. When I lived here for a few years with my first husband, Guy, we had a large house and an acre of gardens, which was one of the reasons I enjoyed being there so much. Rarely a month passed without friends or even second-tier acquaintances showing up for a visit and a tour guide (except, of course, in the dead of winter, when we could have used some entertainment and diversion). My longtime friend Fran Morris came from Oklahoma, and she and I indulged our lifelong garden addictions with visits to Powerscourt and Mount Usher Gardens in Wicklow, the National Botanical Garden, and we strolled through countless nurseries in and around Dublin. A couple from our hometown, Cambria, California, stopped in for a few days, and our daughter Robin came and loved it so much that she took some time off from college to stay for nine months with us. Friends of Guy's from Texas found their way to our house, and our well-used guest room sheltered two young friends of our daughters on their first trip abroad.

Indeed, during those days I traveled to Glendalough so many times that the woman running the visitor center would say, "Good afternoon, Mrs. Deel," when I appeared, which would astonish whatever little flock I herded that day. It was nice to be back here again, so many years later, and see it with fresh eyes.

As we moved along, the natural beauty of the mountains, lakes, streams, and ancient forests enthralled my flock of one. St. Kevin, the hermit, founded a monastic settlement in the sixth century. It continued until the fourteenth century, when the English decimated it. The lovely twelfth-century ruins are one of the most viewed sights in the country. Hardier people than we hike above the upper of the two lakes to the place where St. Kevin lived. There, they also find a Bronze Age cave, one of the earliest works of man in Ireland.

We ambled along an easier route through the forest, where the trees are so thick with moss that it's impossible not to believe that fairies live there. We wrapped up that lovely afternoon with a Sunday "joint" (here we go again) in a nearby pub, surrounded by Irish couples who brought along their children, dogs, and grandma for a jolly autumn outing. Not all Irish conversations are conspiratorial, and we enjoyed being among families enjoying one another on a beautiful day out. Ireland was definitely agreeing with us, and I was having a wonderful time sharing places I loved with my darling Tim.

Back in our Georgian apartment, we wrote most mornings and tried to balance our increasingly busy writers' lives with outings, whenever we could get away. Tim searched for more blood spatter and clues as he wrote his crime novel, while I banged away at what would be the first chapters of this book about our experiences. I finally accepted the fact that I would give this writing thing a serious try, and Tim encouraged me every day to work at it. I was actually having fun telling our story, and writing felt good.

To sell it, though, I would need a book proposal. I had been fiddling with it for quite a while and wasn't getting far. I bought several books of instruction about how to approach the project, but the result was utter confusion. Each writer had a different idea of how this essential tool should be created, and every time I tried to compose an element like a biography, a description of the book, or even a cover letter, I was disappointed and frustrated with the results. The task seemed insurmountable, and I began to doubt that I would ever pull together something good enough to submit to an agent. Tim sat at our little dining room table, and I had commandeered the coffee table for my desk. Neither of us could refrain from glancing through the tall Georgian windows to the view. Every morning, we watched the horses being led out to the field along the wall below our gardens, beyond which the Irish headland jutted into the sea. Autumn declared its presence more dramatically as vivid magentas, oranges, and reds enveloped the landscape. It was outrageously beautiful—which made it very hard to concentrate on our work!

One morning, after a long, fruitless session, I closed my computer. "Tim, I'm using five different book proposal textbooks, trying to pull the elements together into something an agent or a publisher would consider reading, but I'm really frustrated! Everything I do looks homemade and amateurish to me. I just can't get a handle on it. Maybe we should consider getting some professional help. I don't want to embarrass myself."

He turned from his keyboard. "I think you're right. If the article in the *Wall Street Journal* generates any interest, you should have a proposal ready to go. Things move fast in the publishing business, so we'd want to take advantage of the buzz." As usual, Tim had a solution in mind. "Remember Bob Yehling, the guy who did such a good editing job on [the novel] *Mental Hygiene* for me? We could see if he has time to help you."

A series of lucky breaks followed. First, Bob agreed to take on the project. He was a very busy man and a book author in his own right, but he understood our sense of urgency and agreed to plunge into it immediately. Bob would write the bio, the cover letter, and all the other parts of the proposal that would have taken months for us to do ourselves.

My wonderful, sweet muse also pitched in, doing research about other books in the genre of travel and retirement, and providing excellent fodder for Bob's efforts.

Since I became so involved in chores like the table of contents and sketching out proposed chapters while providing other material Bob needed, Tim started to take over more of the household duties I had been performing. Later, Tim would joke that if we were both writing full time, we'd starve to death and go naked because no one would ever get to the market or wash our clothes.

After a few intense days, I responded as I always do when overwhelmed with a project: I ran away and made plans to do anything but the proposal! So many sights and experiences still awaited us in Dublin, and I couldn't very well write a chapter about something we hadn't done, could I? I found some interesting ways to procrastinate in the name of "book research." It wasn't too hard to persuade my darling spouse to play, since watching a person grind away at a computer keyboard isn't very scintillating.

During my previous two years in Ireland, I made several good friends. One, Brooke Bremner, reared her children there. She had since moved back to the United States, but the charm of Ireland drew her across the pond again. Now, she and her husband, David Glueck, divided their time between Kenmare, Ireland, and their other home in Chicago. They were stopping in Dublin on their way home to Chicago, so we arranged to see them. It was wonderful to be with old friends after such a long time on the road. The four of us took a walking tour of locations made famous in the Easter Rising in 1916 and the Rebellion in 1921. We attended the Irish Theatre Festival to catch *The Talk of the Town*, a lovely play by Emma Donoghue, whose book, *Room*, we had all enjoyed. Irish poets, writers, artists, and composers enjoy the kind of financial and emotional encouragement that I wish we would emulate in our country. In Ireland, the earnings made by visual artists, composers of music, and writers are tax exempt. The country's rich literary and musical history is evident everywhere! Tim and I later enjoyed two other performances at the festival, and we loved seeing the packed houses and intelligent audience responses.

We chose to stay in Bray because getting into the city was easy with the DART rail system's convenient runs into the city. Once there, it was a quick walk from the main station to almost any Dublin destination. We found street parking near the station easily, a nice beginning to our pleasant twenty-minute commute. The train wound along the beach, and on every trip we saw something new—a tower or home we had missed, people playing on the sand, a storm moving across the Irish Sea en route to Britain, or clouds lit afire by the setting sun. Always something going on! Every ride in and out of the city was a joy to us, and watching Tim become enthralled with the country added to my pleasure.

Although Dublin is an ancient city and its historic monuments and landmarks remain the same, I noticed some dramatic changes. The National Gallery of Ireland had expanded from its intimate building on Merrion Square by adding an enormous space filled with a world-class collection. I was thrilled to see that the country had made such an investment during its economic growth! It was one more indication of its respect and appreciation for the arts. It made me proud. Grafton Street and its surrounding area, the shopping and street music hub of the city, looked almost the same, except for new trendy restaurants and brand-name stores we saw in all the big European cities we visited. Street musicians, many of them first-class entertainers, made music on every block. Flower stalls, mimes, and busy shoppers made the scene lively at all hours. Marks and Spencer's downstairs food court marked the perfect place to pick up a tasty dinner for our return train ride home. I was happy to see that the worldwide economic downturns and the decline of what was called the "Irish Tiger," the ascendency of the Irish economy in the nineties, had not diminished the city. If anything, it felt livelier and more cosmopolitan than I had remembered it being.

Aside from Brooke and David, we saw other old friends of mine who made us feel welcome, right at home again. We didn't have to look far for new friends, either; it turned out they lived right next door to us in Old Connaught House. We met Alan Grainger one day while we were lugging grocery sacks into the building. With his neatly trimmed gray beard and natty sweater vest, he looked and sounded like the distinguished British gentleman one would imagine living in such an elegant manor. We took the elevator together, realized that we shared a small hallway, and talked about getting together during our stay. As we put away groceries, I said, "Oh, I hope Alan's wife is as charming as he is. Wouldn't it be great to know the neighbors? I'll bet they know everything about this house and Ireland, for that matter!"

The next day, Tim had just settled at his "desk" to begin researching some facts Bob wanted when I said, "You know what, honey, the sun is shining and the forecast says it's going to get rainy and cold tomorrow, so maybe we'd better go up to New Grange today. I don't want you to miss it, and it would be lousy up there in the rain."

He grinned at me. "Boy, are you transparent. You really don't want to settle down and work on the table of contents, do you?" It seemed as if he was taking his new role seriously.

"I'm working on it," I lied. I tapped my head and continued, "It's all ticking away in there, and when I sit down to do it, it will just flow right out." In all honesty, I did hope my little white lie would prove to be true.

"Oh, come on then, kid, we'll go up there, but tomorrow, you really need to knuckle down and get on with it. The article comes out next Monday, and we have to get that proposal in shape, just in case!"

Naturally, the rain arrived earlier than the weather forecast predicted, leaving poor Tim to again dodge oncoming traffic on sloppy, slippery two-lane country roads. It was my penance for procrastinating once again. As we sloshed along, I filled him in on Newgrange. "The thing that knocks me out is that it was built in 3200 BC as a burial site, which makes it older than Stonehenge and the pyramids in Egypt," I said. "When we get there, you'll see that it's a long passageway dug into a huge circular grassy mound with white stones covering the outside. When you look at the mound, you have no idea what's inside. The outside facing looks like a bad 1970s imitation stone fireplace, but it was really how the Neolithic people covered the outside wall of the hill. Those white stones had all fallen off and the archaeologists found them around the mound and put them back!

"I'm a little concerned about your going into the passageway," I continued. "It's pretty tight, and there will probably be a lot of other people there." Tim nodded silently and then swerved hard to avoid a pothole.

When we arrived, about twenty people waited at the entrance, staring up at the space above the opening where the sun enters. It shines straight through and strikes the middle of the chamber precisely at dawn every December 21, the winter solstice. After three thousand years of the planet's slight course changes, it's moved a bit, but it's still on target. Every year a select group is privileged to witness the event. We waited until everyone else had moved ahead, so Tim was able to enjoy the reenactment of the solstice performance before we hustled down the narrow passageway to the drizzly October day outside.

When we returned, we saw a note underneath our door. "Please come for cocktails at 6 p.m." It was signed, "Maureen and Alan, the people next door."

We searched our pitifully small stock of outfits to wear for the occasion. Tim's ancient black wool Pendleton shirt (which we call his "wubie" because he wears it all the time like a little kid wearing his security blanket around him) was just the thing. Maureen and Alan saw me in a long sweater and tights, the bottle of wine in my hand my most significant accessory.

Maureen is one of those mature women whose features are so beautiful that you know she was drop-dead gorgeous in her youth. She was still stunning. Her silver bun was arranged perfectly, and her wide blue eyes were full of intelligence and mischief. We all talked at once, crowding into the entry hall in an immediate lively conversation that, to our subsequent delight, never stopped the entire time we lived next door.

Their place was a different world from ours. They had combined two spaces at the end of the building, so the lofty Georgian windows ushered in light from three sides. An interesting variety of excellently framed paintings decorated the pale green walls, and the etched French doors to the dining room brought in even more light. The carpets were luxurious, and double silk drapes framed the windows. Deep crown molding and formal lintels over the doors brought the rooms together, while the fireplace was a welcome sight on a chilly evening. Family pictures glimmered in their polished silver frames as they sat atop the mantel and several inlaid tables. The sitting room and dining room comprised the entire depth of the building and gave Maureen and Alan an even more exciting view of the woods, fields, and Irish Sea than we enjoyed.

And they had an abundance of our favorite commodity on earth—furniture! Tim and I hesitated before sitting down, not wanting our new friends to think us piggish. When Alan and Maureen gravitated to what were clearly "their" chairs facing the fireplace, we gleefully took up residence in two cushiony velvet wing backs with matching tufted footstools. Heaven.

Travel was an obvious topic we could connect over. We enjoyed stories of their exciting journeys around the world. They, like so many people we had met, had been avid travelers all their lives. "Our health doesn't let us take on challenging trips anymore," Alan said, "so having that rental apartment next door has been a joy to us! We get to sit tight and enjoy people from all over the world who come to stay there. It's a great way to travel—no packing, and it's free, too!" he laughed. We were delighted to once again find kindred spirits, people who were always on the lookout for expanding their world view and found ways to keep learning and experiencing new places, even from those armchairs!

We would spend many more evenings enjoying good wine and conversation (*craic*, as the Irish call it) in that appealing room. Maureen, who was Irish, and Alan, a British transplant, had three daughters and many grandchildren. Alan was a writer, with twelve books to his credit, and he was working on his latest, *Blood on the Stones*, a spy thriller with its roots in the Holocaust. Alan shared Tim's facility for remembering absolutely everything. He proved a bountiful resource for historical fact, legends, and hilarious tales. After a little wine, the dignified Maureen, who at first appeared to be rather formal, told some righteously funny stories, too, mostly about the colorful branch of her Anglo-Irish family who rattle around in a three-hundred-year-old castle in the wilds of western Ireland with muddy dogs and crazy farmers tracking dirt all over exquisite Irish stone floors and ancient oriental carpets. As we left their house, I said, "We have had a marvelous time and we're so happy you invited us! We would love to reciprocate, but as you know, our apartment has terrible furniture. Could we possibly bring the food and wine to your house and pretend that we're returning your hospitality?" The plan worked out well, so we were able to spend time with them without feeling like bounders.

We had such a good time that we were over-stayers, and stumbled the five feet to our house too late to cook dinner. We settled for canned soup, crackers, and a re-hash of the evening's most entertaining moments. We congratulated ourselves on our good fortune. Who could imagine finding intelligent, hilarious neighbors who were willing to make friends with itinerant souls like the Martins! What a country.

Several days later, Maureen and Alan invited us to join them for a luncheon party that would include the father-in-law of one of their daughters, who lived in the wilds of Scotland. Like his hosts, he had many tales to tell. He had climbed mountains and seen sights we loved hearing about. We rolled into high gear as we ordered wine in a sophisticated restaurant we would never have discovered on our own. As the decorous waiter distributed menus, I looked across the autumn flower arrangement that echoed the colors in the china. Maureen extracted a gold-framed monocle from a small leather case in her purse. She popped it into her eye socket and began to peruse the menu. I had never before, except in the movies, seen a person use a monocle! It was imperative that I not make eye contact with Tim, whom I could tell was also choking back a chuckle, or the game would have been up. After she made her choice, Maureen slipped the glass back into its holder and daintily tucked it into her pale leather clutch bag, and I could finally exhale. We didn't embarrass ourselves at all.

Later that afternoon, I started working again on the book

proposal. Bob had sent several pages for review, and I wanted to get them back to him as soon as I could because the next day the *Wall Street Journal* article was to publish my first article. We had no idea what would happen when it came out.

We were so excited that concentration was difficult, so we tried to relax with some mindless TV. "Well, sweetie, I think it's time for bed," Tim said, switching off the set as he headed to the kitchen to make coffee for the next morning.

"I'll just check my emails," I said. California time is eight hours behind Irish time, so we often received messages from home late in the evening. When I opened my email account, I squealed. Embarrassing, but yes, I squealed.

"What is it?" Tim asked.

At first I was alarmed at the sheer number of messages in my box. "I don't have any idea, but there are about twenty new emails here from addresses I don't recognize. Do you think I've been hacked?"

"Wait a minute." He dropped a towel on the counter and hurried over. He looked at the entries and started laughing. "You know what this is? These aren't hackers…these are readers, honey! Look—there aren't any suspicious attachments and their names look normal. They must be *Wall Street Journal* readers. The online edition must have broken already! Open one and see what it says," he said excitedly.

"'Inspiring' is the subject line?!" I croaked, almost too excited to read. "Dear Lynne and Tim, I just read your article and I want you to know that you are my inspiration, my heroes! You're proving that people really can do anything if they have the courage. Keep on traveling. Bob."

"Well, I'll be damned," Tim said. "Go on, open another one."

"Listen to this," I said, getting more and more excited. "'Just finished reading the article in the *WSJ*. How I envy you! Look forward to following your blog and your book. How do you manage the language barrier? I'm so attached to our home. Been here forty-five years! I'm sure I'll find all the answers as I read past blogs. You have inspired us! Keep writing! Julie.'"

Letters continued to flood my inbox as they were routed from our website contact page, and I eagerly opened them all, soaking in the thrilling notion that perhaps our story, our life, had actually touched other people's. Finally, sometime after 1:00 a.m., we forced ourselves to quit reading and get to bed, but we were so stimulated that we both read our Kindle books for a long time before we slept.

The next morning, we dashed to the computer. Almost two hundred emails sat in my inbox. "Check the subscriber list on your website," Tim said. Aye, aye, sir! Readership had jumped from thirty to a hundred and ten overnight.

We didn't need Tim's strong coffee that morning. Our hearts already pounded.

I read the emails. "Tim, I have to answer these folks. They're saying things that deserve a response, and almost all of them have questions about repositioning cruises or house rentals or something."

"You're right," he said. "If it gets to be too much for you, I can help."

I laughed. "Sure…I can just see you writing my kind of prattle: 'Dear George, thanks a billion for writing to me. I've attached five hundred articles about repositioning cruises, plus instructions about how to get a passport. Give my love to your wife and entire family. I will love you forever, your best friend, Lynne.'" (If you can't tell by now, I am a very enthusiastic person.)

He did have to help me, though. He still does. He doesn't prattle but is definitely the expert on practical matters. We committed to answering every email, and we still do that, but there were so many that it sometimes took us quite a while to get back to people.

As the day continued, the flood of mail only intensified. We both hunched over our computers for hours at a time, responding to good wishes and encouragement, answering questions about all aspects of our life on the road. We were ecstatic that people found our story inspirational, that we were on the verge of really making a difference, and that so many people were interested in us. It was an unbelievable experience. As we typed, we brought each other finger food when we thought about it, things we could munch on without missing a beat. It was an emotional whirlwind, and we couldn't help ourselves. Each email filled us with delight and awe.

Suddenly, Tim gasped and then sputtered. "Oh my God! Get over here. This is unbelievable!"

I raced to his side. On the computer screen, I saw the front page of *Yahoo*. Across the five-story crawl at the top, there were the Martins, grinning with the serene roses of Notre Dame Cathedral's garden blooming in the background, the caption "How One Retired Couple Travels the World" emblazoned beneath us! The crawl moved us right along, sandwiched between an article about China and another about a football player's special gift. Neither of us had ever dreamed that *Yahoo* would pick up our story. "This is the wildest thing I have ever seen," he exclaimed.

We were amazed that our grinning faces continued to appear on the crawl for the next three days. Our website readership and email list subscriber numbers went through the roof, a result that had never even occurred to us. When the online version of the *Wall Street Journal* appeared, most comments were positive, but there were some heated debates. We stayed out of it and let those folks talk among themselves.

We answered every one of the emails. Apparently, we had delivered a message to which people could relate. From the responses we got, it seemed that those close to retirement saw our idea as a fresh way to approach the last third or half of their lives. Some told us that they had felt trapped, and our notion gave them the push they needed to begin thinking of their future in a different way, to seek a plan that would allow them to move beyond predictable behavior. People who couldn't travel for health or other reasons said they enjoyed hearing about our plan and looked forward to more blogs and a book. (My first reaction to that was "Wow!" followed quickly by "Eek!" when I remembered the state of my book proposal.) A surprisingly large percentage of our correspondents were young people, some of whom traveled while in their twenties but were now involved in raising families. It tickled us that people our children's ages found our story of value, too. Many told us we gave them hope that they would be able to travel again once they fulfilled their obligations to their children. Others requested more specific information about the nuts and bolts of Tim's massive planning, and we were happy to comply. Readers called us "inspirational," "heroic," and "brave." Not a single person was insulting or negative. And that was inspiring to us as well.

Something else arrived on our email: requests for interviews by bloggers, newspapers, magazines, and television. Each query caused a flutter of excitement between us, followed immediately by terrified discussions about how to proceed. I was in the "don't do anything until you have something (like a book) to sell" camp, because that had always been a guideline when I was in the PR business years before. Tim bivouacked in the "strike while the iron is hot" sector. Late one night, after a particularly intense debate over how to respond to these, he said, "Now, don't get defensive about what I'm going to say, but Rick Riccobono suggested that we call Sarah McMullen. As you know, she's a moxie public relations person, and I'm sure she'd have some good advice for us." Rick, who is one of Tim's dearest friends, and owner of the comfortable leather chairs we so enjoyed in London, is a digital media rights expert and works internationally in the music industry. He was a wonderful source of information and encouragement for us as we stumbled through this new experience, and we'd already had several phone conversations with him about what was happening to us. His suggestion was good enough for me!

"Hmmm…that's a good idea. I know she's so smart. You've told me in the past that she worked with Elton John for all those years. She's not only talented, but she's gotta be one tough cookie to have survived that."

We phoned her and laid out our quandary for her. "Oh, y'all," she said from her office in Houston, "I think Lynne's right. For the most part, saving the big interview shows for later, when you've got a book coming out, is a better strategy."

I fell for Sarah during that conversation, not because she said I was right, but because she proved to be all the things I knew and imagined: smart, funny, sweet, and generous. We have become such great pals that Tim leaves the room, shaking his head, when she and I get into serious BFF conversations about hair and shoes! Her guidance and sincere excitement over our newfound notoriety made our fifteen minutes of fame even more fun. Both she and Rick made themselves available to us, serving as our cheerleaders and offering sagacious advice when we asked for it. They were our lifeboats in a sea of uncharted waters, and we will be forever grateful to both of them. Over the next few days, we were so involved in answering emails that we barely spoke to one another, except to read aloud particularly touching or amusing messages. Of course, we sent a link to the article to our friends and family, so we enjoyed a flurry of communication on Skype and FaceTime. We hardly slept and procrastinated about showering until late in the day. Our obsession grew so intense that we resented stepping out for groceries.

One afternoon, I looked around our littered living room and

burst into crazy laughter. Tim slowly tore his eyes from his screen. "Yeeesssssss? What is it?" Along with his two-day growth of beard, he obviously had not checked his hair in the mirror that morning. I looked even worse. We both were still in our jammies at 11:00 a.m.

"Look at this frat house! We're messy all the time, but we have sunk to a new low. We've gotta stop and clean up this joint!" I exclaimed.

Let me illustrate my point. My coffee table "desk" held not only my computer and notes, but also a half-finished peanut butter jar with a knife standing straight up in it, cracker crumbs littering the paper towel under it, and a browning apple core on a saucer. Several empty Coke cans, a flat non-alcohol beer and an abandoned wineglass were scattered around the room. Soaking in the sink, waiting for someone to deal with it, sat a saucepan that had been used for heating canned soup.

"Oops...you're right. Just let me finish these three from yesterday and we'll get on it," Tim said sheepishly.

We spent the next few hours cleaning up our home and ourselves. When we returned from the grocery store, we found another note from Alan and Maureen. "Haven't seen you in days. Time for a break. 6 p.m.! *Sláinte* [cheers in Irish], A and M."

It was just the nudge we needed. Alan and Maureen became our ballast as we plowed through the waves of excitement that washed over us. For several days, they were the only respite we gave ourselves. They greeted us at their door with hugs and kisses, and ushered us to our red chairs in their beautiful sitting room. Alan poured Tim his drink and handed me a hefty glass of red wine, and they listened indulgently to our latest tales of neophytes awash in the current of sudden media attention. The fire snapped and sputtered and the wind swirled around Old Connaught House that night. We could see that immense changes would occur in our lives, not all of them easy to navigate. Our advisors, Bob, Rick, and Sarah, kept talking about books, TV, interviews, a future that looked terrifying from where we sat in our little apartment in Ireland.

That night, after our refreshing evening with Alan and Maureen, we managed to put together another bowl of soup with crackers. In the next couple of days, as the torrent of letters continued, I was asked by the *Wall Street Journal* if I would write a short piece, answering some of the most-asked questions readers had posed. I was thrilled to accept their invitation.

✳ ✳ ✳

The pressure of making decisions mounted as our days in Ireland came to an end. Several agents had expressed interest in representing me, and a major news program contributor had made overtures about featuring us in a segment. Every day brought some new challenge that needed to be addressed, and our team of advisors became more valuable with each volley. We tried to keep food in the house, make our living space sanitary, and clean our clothes for traveling while simultaneously thumping away on our computers and talking on the phone late into the nights. The eight-hour time difference to California suddenly became a real problem because just as we would end a long, hard-working day, the people there would be just starting theirs, ready to talk, ask questions, and make plans. The days evaporated.

So did our wiggle room. We had none. Our reservations for a week in Marrakech, Morocco, were nonrefundable, so we had to take this show on the road without knowing what our Internet situation would be. Our repositioning cruise, which sailed from Barcelona, was an immutable climax for our travels, a deadline that could not be postponed because of all the reservations and plans made around it. We woke up early and went to bed late, both of us exhausted from stress and excitement. As we prepared to leave Ireland, we left those coats with a friend and donated other cold-weather gear to a local charity shop. And I signed a contract with Dana Newman, an effective, enthusiastic literary agent and attorney with a solid track record of success with nonfiction authors. It was a moment I never could have imagined when we printed those cards in Mexico!

We left Ireland for Africa just before winter roared in from the Atlantic. And as we did, even more publishing mayhem rumbled into our lives, as furious as the Irish Sea in October.

Chapter 11
Morocco

The Muslim call to prayer erupted from a speaker mounted on the ancient tile roof across the street, answered by a hundred others throughout Marrakech. Smoke billowed out of doorways where men seared meat over charcoal stoves, and I glanced up just in time to avoid running into a donkey cart that had appeared from nowhere. Drums, snake charmers' flutes, shouts from vendors, and Arabic music blasting from boom boxes competed frantically. It was chaos.

We hurried along. Tim walked particularly fast, his shoulder almost touching the peeling terra-cotta wall. I followed as closely as possible without stepping on his heels, my eyes downcast, trying not to trip on the uneven cobblestones. I flinched when the pink sleeve of a woman's robe touched my face as she roared past me on her motorcycle.

Without turning his head or slowing down Tim shouted to me, "We sure are brave! We may finally be too old for something!"

"You got that, buddy!" I shot back without breaking stride and then giggled, "What's wrong with us, anyway? We are too old to be doing this! We should be home babysitting grandchildren or something." Crosby, Stills, Nash, and Young kept singing "Marrakech Express" into my mind's inner ear.

Tiny shops, their tattered awnings meeting in the middle of the narrow lane, offered trays piled with silk purses, leather goods, jewelry, fruits and vegetables, water pipes, bolts of cloth, and pottery, making our passage almost impossible as we headed for the center of the city. Storekeepers vied for our attention, some touching our arms, imploring us to look at their goods. We dodged donkey carts, tourists, Africans in robes and swirling burkas, men in fezzes and skullcaps commanding us to follow them, and women and children begging for money. The cacophonous moment, the calls to prayer echoing over everything, the confusion of odors—spices, searing meat, baking bread, sour bodies, sweet incense—made us breathless with excitement.

The dark narrow *souk* (market) street ended, and a blinding sun startled us at Jemaa el-Fnaa, the gigantic, chaotic square, one of the largest in the Arab world. It is the heart of Marrakech, where snake charmers, fresh orange juice vendors, men with chained monkeys, magicians, fortune-tellers, rug merchants, jugglers, and drummers all gather to conduct their business wherever they choose to squat. So do men in colorful Berber costumes, with their coned woven hats and brass cups dangling like necklaces, henna tattoo artists, and people selling jugs, hats, maps, and postcards.

We stopped to stare. Big mistake. We were assailed by these people, who wanted us to either buy something or hire them to guide us somewhere. We learned very quickly not to make eye contact but to keep walking purposefully, grabbing furtive, sneaky glances at the surrounding low faded terra-cotta buildings, the towers reaching upward here and there, and the purple mountains in the distance.

Tim spotted a restaurant with umbrellas, grabbed my hand, and half-dragged me through the crowd to a table, where we would have ordered anything just to buy time to get our bearings. When the waiter arrived, Tim gestured to the items the people at the next table were enjoying, and nodded. The waiter understood. He returned quickly with a filigreed teapot, two jewel-colored glasses, and a plate of honey-soaked phyllo pastries full of nuts and spices.

We had arrived in Marrakech.

"This city is breathtaking," I breathed, sipping the strong tea. "I love being in such an exotic place, but I'm so glad we decided to try it out before committing to a whole month here. Of course, we did choose to be in the medina, the oldest part of Marrakech, not the more modern section of the city, but still…"

"I thought we'd go over to that part of the city tomorrow to just get an idea of how the Europeans live here," he said. "It's funny—we started this trip in Istanbul, which is a pretty challenging place, and we're ending it here in Africa, which is even more daunting!"

We retraced our steps to our riad, this time more at ease. (A riad is a Moroccan home that has been converted into a hotel.) We enjoyed looking at the performers, the buildings, and the vendors' wares. Marrakech enveloped our senses completely, but only after we surrendered to her manic pitch days later did we begin to catch her rhythm and negotiate the streets with a modicum of confidence.

Here are a few basic facts about Marrakech. Facts that increase your chances for survival. Traffic never stops in Marrakech, the streets are dangerously uneven, and there is always the temptation to stop paying attention to what you're doing. A fall or a collision awaits the unwary. It's also easy to get lost in a thousand-year-old city whose streets all look the same to a foreigner. Fittingly, the owner of our riad had given us the sort of directions in a language we now expect in countries where street names mean little and can change every block: the language of landmarks. "Walk down the street until you pass the square with the drugstore on the left. There will be two arches. Take the left one, and follow that street until you get to the big mosque. Go to the right, around the mosque and on to the next set of arches…"

You get the idea.

We walked along a narrow street that would barely accommodate one car, but skillful drivers, all masterful at the one-lane tango, rarely touched each other as they edged along. We turned, went down several tile steps into an alleyway less than ten feet wide, and came to our formidable studded iron gate, which was twelve feet high. After a moment, a small door within the gate opened. We ducked to enter, while Marika, the pretty cook for the house, stepped aside. The aroma of spices and roasting meat followed her from the kitchen. I would have gleefully eaten dinner right that minute! My mouth was watering. The low-ceilinged entry hall heightened the surprise I felt every time we rounded the corner into the courtyard.

Our riad sat within a four-story square in which ten rooms and suites surrounded the central courtyard. Our roof was open to the sky, but its system of canopies closed in the rain. Colorful tile decorated the walls, and intricate white trim and shutters accented the round Moorish arches above the doors and banisters. Lacy olive trees and large potted plants added softness and texture, while lively tapestries decorated the walls. Ancient tiles protected each level of the hallways overlooking the patio, their colors enriched with time and exposure. Hand-woven cushions were piled atop built-in concrete seating, and patterned carpets softened our steps.

Patricia, the housemaid, silently lit candles on tables and in gorgeously filigreed iron and tin sconces hanging from the ceilings and mounted to the walls. Huge candles sat in the alcoves and along the pool. The riad glowed with flickering light, reflected in the glittering dark blue water. Elaborate tin lampshades and chandeliers glittered in the early evening.

Abraham, a very tall and handsome houseboy, greeted us in his white linen Muslim garb with a little bow. Speaking French, he asked if we would like tea, then gestured questioningly toward the rooftop balcony. I mumbled something in my terrible French and indicated that we'd be there shortly. He went to the kitchen, directly across the patio, and we opened our room.

Two German women had checked in to their room next to us, and it was impossible not to hear them chatting away. Voices came from rooms on the second floor, too. Tim shut the wooden doors to our room, and I closed the frail shutters over the windows, all of which opened onto the courtyard. He whispered, "It's picturesque as hell, but I feel like I'm living in a dorm! I can hear everything in the building."

"Me too: Abraham is filling the pot for tea, the French people are on the phone, and the new people are making plans," I said. "Uh oh, the owner's back and he's about to plant himself in that alcove outside our door, smoke his cigarettes, and call his wife in the Congo. Wonder if they're still fighting about the furniture for their apartment? But Tim, our room is big enough and comfortable, and it's only for a few nights, so we'd better just relax and enjoy it."

At this outburst, Tim laughed and said, "I think you'd better have a little Scotch with that tea. It's cocktail time!"

We ascended the stairs, its risers decorated with tiles and gleaming white filigreed railings. "Hey, have you noticed how much at home we feel here?" I asked. "Look at these punched tin lampshades, the tiles, arches, concrete furniture, patterned cushions, big glazed planters, tile floors…we could be in San Miguel!"

"Of course," he huffed as we reached the top floor. "Think about it—the Moors occupied Spain, then the Spaniards went to Mexico and took their culture with them." Now, I know that somewhere in the back of my mind I knew those facts about human migrations, but the beauty of travel is that now I knew those facts in a way that only being on the ground and experiencing them offers a person.

He collapsed on a rattan chair and we surveyed the rooftop space. "Oh, Tim, look at the city! And the moon is rising right over there! This is divine," I gushed.

The balcony was a Moroccan dream: comfortable sofas and lounge chairs were within easy reach of brass tables. Candles flickered everywhere. Fragrant flowering plants draped the stucco walls, and small trees offered a feeling of privacy. An awning along one side of the garden sheltered tables laid with crisp linens, polished cutlery, and china for dinner. The low city spread out before us, pink terra-cotta buildings with rooftop balconies like ours, mosque spires punctuating the skyline, and puffs of smoke rising from fires and grills, the sumptuous scents of meats spreading all over the city.

Abraham brought the tea and glittering glasses, along with several plates of olives, cheese, and tiny sandwiches. I thanked him in my lousy French and he smiled. As Tim poured my cocktail, Annette and Gabrielle, our neighbors on the first floor, whom we had met as they were checking in earlier that day, arrived on the roof. Annette accepted my offer to share my Scotch. Gabrielle brought wine with her, so our cocktail hour was off to a lively start. They were longtime friends whose lives led them to opposite sides of Germany, so they traveled once a year together to catch up and enjoy a respite from their children and jobs.

Annette, who was a head nurse from Hamburg, spoke almost perfect English. She was one of those people very comfortable in their own skins, sporting a ready smile beneath her short black hair and bright blue eyes. I never saw her having anything other than a great time. Meanwhile, her friend Gabrielle, who lived in Bavaria, had English as sparse as our German, so we didn't get to know her very well. She was blond, wore wonderful jewelry and scarves, and laughed a lot…always an attraction for us. She was also game for anything the rest of us dreamed up, another trait we're fond of. She was the fourth person we had met from Munich during our travels. They all loved to have a good time!

"We had a wonderful time today," Annette exclaimed. "We

shopped all over the *souks* and had an amazing lunch in a beautiful French restaurant we found near the square! We're trying another place tonight that a friend told us about."

As we chatted, we speculated about the new owner, Renauld, who said he was Swiss but didn't speak German at all. Annette and Gabrielle found that suspicious. He spent hours at the table outside our room staring at his computer, fiddling with numbers. We were never quite sure exactly who and what he was, why he bought the hotel, and what the story was with his Congolese wife. But from all of these random tidbits, we developed delicious gossip, fueled by the atmosphere of Marrakech itself. Its mysterious, slightly dangerous atmosphere gives rise to all kinds of romantic notions. Notorious spies and nefarious activities occur to visitors in this extravagantly dark and dangerous-looking part of the world.

The other player in our little hotel cast was Jack, a good-looking forty-something man who seemed to speak every language. The hotel manager for years, he was very sophisticated, even though he always wore jeans and a T-shirt. The new owner was in awe of Jack because he ran the hotel perfectly and the staff did his bidding without hesitation. He rattled away in German with Annette and Gabrielle, spoke rapid, exquisite French with the handsome couple upstairs, gave instructions to the staff in Arabic and French as needed, and talked to us in perfect English. Privately, we called him Jack-who-knows-everything. Because he did. No matter the question, whether about Marrakech, Paris, or the stock market, he had an answer. He had lived in Marrakech for ten years, and he was discreet about his living arrangements. His partner was an architect; I envisioned a very sophisticated older man who owned a lavish villa. I decided that Jack kept his day job to stay busy. It was as if we were living in Armistead Maupin's apartment building in *Tales of the City*!

That evening, Tim and I enjoyed a romantic dinner under a large moon on the terrace, a perfectly prepared lamb tagine. It was served impeccably by Abraham, who didn't seem to mind trotting up and down four flights of stairs. Our meal was so delicious that I asked for the recipe, which Jack-who-knows-everything supplied the next day.

Nearly all of my mornings were occupied writing new parts for the book proposal and completing the articles I committed to write, but in the afternoons, we explored the wonders of Marrakech. A highlight was Yves Saint Laurent's blue Majorelle Garden, designed in the 1920s by Jacques Majorelle, a French expatriate painter. Saint Laurent and his partner, Pierre Bergé, restored the gardens after they had been left in ruins for many years. This haven sits in the midst of Marrakech's madness. Majorelle's electric cobalt blue, which YSL used on buildings, walls, fountains, and bridges, creates a stunning backdrop for the silver-green of hundreds of plant species. Within a walled garden on the grounds, we enjoyed an excellent lunch and were fascinated with the small museum's collection of Moroccan art.

We then ventured over to Marrakech's modern section, Guéliz. Had we chosen to rent an apartment for a month, we would probably have chosen that neighborhood. While we found Guéliz interesting and things there were much less frantic than where we were staying, it was far less enticing or exotic. It contained the same stores we found in almost all other European cities, and little else. The wide streets were lined with much more European-looking buildings, and the ample sidewalks allowed us to meander along without having to worry about being knocked down by a fast-moving vehicle. We found a little Parisian bistro with outdoor tables and we might as well have been lounging about on the Ile de France! Although it was easier to negotiate and not nearly as challenging, we were more than ready to return to our more exotic neighborhood. After all, adventure was our goal in coming to Africa in the first place.

✶ ✶ ✶

That evening, on the roof, we had cocktails with "the girls," as we called our German friends in our private conversations. As we chatted, Annette looked over at Gabrielle and back at Tim, and said hesitantly, "We have a big favor to ask."

"Certainly," Tim replied.

"We would really like to go to Jemaa el-Fnaa for dinner. The square is supposed to be fantastic at night—a whole different world. The daytime performers are replaced by huge tents with hundreds of small restaurants. We want to go, but to tell you the truth, as two women alone at night in a Muslim country, we feel uncomfortable. Even during the day, we sense disapproval, and wading into that scene without a man makes us nervous. We wonder if you'd mind coming along with us?"

Many times, Tim and I had discussed the plight of women in some Muslim countries, where they can't move about freely, drive, or have much of a say about what happens to them, let alone meaningful careers outside the home. We rarely saw women enjoying themselves in sidewalk cafés, which were filled with men. We agreed that we felt the presence of fundamentalist repression much more strongly in Morocco than in Turkey.

"I'd be delighted to be your escort," Tim said. "We had planned to go there anyway. How about tonight?"

When we entered the square, all four of us gaped in wonder. Smoke from a hundred charcoal fires drifted upward into the night sky, and candles blazed everywhere. The aromas of fish, meat, and spices tantalized us. Drums, flutes, and human voices blended into a crazy melodic tide that rose and fell almost as if there were a conductor. Storytellers, snake charmers, monkey handlers, and fortunetellers, along with spice and vegetable vendors, set up shop around the perimeters of this huge tent city that covered hundreds of long tables full of people. Families, romantic couples, ancient tribesmen, and tourists of every nationality enjoyed what looked like a gigantic church picnic together. I was floored with the spectacle, completely caught up in being a part of such a sea of human activity. It was one of the most amazing travel moments of my life.

As we walked down the aisle, hawkers from each of the "restaurants" assailed us good-naturedly, waving their paper menus and shouting the virtues of their particular offerings. We joked with them as we watched diners at the long paper-covered tables consuming fried fish, chicken, beef, lamb, potatoes, eggplant, salads, and oceans of tea, colas, and water. Of significant note was the absence of alcohol, which is not served in Morocco's public places, although it is available in hotels and upscale restaurants.

Tim and his harem of three chose a table. Immediately, the waiter brought little plates of olives and bread and menus. We feasted on crunchy fried fish, skewers of chicken, lamb, and vegetables cooked over charcoal, eggplant and tomatoes drizzled with olive oil, and pita. We also tried sauces none of us recognized nor could identify the flavors. We ate everything with abandon.

A few feet away from me, a woman dressed in traditional garb gave orders to the boys who ran the food from fires to customers. All collected money was brought to her, and she doled out the change to the running boys, who returned it to the customers. As she sat, her eyes moved everywhere. A gruff woman, she shouted disapproval or encouragement to each employee, not sparing the cooks or anyone else from her eagle-eyed domination. From afar, she seemed to be an employee's nightmare, a monster overseer, but as I watched her, I saw the sparkle in her eyes and realized she was enjoying herself enormously! Her affection for the young people working there was evident, and she clearly viewed them like her own children. She and

I smiled at each other, and I nodded in that silent understanding mothers share.

As we rose, I asked if I could take a picture of her. She assented, I snapped, and she motioned that she wanted to see it. The photo pleased her. I walked behind our little group feeling as if I'd made a friend.

We wandered through the square and stopped at a stall, its three ten-foot walls packed with hundreds of backless, pointy-toed, tooled leather shoes cunningly arranged, toes up, on racks. They looked like the world's largest, most colorful box of crayons. Gabrielle wanted to buy some. The hunt was on! After fondling many shoes, she selected two pairs and prepared to pay the vendor, who had been encouraging all of us to buy. Annette, the enforcer, stepped into the conversation, told Gabrielle to hold on to her money, and began the haggling dialogue that Moroccan sellers and buyers expect in just about every transaction from cab rides to fine jewelry purchases. Every tourist guide exhorts visitors to negotiate prices in Morocco, but I doubt if many were as adept as Annette. She countered with a ridiculously low price. He scoffed and knocked 5 percent off the posted amount. She persisted, bringing her own figure up 20 percent. He laughed and came down 15 percent. This went on and on, over a $20 pair of shoes. She later confessed that she had been observing the locals that day and had caught on to how they operated! It was quite a performance.

Eventually, I grew bored (you can bet there were no 11½ AAA shoes in that store!) and wandered away to inspect the shimmering stained-glass lanterns next door. When the other three joined me, Annette had prevailed. Gabrielle acquired two pairs for $20, instead of $20 each, one in a fetching animal print, the other in screaming pink/orange. Not a bad savings for ten minutes of light-hearted conversation!

From that moment, Annette became our official negotiator. When anyone in our group wanted to make a purchase, we'd hand the item and money over to her, and she'd march up to the shop-keeper to make the deal. We loved watching her work!

One afternoon, Annette and Gabrielle came into the house and sat down at the table where I was working. I stopped for a chat. Abraham delivered tea on a beautiful tray. "We've been looking into henna tattoos," Annette said, popping a flaky little pastry into her mouth. "Jack told us that the people who do them in the square sometimes use inferior paint that can irritate the skin, so he suggested a place that's over a tea room not too far from here. Would you like to go with us? We have an appointment this afternoon."

I had watched the local women paint intricate designs on people's arms and hands but never had enough time to watch the entire process. "Yes, I'd like that very much," I said. I deserved a break from writing. I had been fascinated with the tattoos and thought it would be great fun to have one, especially since I'm much too chicken to have a real one!

We set off through the ever-wild streets, and I was happy they had blazed the trail earlier, when they went there to make the appointment. I would never have found the place. It sat on a tiny street crowded with shops and swarming with foot traffic. A young man admitted us and showed us up a dark hallway to a rooftop balcony, shaded with colorful textiles and cooled with potted ferns. He produced tea and several books of henna tattoo designs. We were sipping and admiring the pictures when a woman, her head covered in a leopard skin silk scarf, appeared with a wooden tool kit. She smiled and pulled up a small stool. Using sign language, we decided that our leader, Annette, would be first.

The woman glanced at the pattern Annette had chosen. She placed Annette's hand on her own lap and pulled a hypodermic needle out of her box with her permanently ink-stained hands. I was alarmed for a moment, until I realized that she had cut off the business end of the needle and was using it as a painting tool. With thick dark brown ink, she copied the filigree pattern onto Annette's wrist and the back of her hand. The woman's practiced freehand strokes replicated the design perfectly. She moved to the other hand. Within fifteen minutes, Annette admired her matching hands. That would give her patients a start when she returned to work the next week!

I chose to get a design on one ankle. That was a good call on my part, since when henna begins to fade after several days, it resembled a skin disease. I wouldn't have wanted to frighten my table companions on the cruise ship home the following week.

When we'd arrived at the riad, Jack-who-knows-everything had said that if we wished to dine at the hotel, to make our wishes known before noon because the staff would need to procure the ingredients. One morning, we mentioned to the owner we'd like to have another delicious meal that night. "Will you please order the hammam dish?" Renauld, the owner, whispered. "It's so much trouble that I don't like to order it for myself, but if you do, they won't mind."

To this day, we still wonder how the dynamics of that little riad group worked. Did Jack-who-knows-everything surrender control to the owner? Did the owner surrender to his wife? We'll never know.

I asked Jack-who-knows-everything if we might try the hammam dish that evening. He asked if we wanted beef. Yes. I asked him how it was prepared. "It's an ancient dish here in Morocco. We put the beef in a pottery urn with lots and lots of lemon slices, then cover the urn with many layers of foil. Then Marika takes it to the hammam, the public bathhouse down the street, where it is placed over the steam the bathhouse generates. It stays there all day, and we pick it up in the evening. I know you will like it." It sounded like a grand idea to me, but of course I'm one of those nut-job foodies who tried haggis in Scotland, so very little puts me off.

Let me tell you—that bathhouse beef is spectacular. The owner of the riad joined us that night on the upper terrace, and enjoyed it more than anyone. It's a dish I can never try to replicate, because I don't think putting it over a hot tub would quite do the trick...

The next day, as Tim and I sauntered along one of Marrakech's many wide, serene parks past a stand of majestic palm trees, he asked, "Did you know that over on the North Atlantic coast of Morocco, there are goats that climb trees to get the fruit?"

"How in the world do you know so much about Morocco?" I realized immediately that I'd been set up.

"I saw *Lawrence of Arabia*," he leered, enjoying my entrapment in his lame joke. "So naturally I know everything about the desert." He'd been dying to use that line.

"Okay, that's just about enough. Time to get out of here. The desert has gotten to your head, if you have to reach that far to be amusing."

Indeed, the desert was getting to us. We operated in such a state of sensory overload from Marrakech's turbulent atmosphere that after a few days, we craved an evening behind our shutters with food that tasted like home. We asked Jack-who-knows-everything if he could possibly manage to find a pizza place (of all things!) and order one for us. It was the first pizza take-out in the history of the hotel, and it was terrible, but we were so happy to spend an evening of downtime that we didn't care! We ate our pizza and watched a movie with our computer and earphones. Just another example of how and why it's sometimes harder to be a tourist than a home-free traveler.

✳ ✳ ✳

The night before we left Marrakech, we accepted the girls' invitation to join them for dinner at a restaurant they had discovered. Annette, a great planner as well as a great negotiator, asked Jack-who-knows-everything to make a reservation. Then she figured out how to get there. She took the lead, with our big protector bringing up the rear of our quartet. Annette expertly cut through the tiny streets, their shops still open, the dazzling array of goods looking even more tantalizing beneath and among flickering lights.

It was worth the long walk. The restaurant looked like a Moorish castle, lit with lanterns and guarded with bearded men wearing white linen and somber, serious expressions. We proceeded up a winding staircase to a pasha's paradise. Candles and torches blazed over an enormous roof deck swathed in colorful drapery and flowering vines, with tables set invitingly. An enormous orange desert moon was rising, adding the final touch of romance. We savored the national favorites: lamb tagine with tender vegetables and exotic spices, couscous, eggplant, cucumber salad, and fabulous phyllo pastries for dessert. We toasted one another with lovely French wine.

After the call to prayer rang through the city, we opted for a taxi to take us home. As we approached the line, the negotiator stepped up to talk to the first driver. They agreed on twenty dirhams, about five dollars. Tim rode shotgun, and the two girls and I jammed uncomfortably into the backseat.

Before he started the car, the driver announced he would double the fare to forty dirhams because it was illegal for him to take more than two people.

"No," Annette said.

He insisted. She said, firmly, "That's it. Get out of this car, all of you."

We protested. She commanded. We obeyed.

As we struggled out of the little Nissan (none of us were lithe, tiny, or young), the driver leaned out the window. "Okay, madam, twenty."

We repeated our circus act and managed to squeeze in again. Without the wine, we probably couldn't have done it at all. By the time we reached our alley, we were all great friends with the driver—and Annette gave him an extra four dirhams (about 50¢) anyway. Negotiating is part of life in Morocco.

The next morning, Abraham loaded our gear near the front door. Flanking him were Marika and Patricia, followed by Renauld and Jack-who-knows-everything. They stood in a line in front of the pool, shaking hands with us as we thanked them for their hospitality. We all enjoyed our colorful week together.

The taxi bumped through the crowded cobblestone streets, the driver swerving to avoid bicycles, carts, motorcycles, and unwary tourists. "Well, I'm glad we came," Tim said. "It's definitely a place that we needed to see, but I think a week was just enough time for us. I'm exhausted and looking forward to a hotel room with a door that really closes, where I don't have to listen to Marika and Abraham telling jokes while they wash the dishes until midnight."

"I'm tired, too, and really looking forward to getting on the ship after Barcelona," I said. "It's time to go home and burn our clothes. That blue skirt and black top have got to go, and if I see you in that faded lilac shirt in California, we're through!"

The large, modern hotel at our next stop, Barcelona, didn't disappoint. Its big, heavy door shut firmly and didn't invite eavesdropping. When you're home free, little things sometimes take on a larger meaning! The bed felt great, too, offering a level of comfort we sorely missed in our beautiful but simple riad.

As he turned out the lights, Tim said, "You know, I'm ready for some downtime. I'll be happy to let someone else make the decisions for twelve days, and I'll really be happy to see the kids. I know they've all changed in seven months. Do you think we've changed?"

"I don't really know," I mumbled. "I'm too tired to think about it right now."

"I guess we'll find out when we get there." He drifted off.

Chapter 12
Return to California

"What happened to all of those interesting people who sailed with us in May? Looks like we're in for a long, dull twelve days," I said as we took our initial tour around the *Grandeur of the Seas*. It would set sail from Barcelona to Miami in a few hours.

"Maybe the fun people went home already or they decided to stay in Europe through the Christmas holidays," Tim replied. We ducked out of the chilly November wind. "I'm beginning to wonder if this is the much-touted Royal Caribbean Assisted Living Cruise."

Pleased with his quip, he held the door for me to enter the ship's main lounge. I rolled my eyes in response.

The reason for our griping? Canes, walkers, and wheelchairs everywhere. Now, we are not spring chickens ourselves, but let's just say that these guys made us look young. The passengers this time looked older and less dynamic than the lively cast on our last transatlantic cruise to Europe. Fewer were animated. We settled in one of the bars to watch people coming aboard. "It reminds me of that Norman Rockwell painting, the one where the family's going to the beach. They're happy and laughing: kids and grandpa, mom and pop piled in the car. Even the dog's smiling, his head hanging out the window, ears flying. You remember that one? I think the pooch was a cocker spaniel."

Tim laughed. "And in the bottom panel they're coming home from the beach, sunburned, exhausted. Everyone asleep except the poor dad, who's driving."

"Well, think about it. When we left Florida in May, people were boarding a transatlantic cruise, the thrill of a lifetime, with adventure ahead of them in Europe. Now it's November. This crowd has been there and done that—on a tour or a cruise, whatever. They're tired, they need haircuts, they're sick of their clothes, and they're going home, where bills and kids and business as usual is waiting! No wonder they don't look too happy."

"Well, I can sure use a haircut, and I know you'll be happy to get a little color job before we get to Florida." Tim ran his fingers through his curly mop.

After seven months of home-free living in Europe, we were ready for a United States "fix" and we were really excited to see our children and grandchildren. A fast-food delicacy for those who live in California and other western states, an In-N-Out burger sounded like culinary bliss. We were looking forward to American TV, garbage disposals, grocery stores, familiar faces and accents, big cars, wide roads, and parking lots with big spaces. In our slightly world-weary state, that all sounded like heaven.

I kept having flashes—whether flashbacks or vision-flashes into the future, I'm not sure—in which we'd be going HOME to our old house. Then I would shake my head and remember that HOME consisted of a rented apartment near our daughters Robin and Alexandra. When I mentioned my momentary lapses, Tim said he'd experienced the same ones. Moving around as much as we do, it's easy to forget at any given moment where you are and where you're headed, let alone the day of the week or the street you're living on. It was confusing. We had been on the road so long that we weren't sure if the United States would feel like another foreign country! It worried me sometimes to feel so disoriented.

We gave up people watching and returned to our cabin to find places to stash our gear. The stateroom was mid-ship on deck two, a place Tim had chosen in anticipation of the heavy mid-autumn seas that roil in the North Atlantic. A few days later, when waves crashed over our porthole and even some of the crew looked a little wan, we were happy to rest in that stable spot. Tim's more than just a pretty face.

As we unpacked, I noticed the phone light blinking. It was a message confirming our dinner date with a couple from Atlanta. After the *Wall Street Journal* article appeared, a woman emailed us, saying she and her husband would be aboard this very ship, sailing from Barcelona. They wanted to meet us, so we arranged an evening in the ship's specialty Italian restaurant. We were excited to meet people who had read about our travels, and looked forward to hearing about their experiences, too. This author thing was turning out to be fun!

Cruise ships usually provide several theme restaurants, which give passengers opportunities to change their pace from the large dining rooms where dinner is served every evening. There is a nominal extra charge, but well spent for the personal restaurant service and more intimate setting. Our ship housed Italian, steak, and Asian restaurants.

We met at the restaurant. Ginger and her husband, Tom, were on their way home after a ten-day Mediterranean cruise. We enjoyed an excellent Italian meal with this animated, attractive couple while swapping family information and travel tales. We found each other's company delightful, and Tim and I were always happy to make new friends.

After the main course, as we tasted our decadent dessert, Ginger said, "I have a thousand questions for you! I'm dying to know how your home-free life is all working out."

"Fire away, we don't mind at all," I replied.

"Well, I don't mean to pry, but I just wonder how you cope being together all the time? I mean, you don't have outside activities to distract you, because you're not anywhere long enough to be involved in the community. You must spend almost all your time together. Don't you get on each other's nerves? Tom and I would drive each other nuts!"

Good point. Tim and I looked at each other. "Sometimes we do," I said, "but Tim is such a gentleman that he pretends that I'm interesting all the time. I, on the other hand, am probably very trying to be with every day." I smiled sweetly at Tim. "Seriously, Tim, don't you think that being out there without anyone else to rely on has made us closer?"

"We have our moments, my dear," Tim laughed. "Remember driving in Italy?"

I laughed in agreement and with that, Tim was off to the races—figuratively speaking. This time, he regaled Ginger and Tom with stories about Victoria, the astonishing hairpin turns in Florence, and our wild moments in Cornwall. We certainly shouted enough in some of those cliff-hanging moments! As the laughter died down, he added, "Really, though, we are lucky to be so compatible, and I'm sure that being out there without a net could be a challenge to a lot of couples."

"I love your stories, but I can't imagine how you do this," Tom said with a shrug. "Aren't you worried and a little scared about what will happen next? I mean, what if an apartment is awful or the car rental doesn't work out, or one of you gets sick? All kinds of stuff occurs to me—civil unrest, that volcanic ash thing a couple of years ago, tsunamis, bird flu. Doesn't that stuff drive you crazy?"

Tim broke into a knowing smile and glanced at me. He paused, looking for the exact phrases he wanted to use, his brown eyes focusing and refocusing as he plumbed his big brain for answers. "You know, just last night we were talking about that very thing, how we're less worried and more relaxed than we were when we started out. Maybe it's because we're more experienced now. Situations have arisen, but we've managed them well. Of course we're scared sometimes. We worry about accidents, whether we're too old to be doing this, all sorts of things. But lousy stuff happens everywhere. Lord knows, we come from the land of earthquakes. Life's full of risk, no matter where you are."

I took advantage of his pausing for breath and jumped in. "We really do laugh off most of the little trying parts, and if things get really bad, we've either fixed it or moved on," I said. "Of course, we're very lucky that we've been well and haven't hurt ourselves along the way. So far, we've avoided natural disasters, unless you count heat waves and cold snaps. But really, we're not in any more danger than we are at home, when you think about it."

"I guess you're right," Tom said. "Driving in Atlanta is probably just as daunting and dangerous as driving in Cornwall, but at least it's on the right side of the road." I laughed as a vision of our first day in England, when we stopped the car on that muddy road to nowhere, flashed through my mind.

We got together several other times during the trip, but our social activities were limited by my increasingly busy writing schedule. I was under orders from Dana, my spanking new agent, to start writing that book immediately. By then she was talking to several publishers, and one had suggested that they might require a March deadline for the manuscript. I'd also taken on that essay for Mark Chimsky for his book, and *International Living* had asked me to write an article for them. It also, finally, occurred to us that, unlike the vacationers who viewed the cruise as a floating resort, part of their holiday, this was our floating home that happened to be taking us to our destination.

One day, as I was typing away at my computer, Tim returned to the cabin from a walk around the deck. I jumped up. "I'm beginning to know the meaning of cabin fever! I've gotta get out of this room, but there's nowhere else to work because this tub doesn't have a library!"

"At your service, madam," he said with a grin. "Come with me, and bring that machine with you."

Leave it to Tim to discover a large restaurant/bar high on the stern of the ship. It was empty and quiet in the afternoons, so I camped there every day, pecking away, looking up from my work to see the ocean, our churning green wake disappearing into the horizon. Actually, it wasn't a bad office—it had some view. On stormy days, the white caps and fantastic cloud formations added more drama. I'd remain in my private library until cocktail time, when Tim dragged me out to have some fun. It was quite an effort to stay focused. The pattern of his great care and kindness to me as I explored his realm of creative writing was just beginning. His ability to graciously shoulder the job of being the muse while I spent most of the next year deeply mired in the process of writing this book would give me even more reason to love and respect this marvelous man.

Finally, the ship docked in Miami. Imagine our thrill at seeing Tim's daughter, Amandah, and our precious grandson, Sean, waiting for us! I felt as if we'd stepped out of a train, not sailed thousands of miles on a ship. Isn't it strange how human beings grow accustomed to familiar faces and places so quickly?

Amandah and her husband, Jason, made us feel instantly re-rooted in our American life. We started by celebrating in grand style in their newly decorated home. Theirs is the ultimate Florida life: a screened-in lanai and pool with a lake at the bottom of their garden (I didn't see any alligators crawling around, but there are alligators in those backyard lakes), with cool white tile floors and high ceilings that work well in the sticky, humid Florida weather. Our ensuing Thanksgiving feast measured up to expectations, a relaxed family affair: great food, football on TV, and cuddles with Sean, the beautiful youngest child of our family.

* * *

After a few days with Amandah, Jason, and Sean, we flew to see our Texas tribe: Tim's daughter Alwyn, her husband Jeff, and her two amazing children. Jackson was a sprouting young teenager, while little sister Faith was her usual multitalented, always entertaining creative self.

We were surprised by the sheer size of everything—big cars, houses, comfortable spaces between them. The lack of scooters was interesting and the noise level was appalling to us for a few days because we had been in countries where things were quieter for a long time. The constant loud music everywhere in public places was an irritant, but hearing American English swirling around us was a treat. We could eavesdrop without effort!

In their Texas-size home in Austin, we were treated to our own private suite with a view of the rolling Texas hills. A highlight was a good ole' "Amurrican" feast of ribs and sausage, steak and chicken with all the trimmings at The Salt Lick, an enormous, wildly popular barbecue palace featuring live country music and cauldrons of food served up family style. The evening and atmosphere provided a perfect segue for our next stop in Central California, where cowboys and wine rule.

A few days later, we arrived at our rented apartment in Paso Robles, not far from our two California families, and quickly settled into our routine. Although we love the road and have adjusted to staying in other peoples' places, using their things and living sparsely, it felt wonderful to retrieve some of our own pots and pans, our favorite coffeepot, and familiar linens and pillows from the storage facility. We dug out "new" clothes, jewelry, boots, and coats from our storage unit. My big, fluffy, warm terry bathrobe felt as welcoming to me as a mink coat. Those things don't pack very well!

Suddenly, all things American excited us. With renewed enthusiasm, we embraced the prospect of living for two months in our home country. Silly things like hopping in the car and driving without thinking about which side of the road we were on, or puzzling over the configuration of a roundabout thrilled us. Understanding the labels on every item in a grocery store and then just tossing the groceries into the car without lugging them several blocks was a treat. American TV news was a double-edged event: we could understand all the words, but many times the stories were so inane that we'd switch to the BBC. Most of all, we were home and overjoyed to be with our friends and family for the holidays! The view from our small apartment stretched across the town and into the vine-covered hills beyond it. People think of the Napa area of Northern California as the wine-growing capital of the state, but the Central Coast is catching up fast. More than 140 wineries snuggle among them as they step back from the ocean, with new wine tasting rooms sprouting up almost daily. The restaurant and bar scene has become sophisticated, and McMansions dot the countryside. Cattle and vineyards vie for space in the landscape.

We had dreamed of some downtime and many relaxed evenings with my daughters and their families. But while we certainly enjoyed lots of family fun during the holidays, in California, time seemed to speed up. We found ourselves far busier than we ever were on the road, and the days evaporated with social events and chores.

My daughter Alexandra and her husband, Lee, had bought a twenty-nine-acre gentleman's farm in Templeton, California, just south of Paso Robles, while we were gone. The approach to the property, through rolling hills covered with California live oaks, is stunning. Their spread was complete with a pool, as well as heart-stopping views of vineyards and ranches. Ethan, who had entered a new middle school in the community, and Elizabeth, a beautiful ten-year-old whose school was just a mile from the farm, were thriving in their new environment. They loved their new chicken-tending, pool-cleaning, farm-rambling life! The farm became headquarters for Christmas and New Year's Eve parties for all of us and our friends, even with the dust and grime of remodeling insinuating itself into everything from toothbrushes to kids' homework papers.

Meanwhile, my daughter Robin, who owned a small business on the coast in Cambria and kept busy with her two daughters, Fiona and Rory, hosted traditional family parties like our annual cookie day and the Christmas Eve feast.

One morning, during these mounting family events and my writing schedule, I brandished a yellow pad and pen. "We'd better get with it. Our calendar is filling up," I said to Tim. "I've made checkup appointments with just about every doctor in the county, so we can leave knowing we're okay."

"Do we REALLY have to go to a dermatologist?" he asked, not wanting to be bothered with yet another appointment. "I've never been to one in my life, and I hate wasting the time to go all the way to San Luis Obispo to his office."

"I know. That's the point, we haven't been before," said Bossy. "But at our ages, we really need someone to look us over, just to be sure."

"Oh, I know you're right, but seeing the internist, the dentist, the mammogram radiologist, the proctologist, hair dressers, manicurists,

and with guests coming to town to say hello while we're home, parties and the Christmas holidays, we're too busy to think." He sighed
and poured us another cup of coffee.

I reached for a stack of mail-order catalogs. "This is some 'rest,'
huh? We've also gotta decide what clothes and other stuff we need
to buy before we leave. We'd better start ordering clothes for our trip
in the next couple of days or they won't get here on time." While
San Luis Obispo County offers unparalleled beauty and great wine,
the shopping opportunities are limited.

I added, "And then I've GOT to find time to write!"

The pressure surrounding the sale of my book grew more pronounced every day. Dana had submitted the proposal to several
publishing houses that she thought would be a good fit. There was
a surprising amount of interest. It seemed that each one wanted a
different tweak: one wanted expanded chapter descriptions, which
took me days to accomplish; another wanted a full third chapter,
which meant I had to finish it, send it to Bob for his editing, re-
check it, and have it incorporated into the mix. All the while I had
that March deadline in the back of my mind, which made me feel
terribly pressured. While we were grateful for so much interest, the
drama of revised proposal requests and the question about whether
any interested parties would offer a substantial contract fueled an
already tense, suspenseful situation. We tried hard to remember that
the hoopla concerning our story was incidental to our real life, but
we found it difficult not to get caught up in the excitement of the
attention suddenly pushed our way.

"And remember, we still have to gather up the things the French
Consulate requires for an extended visa. We have to make the plan
to get to LA for that meeting. We'll have to stay overnight," Tim
said. I added those items to the long list.

For the next few weeks, we raced from doctor to doctor, while I sandwiched in minutes and seconds to write the new materials we needed. Tim gathered proof of our financial stability, our lack of criminal activity, proof of citizenship, and the status of our health, so the French authorities would let us remain in the EU for longer than the ninety days allowed by the Schengen Agreement. He also handled the mundane issues of our life, like banking, taxes, updating our trust—and, not to be forgotten, planning the details of our next year or two on the road. Since I was writing most of the time, he was also tending to groceries, laundry, and our daily life. This was not shaping up to be the rest and relaxation break we had anticipated.

We were learning that the home-free life is not really as carefree as it might seem. All the minutiae of living still must be addressed. However, for people on the road for many months at a time, a year's worth of life's details must be handled in a matter of weeks. When we're abroad we have no family obligations other than some delightful phone conversations. At home, we find ourselves happily involved with events with family and friends. It's a pleasure, but parties do eat up time. There is a trade-off: independence and total control of our activities versus the warmth and joy of being with our people!

Along with his own projects, poor Tim was kind enough to listen to me read my daily output every afternoon, offering his insight and commentary. He never once rolled his eyes with boredom as I doggedly carried on writing page after page of new material. I do not know how he found the patience to live with this new situation.

As if all this weren't stressful enough, we were suffering from claustrophobia. We had rented the tiny apartment the previous spring. Since we did not anticipate my needing a quiet, private place to concentrate while I worked on a book, we felt a tiny one-bedroom apartment was enough. While attractive and providing a spectacular view, it was so small that we could hear each other breathing through the closed door. Tim couldn't watch the news or make a phone call without my hearing it. A bad situation. We considered renting a small office space, and I even spent some time at the public library trying to write. It almost worked, but the chairs were worn out so my derriere ached after a little while sitting there, and some library visitors couldn't control their chitchat, the shushing librarians notwithstanding.

As the days stretched with us both cooped up in our small space, Tim was growing understandably testy. I was downright mean.

One day, while I was sequestered in the corner of the bedroom with the paper-thin door separating us, Tim shouted, "I've GOT IT! How stupid can I be? Why didn't I think of this?"

The door burst open. There he stood, grinning for the first time all day. "What in the world is wrong with you?" I asked, petulant and cross, because he had just interrupted some great thought. (Not that I can remember it right now. It's truly amazing how a person can begin to take herself much too seriously.)

His smile grew. "I've solved the problem—tomorrow you will be able to write and nothing will bother you."

"How is that possible? Did you buy a bomb shelter?"

"No, I've ordered you the heavy-duty Bose noise-canceling headphones. The top of the line. Merry Christmas!"

It was a perfect solution. I gasped, and then lunged at him for a big kiss. We went out to dinner to celebrate.

The next morning, I waited at the door like a kid ready to surprise Santa Claus at midnight for the FedEx guy to appear with my headphones. Tim had changed my life again!

At last, I was able to tune out and write wherever I wanted, including the long car rides when Tim happily listened to music and drove us to and from Los Angeles for our meeting with the French Consulate. Both the book material and the visa request worked out just fine.

Since then, I have written proposals, articles, and this book in cars, planes, trains, on ships and ferries, in hotels, apartments, and an Irish cottage (which was sublime since it required no earphones). One afternoon, I plopped down in the lounge area of a Portuguese shopping center and wrote almost 1,000 words of Chapter Five while Tim shopped for sweaters for us. People swirled around me, laughing, talking, and pushing baby carriages and shopping carts. It made no difference to me: I happily sat there writing about Morocco's swirl of color and dust while listening to Mozart sonatas in a sparkling clean shopping temple full of Europe's ubiquitous C&A, Zara, and Sephora stores.

* * *

All the hard teamwork paid off when the new proposal content was well received. Before we returned overseas to the next phase of our home-free life, I secured a book deal! Stephanie Bowen, an experienced editor at Sourcebooks, Inc., the publisher we favored all along, decided to buy the book, and Dana artfully arranged a contract that satisfied all parties. It was a thrilling moment, proof of our extraordinary luck in gathering a team of smart people who contributed their experience and energy to helping us tell the world about our home-free life! Rick and Sarah, Dana and Bob, and so many others had conspired to bring us to such a delightful place in our lives.

After we indulged in jubilant phone calls to everyone we knew who really cared about the project and some who probably didn't, but were polite enough to be encouraging, we took ourselves out for a luscious meal and a very, very nice bottle of local Paso Robles Zinfandel. We stayed up late crowing about our great good fortune and imagining what the future would bring.

We were overjoyed to have this major event completed before

we left the country again. Right from the start, Stephanie and I were on the same page. I was as nervous as a schoolgirl when we had our first conversation, but right from the beginning I knew that our collaboration was going to work. She was so enthusiastic about our story, and her warmth and obvious expertise inspired the level of renewed inspiration and confidence I knew would be needed for me to accomplish the job. And guess what? The March deadline was lifted. Sourcebooks, in its wisdom, had given me until June to complete the project. At that moment, it felt as if a boulder had been lifted from my shoulders. I still had a mountain to climb, but at least I didn't have to do it in three months!

A few days later, after we had recovered from the news, I shouted, "Hey Tim," from my bedroom office, where I was tethered to my laptop.

He jumped with alarm and almost dumped his computer off his lap. A harpsichordist was banging away to a Bach piece through my earphones, so I hadn't realized how loudly I'd spoken.

I looked through the doorway to see him pointing to his ears, grimacing. I apologized, took off the equipment, and said in a normal tone, "I just got an email from Judy Butcher. She's coming to town on her way to San Francisco. Won't that be fun? We can take her over to Cambria to meet Robin and up to the farm, too. I think she'd like that, don't you? I'll bet she'll like that swanky Argentinean restaurant that's opened over there by the park."

He nodded his approval and motioned for me to get on with my work. Is muse another term for foreman?

After we roasted together in Florence, Judy spent the late summer in Germany before touring around Europe visiting relatives and pals. We were anxious to catch up with her. A few evenings later, while enjoying Malbec and some really tasty South American food, we chatted about our experiences and shared our plans for the future. Our conversation somehow seemed easier and more natural than our talks with family and friends. Of course, our family was interested in our adventure. However, it seemed hard for them to relate to our free-floating life, in which we talked about meeting someone for lunch in Berlin as casually as if we were meeting them in Los Angeles or San Luis Obispo.

It began to dawn on us that we had fundamentally changed since our decision to live home free. Our worldview had become larger and our place in it more fluid. As we talked with Judy, who had lived internationally for much longer, we realized that living home free had unfettered us in more important ways than leaving pots and pans behind. We were much more intrepid and felt completely comfortable about being in new situations, living in countries whose languages were unknown to us, finding friends to amuse and inform us. We had more confidence in our ability to be in the world, and it certainly took a lot more drama to make us upset nowadays.

Later, we introduced Judy to the girls and their families. While she was with us, we plotted how we'd meet the following summer in Paris; she planned to take one of her granddaughters on an expert's tour. Judy gave us some excellent contacts for our search for an apartment in Berlin the following August, and we tweaked our schedules so we could enjoy a few days together in that city, too.

Finally, the time came to part ways. After we dropped off Judy at the train station in San Luis Obispo, Tim said, "You know, this is something we didn't expect, a surprising bonus. We meet people all the time who share our love of being on the road. And the best part is that we're staying in touch with a lot of them, looking forward to finding one another again. We've seen Judy Butcher in, what, three countries now? And by the end of the year it'll be five. Wouldn't it be wonderful to try to hook them all up somehow? What a great party that would be!"

"What an idea!" said the gal who is always ready for a party. "If we really worked at it, maybe we could round up a lot of the new friends we have in someplace central. Maybe London or Paris. I'll put that on my list. Lord knows we've pulled off crazier stuff."

We spent the next few weeks tearing around the county, visiting our medical people, our attorney, and talking with our tax guy and our brilliant financial advisor. We checked out medically: absolutely nothing wrong with our bodies. We had been in good shape when we left for Europe, and it appeared being on the road agreed with us, because we returned even healthier. Our financial checkups were good, too. Our plan was working, and we were staying well within the budget we'd agreed upon, but that was no surprise. We had expected it to work all along. Most people our age have learned to stay within a budget!

Things we had ordered from catalogs and stores arrived every day: shoes, bags, easy-care travel clothes, all the things we needed to begin another odyssey. This time, we packed even lighter, and replaced essential items: a new blazer for me, new jeans a size smaller (ahem) since I had successfully shed a few more pounds from all the walking we had done, and a long raincoat with a zip-out lining I would need in Portugal and Ireland during some seriously cool, rainy weather. Tim bought a new blazer, too, and his Irish cap scurried right back into the suitcase, along with some new comfortable walking shoes. After days of debate, he popped his beautiful summer Panama straw hat on his head decisively. "I'll wear this hat in Paris this summer if it's the last thing I ever do," he said. *We'll both live to regret that decision,* I thought to myself.

In a few weeks, while traveling again, Tim and his beige straw hat with the black grosgrain band became easy to spot in airports full of people wearing dark winter clothes and tweed hats. Our efforts to find a safe place for the thing on planes, ship cabins, trains, taxis, and ferries drove us crazy, but he was too stubborn to mention it. I certainly didn't want to antagonize him by complaining. It became of those silent "gotcha" jokes familiar to all couples!

We made our agonizing decisions about what to cram in the duffels, and shoved the rest of our gear into storage. We deposited our car at the family farm, tearfully departed from our beautiful people, and found a hotel near Los Angeles International Airport—where we were treated to an impromptu jazz concert.

The next day, we sat across the aisle from one another on a plane bound for Florida. Tim's straw fedora rested comfortably in a spot he claimed in the overhead compartment. I watched a fellow passenger give him the stink eye for taking up valuable space, but I buried my head in my Kindle book and didn't say one word. That hat was his problem, not mine.

Sometimes, gotcha moments aren't at all worthwhile.

Chapter 13
Portugal

Destiny brought Tim and me together after decades apart, but eighteen days aboard Carnival Cruise Line's ship *Destiny* thoroughly tested fate's wisdom and our devotion.

The minute I saw the chocolate brown main salon swathed in golden disco lights, I suspected we had a problem. I hadn't seen anything like it since *Viva Las Vegas*. "Do you think Ann-Margret's going to come strutting down that staircase?" I asked

Tim cut his eyes at me and kept walking, harrumphing under his breath. Further inspection revealed that the ship, when built in 1996, was the largest cruise vessel in the world. It had plied the Caribbean for sixteen years and it was clearly in need of more than a paint job and new drapes.

Carnival's sales materials had not even hinted that this would be *Destiny*'s last voyage…nor her first ever transatlantic crossing. If that wasn't enough to concern us, we were to learn some other "interesting" facts while sailing across the ocean: neither the ship nor its crew, nor any other Carnival vessel, had ever undertaken such a long journey. Her destination wasn't really Venice, but a shipyard in Trieste, a half day's sail farther on. We were later informed that, upon arrival, all passengers would be hustled off the ship by ten in the morning, which meant the start of debarking just after dawn. After dumping the guests, she would steam away for her $116 million heart/lung and hair transplant, along with a much-needed nose job and face-lift.

We were not encouraged. In addition, almost every passenger we met felt like dates for whom we'd bought dinner and drinks, but didn't even get a good-night kiss! We just didn't have any chemistry with those folks. It looked as if it would be a long, lonely voyage.

Yet, we were home-free adventurers and seasoned travelers, so we were determined to make ourselves happy and at home instead of sulking. We moved in, admired our light, bright stateroom with its tiny balcony, stowed our gear, and set up camp, determined to make the best of it.

Eighteen days inside a thousand-foot-long deteriorating capsule full of bored people was an endurance test, not only for passengers, but also for the crew and especially the kitchen. One night, we were served escargot in the regulation porcelain six-divot plate, each containing a shell crammed with a tasty morsel. It was a delicious appetizer. Evidently they weren't a big hit with the rest of the passengers, so the next night, the thrifty chef presented them without the shell in little bowls. This time, they were tossed with herbs to enliven them. I could imagine his staring at the little brown pile with green flecks thinking, *hmmm...that's dull. How can I make this look more interesting?* His solution was to garnish his creation with one potato chip standing on end in the middle of the pile. It didn't work out too well visually, but they tasted good, and Tim and I were happy enough to get escargot two nights in a row in any configuration. I did feel for the poor chef, though. Trying to come up with something attractive for fifteen hundred guests eighteen nights in a row would drive anyone over the edge. Let's say I have now tasted salmon prepared in every conceivable manner except mixed in my toothpaste.

Just before our dessert arrived every evening, the maitre d', a Nicolas Cage look-alike, would grab the microphone at his front desk. In his Eastern European accent, he'd announce, "Ladies and gentlemen, it's shhhhhhhowtime!"

Several fit young women, garbed in Caribbean ruffles, bounded into the dining room and jumped atop four strategically placed marble plinths. Mr. Cage cued the pre-recorded steel drum band and the young women gyrated for about five minutes. After a few days or so, even the most polite passengers were finding it difficult to feign interest.

About every third evening, Mr. Cage would command the wait staff to drop their duties and arrange themselves around the large room, lining the stairs and balcony railings to serenade us with the ditties they'd been required to learn phonetically. The performers pretended to enjoy themselves, and so did the diners, but I knew they were humiliated. A group of reluctant Indonesians warbling "O Sole Mio" creates an unusual theatrical experience, to say the least. We were embarrassed and pained that they were forced to do this.

Happily, the food was good, and since we'd asked Nicolas Cage to give us a table for two, we weren't required to socialize. Unhappily, there were no specialty restaurants aboard. A steak house or Italian restaurant would have offered a nice change of venue and certainly improved the situation. On several evenings, we resorted to room service rather than facing the entertainment. We don't mind propping up on our bed, munching BLTs and potato chips while watching *Lincoln* on the ship's closed-circuit TV for the third time. At least it beat the reruns of *Love Boat*, our other choice.

I frequented the ship's library when it wasn't filled with clicking Knitting Club members. Tim would deposit my Bose earmuffs, along with me, and fetch me when it was time for food…or better yet, cocktails. Thus, we endured *Destiny's* last hurrah and we were grateful to arrive safely in Italy without needing to test the whistles on those orange life vests. Although I am not fearful by nature, I do have a healthy respect for the sea. Arriving at our destination without incident always deserves a silent thanksgiving.

When we docked, a dusting of snow covered the ancient wonders of Venice—an exciting, unusual phenomenon. However, it was much too cold to venture out and we had an early flight to Lisbon the next morning, so we luxuriated in a stationary bedroom for the first time in weeks and a dinner without Caribbean ruffles or singing waiters.

To our delight the next day, everything went smoothly, a sign of good things to come. Even doing the airport drill—getting the bag trolley, finding the luggage and the car rental desk, locating the car itself, and starting out in the right direction—was indicative of the following five weeks. It was all EASY.

Once in Portugal, Victoria adjusted instantly to her new home and started butchering the Portuguese language without a hitch. As we crested the first hill overlooking Lisbon, I was riveted on the GPS screen, trying hard not to muck up such an easy arrival. Tim commanded, "Look up from that thing. I don't need any help right now and I know where we're going. Look at this city! I've been dying to show it to you!" Tim had visited Portugal years earlier and had longed to return.

I looked up. What an incredible sight. "Oh Tim, it's even better than the photos. It's Istanbul meets San Francisco!"

Lisbon seemed to blend the best of those two astounding cities. We drove under the tremendous, graceful Águas Livres Aqueduct, built in the late 1700s. Beyond it, red tile roofs topped buildings painted in Easter egg colors. In the background was the wide Tagus River, flowing into the Atlantic. We approached one of the world's longest bridges, painted the same rusty shade as the Golden Gate Bridge, which connected Lisbon to the communities on the other side. An elaborate castle topped a big hill in the distance on our left, and across the river, not far from the bridge, stood Christ the King monument, a replica of the larger one in Brazil. It was a sensational view which, of course, Tim couldn't enjoy much because he was trying to get us onto that bridge without taking someone else's bumper with us.

Our charmed day continued with Victoria flawlessly directing us over the bridge toward Costa da Caparica, a little beach town, our new home. Within twenty minutes, we pulled up beside the property manager, who hopped out of her car and opened our gate. We hadn't been on the ground for more than an hour. Believe me, this is a statistic worth noting. It was the easiest transition we had made from airport to target destination in our many years of traveling.

We always try to remember these really good days when things aren't going so well!

We were in great spirits. When the property manager opened the door, we were even more delighted. The house was large, a treat after the restrictions of our diminutive digs in California and the shipboard cell that had been our "destiny" for eighteen days. It included a large private fenced patio, a good-size living room with a wood-burning fireplace, and a dining room that seated eight. The kitchen was excellent and it had a dishwasher. There was even a covered laundry area outside the kitchen, and a washing machine. No dryer, of course, but it had a big clothesline, so the laundry guy was in business. Nice bedrooms and a full bath awaited upstairs.

It seemed like luxury living to us, and it was clean and, more importantly, cheap, well below our monthly housing budget. In this and many other ways, Portugal surprised and pleased us. The streets, bathrooms, trams, buses, and tourist venues were scrupulously kept. Of course there was plenty of graffiti and there were run-down areas. The country showed signs of wear and economic distress, but it stood out as one of the most hygienic places we had visited.

Katarina, the manager, ticked through our checklist with us before she left. She spoke perfect English, which was wonderful, since the Portuguese language is completely beyond the ability of ordinary people to decipher. It has nothing to do with Spanish at all, and sounds to my ear like some Eastern European lingo. Even our dear friend Clif Garrett, a linguist and language professor of some repute, advised me to save my energy and time because my attempts would be fruitless. I mastered "thank you," "please," and "pardon me." Since almost every Portuguese person we met knew at least rudimentary English, which they spoke willingly, that was enough.

Katarina showed us how to turn on the wall heaters, which were located in every room. "Just turn the switch," she said confidently. "See, the red light is on, so they'll start up right away. They'll keep you warm as toast."

Once again, we quickly moved into our routine, making a grocery list, putting our things away, and inspecting every cupboard and closet to see what the home provided.

Several hours later, the house was still only as warm as yesterday's toast. Although the red lights came on, only one heater worked. The concrete house had been closed up for at least a month, so the temperature dropped precipitously when the sun went down. That night, it plunged to the mid-thirties Fahrenheit, and although the fireplace helped us downstairs, the bedrooms felt like walk-in refrigerators. I went to bed in fleece tights, a T-shirt, my PJs, a sweater, and two pairs of socks. I have no idea what Tim wore because I was scrunched under the covers when he came diving into bed, and I spent the night with my back jammed up against his warm body. We put every blanket in the place on our bed, so the covers were too heavy for either of us to move.

When we first set out on the road home free, we were a little tentative. We might have gone out the next morning to buy some space heaters ourselves, thinking we could speed things up. However, experience taught us that the manager might ask us to wait for the repairman or just put more wood on the fire. We were prepared to be more proactive and insistent about correcting the situation without being inconvenienced. Remember the blue button in Buenos Aires? We had learned a lot since those early days.

We had no phone, but Skype worked fine. By 8:30 a.m. we had reached Katarina, explained the problem, and told her that we wanted it corrected before that evening. We did not want to spend another night dressed like Pillsbury Doughboys. Within an hour, she arrived with two large, effective radiators, a huge pile of firewood and kindling, and a promise that the radiators would be repaired. Although the weather that March was raw, we quickly became cozy. Even better, we had not invested our money in someone else's problem or waited around for hours for some guy to show up and tell us it would take weeks for the part to arrive from Germany, a tale of woe we'd heard from expats in several countries when some piece of their equipment broke down.

The portable heaters worked beautifully the entire time we lived there, and although the owner's electric bill might have been a surprise to him, we were comfortable. Of course, it was three weeks before the repairman appeared. Nice guy, but the parts never came while we were there.

By the second night, we were completely unpacked and into our rhythm. I prepared a tasty little pork roast, some veggies, and a salad, we had napkins in our laps, a pretty bowl of flowers on the table, and even candles to enliven the scene. The heaters hummed along, the refrigerator and pantry were full, and a nice little fire crackled in the living room. Our Internet connection worked fine, and we charged our electronic gear with our plug adaptors. We also tried all of the appliances. They worked well, and we were feeling very proud of ourselves.

We soon found a large supermarket, about fifteen minutes away in a big shopping center. We figured out the parking and shopping drills by watching the insiders, so we were spared a repeat of our Italian humiliation and irritation. We bought a local throwaway phone for about ten dollars, persuaded the clerk to make it speak English instead of Portuguese, located the nearest gas station for future reference, drove to the ferry pier to check out the parking situation and boat schedule, and sent messages to let everyone know we had arrived safely.

In short, we were at home, and our home-away-from-home routine was really clicking. "I can't believe how easy this has been," Tim gloated as he leaned back against the warm stucco wall of our patio the next morning. "Seriously, all of our experience has paid off and it's all come together. I'm proud of us, honey."

"We've surely learned a lot, haven't we? If I can just finish the book, we'll be free to play. Guess I'll go inside and start to work." All those months of making mistakes and learning to cope with almost any situation had really paid off in a big way! We had found out the hard way how to ask the right questions and look for solutions before the problems even arose.

"Wait…what do you say we go out to lunch first?" he asked.

I was on my way upstairs to find my shoes before he finished the invitation. As you have learned by now, it doesn't take much persuasion to distract me from my work, especially if there is food and drink involved.

We walked to the end of our lane, lined with palm trees, enjoying nice-looking houses on either side. Their vine-covered, walled gardens reminded us of Mexico or Italy. When we reached the end of our street, we ducked through a break in a small forest, as we'd noticed the locals doing. We found a sandy path, with wildflowers and bright yellow broom decorating its borders, and we meandered along it toward the dunes. It was a joy to be among trees after having spent such a long time in the sterile atmosphere of a ship. The sound of pounding surf grew louder. Chatting away, we climbed a rickety wooden staircase. At the top, both of us stood there frozen, transfixed by what we saw.

The waves were tremendous! Huge sets started hundreds of yards out and crashed in their green/white/blue fury below us. The beach, which stretched for seven miles, was almost empty, pristine in its winter solitude except for the surfers who enjoyed themselves enormously. I couldn't wait to tell our friend and editor Bob Yehling. In addition to being an extraordinary writer, teacher, editor, marathon runner, and all-around good guy, he is also (of all things) a big-time surfer dude. When we told him about the waves later in a Skype call, he let out a yelp of jealousy. "Do you realize that Garrett McNamara rode the biggest wave of any surfer in the world last year right by there?" he exclaimed. "It was measured at seventy-eight feet."

A pity such excellent surf was wasted on two non-sporting types.

There was a long row of clapboard restaurants, spaced far apart, hunched along the top of the dunes. Each big beach shack included a large covered patio. Brightly colored beanbag pallets were tossed on the sand around low tables, very handy for customers to enjoy. The land embraced the tremendous bay on three sides, and we could see the Tagus River flowing right into the ocean. It was dramatic, exciting, and cold.

We hurried to the Kontiki Bar, the closest of the bar/restaurants, and were delighted to be tucked behind some dunes, seated at a table sheltered from the wind gusts by sturdy glass walls and a canvas canopy. Three generations of Portuguese families gathered on the patio, already enjoying their Sunday lunch: drinking wine, chatting, laughing, and watching their children frolic in an unusually sunny March afternoon at the beach. We could tell from their name-brand clothes and upscale haircuts that these people lived across the bridge in Lisbon, where Gucci and Prada stores coined money in expensive real estate along Liberdade Avenue.

We lingered over our meal and enjoyed a long lunch. I was happy to be in a country where they understood octopus in all its iterations, while Tim was content to munch one of the best hamburgers he had found anywhere. When the skies behind the hills on the other side of Lisbon began to darken, we trotted home in a hurry. The weather changes fast in that part of the world, and we barely beat a huge downpour that would last all night. It made for wonderful sleeping.

The next morning, Tim was distracted. "Do you have the keys? I have the camera. Now, where is that ferry schedule? I just had it in my hand…"

We were in our regular get-out-the-door mode. I threatened to plant a little Post-it list on the front door, but Tim claimed we hadn't sunk quite that far into our dotage (then why don't we ever have a phone with us? I ask you). We were off on our first trip to Lisbon; since the ferries cast off punctually, we raced to get out the door.

"Yes, yes, I have the keys! Please go out and I'll grab my purse and lock up," I said to him, pulling on my raincoat.

As I looked at the keys, I suddenly had a dreadful flashback to Argentina: it was the same medieval-looking brass clunker that had given us so much trouble in Buenos Aires. If you chose the wrong one or inserted it upside down, you were sunk. Of course, the mechanical lock was buried inside a heavy door, so the chore had to be accomplished by feel. We never did get it right on the first try, in either country.

But we loved the ferry. After we walked aboard, we clattered up the metal stairs to the enclosed upper deck so we could see everything. Lisbon looked like a pastel wedding cake gleaming in the sun beyond the big red bridge. What a glorious sight! Cargo ships, guided by tiny tugs, lumbered in from the ocean. Sailboats skittered back and forth on the river, dodging them. Even the locals, who use the ferries as casually as we use our freeways, seemed to enjoy the views.

Lisbon has been a major seaport for more than three thousand years, since Phoenician times. It is the oldest capital city in Europe, easily outdating Rome and London. The place teems with history. Phoenician ruins lie beneath the Lisbon Cathedral, and the statue of Vasco da Gama, the great explorer who found the route to the East from Portugal, commands one of the major traffic circles in the city. The diverse population stems from the variety of conquerors who have arrived and stayed in the country. Muslims, Arabs, Jews, Berbers, and Saqaliba have all marked the population with their genes. Our entire visit felt like an excellent history lesson about a country we'd known so little about.

We had met a couple at the ticket desk while all four of us tried to understand what the man in the cage was telling us about the tickets and schedule. Once aboard, they sat down next to us so we began to share basic information on the ride. Yanni, who was Dutch, had been married to John, a Brit, for thirty-five years. They lived in England and had two grown sons. They were the classic hardy English couple who love to travel, and like so many of their countrymen, they were enthusiastic campers. They had spent the past several weeks on the road, driving down through France and parts of Spain in their caravan (what we call a camper in the United States). They were staying in Costa da Caparica for a few days before heading through northern Portugal on their return trip to England.

Outside, as we moved past the shoreline, there were huge cranes, hulking warehouses (many abandoned), sturdy concrete wharves, and tiny cafés and bars. As we approached Belém, the Lisbon port west of the main ferry terminal, Yanni said, "Look,

look—it's the famous monument to Ferdinand Magellan, the great Portuguese explorer!"

Not only do people in other countries often speak several languages, but they also seem to grasp history, both their own and everyone else's. Many North Americans lack this education. It's embarrassing. I did not want to admit that although I'd attended a good university, I hadn't given Ferdinand a thought since the sixth grade, so I nodded sagely and said I'd been looking forward to seeing it.

"Can you imagine what it must be like to approach this city from the sea?" I asked, in an effort to participate without admitting my ignorance.

We watched a cruise ship make its way up the river to the main docks. I was certain that the passengers would be astonished to see the Magellan monument, which soars 171 feet above the north side of the river, and the bridge, its main tower 623 feet tall, and 3,300 feet long. Just beyond that, the Cristo Rei stood 436 feet above the water, his arms outstretched to welcome and protect Lisbon's inhabitants and her visitors. The soft prettiness of the city served as a backdrop to these massive structures. Even from the deck of a lowly local ferry, it's one of the most beautiful sights I've ever seen.

Yanni and John were camping in a resort only half a mile from our house. Since we were enjoying their company so much, we agreed to have cocktails and dinner together the next night, and we parted at the terminal. They took off to see the sights in Belém, while Tim and I walked a block or two to catch the famous #15 trolley, which would take us into the main part of the city.

Our ferry tickets included trolley and the bus service, so we hopped aboard, flashed our green tickets at the electronic eye, and found seats in one of the cute old-fashioned trolley cars that traverse the city in all directions. The gay "ting ting" of their bells adds to the charm of the place. We got off the trolley and trudged up a very steep hill past antiques stores, designer shops, and small cafés. At the top, we were rewarded by Rossio Square, Lisbon's favorite meeting place, with two enormous identical fountains anchoring each end and a massive statue dedicated to Dom Pedro IV in its center. Black and white tiles decorated the sidewalks, arranged in elaborate designs. These Rossio Square tiles fooled the eye into thinking the ground was undulating. It's a strange experience. Every time we walked across its expanse, we marveled at the optical illusion. "I've been saving this part of Portugal as a surprise for you," Tim beamed as I saw the square.

Nearby, we found the foot of the Avenida da Liberdade and entertained ourselves by gawking at the lovely buildings and storefronts. As we moved up the slight incline of the street, the store monikers became more international and pricey. When the Gucci, Prada, and Burberry signs appeared, we knew where those people we had seen at the Kontiki in Caparica did their shopping.

The entire center of the wide boulevard consists of a long, gracious park. Its graceful trees showed the first hints of budding green, and a man-made stream ran through an attractive garden. Every few blocks, people enjoyed coffee and pastries beneath the trees at small cafés. As usual, we were hungry, so we sat down for our introduction to the famous *pastel de nata*, the Portuguese egg custard served up in an individual round flaky crust. I polished mine off before Tim had finished stirring his espresso. "A little hungry there, sport?" he asked.

I was so embarrassed (not) that I hopped up and fetched another one.

Now we again enjoyed the best part of living home free, the luxury of wandering around without much of an agenda, and getting the feel for a country without rushing to see the sights. We observed that the Portuguese are great lovers of beauty and color, have a happy outlook in spite of their dire economic condition, and that they certainly know how to make a mean pastry. We stopped for a delicious grilled fish luncheon on a street lined with patios full of carefree tourists, and retraced our yellow trolley drive back to the port.

As we watched ferry crew members expertly dock the red double-decker boat, I heard, "Hallo, hallo there!" On the spot, Yanni and John invited us for tea, which morphed into a bottle of mellow Spanish red at their campsite. From their tiny, super-efficient caravan, they quickly produced compact camping chairs, a table, wineglasses, and cheese and crackers. We sat under the trees while John gave us a tour of their home on wheels. It was fascinating. The vehicle had all the amenities of the big RV behemoths we see in campgrounds in the United States, right down to the built-in awning, refrigerator, sink, and heater. However, it was no longer than a normal American car, and narrow enough to negotiate Europe's spare roads. This German marvel of innovation put every inch to use.

We enjoyed playing host the next night at "our" house. Tim drove us to a restaurant he'd found on one of his exploratory rambles around Caparica, our little beach town, while I'd been at home doing battle with the chapter about England. The muse's job never ends. A string of rectangular modular buildings ran along the boardwalk, each an individual restaurant offering its own particular specialties. The one we chose offered up a fish stew with plump fresh mussels the size of meatballs in a cheesy, creamy liquor that we sopped up happily with crusty Portuguese bread.

As we savored our feast, our companions regaled us with tales of their worldwide adventures. "I guess, aside from Kilimanjaro, the craziest holiday we ever took was a four-and-a-half-month camping adventure through South America on a bus with twenty people we had never met before the trip," Yanni said.

I realized, as we chatted, that the friendships we were developing in our travels were different from those at home. Most relationships start from a situational basis: work, hobbies, school, or club encounters. Some last, some don't. Certainly long-standing friendships offer the comfort of shared history, but on the road, there is an almost indefinable moment when we make a connection with people who are kindred spirits. It's a chemistry almost like love, a recognition that doesn't require deep exploration to discover. Meeting other travelers far from home, in whatever country it may be, creates an atmosphere where it's possible to cut to the bones of the friendship; there are no trappings or protocols in the way of just getting to know the person for the person's sake. I inevitably feel a pang of regret when we say good-bye to a new friend whose company we have enjoyed because although we usually do stay in touch and try to find ways to intersect as we move around the world, we're all living such fluid lives that it's hard to know if we'll find one another again.

As I had drifted away with my own thoughts, Yanni had continued talking about their time in South America. I glanced at Tim, who gaped openly at Yanni. "Four and a half months in a BUS?" he exclaimed. We thought we were special for selling our house, dumping our stuff, and traipsing around the world without a home base. But we live in houses and apartments, not a bus, and we certainly don't have to put up with anyone but each other! These astonishing people gave another example of hardy seniors who are flexible and brave enough to make bold decisions and enjoy adventure in their later years.

"But how did you DO that?" I asked, washing down another big fat mussel with a great Portuguese red wine. "I mean, where did you bathe and sleep and eat?"

"It was a kind of bare-bones adventure," Yanni replied. "The organizers provided the bus and driver, but among the passengers, we just arranged a routine that worked. We rotated cooking and shopping among ourselves, so no one had to do everything, and about every third or fourth day, we'd check into hotels to do our laundry, wash our hair, all of that, and then we'd be on our way again."

"Sometimes, it was really difficult to keep our cool," John said. "Some of the people were terribly annoying, one of them downright nuts. But it was the only way we could possibly have afforded to see that much of South America, so we put up with them and carried on."

That night, while a storm raged outside, Tim and I were tucked in our big soft bed, reading our Kindles, our radiator chugging away. "Well, I'm certainly glad we met Yanni and John," Tim said, "and their road trip in South America was a fascinating tale, but right this minute I'm really happy that I'm not in that little camper with that cold wind blowing thirty knots, tossing us around."

Meeting our new friends verified how we learned from each person we met. Everyone possesses her own degree of tolerance. What may seem like adventure to one person might be torture for another. Perhaps being home free is more an attitude than a lifestyle, and what constitutes personal freedom differs for every individual.

✳ ✳ ✳

The weather didn't improve the next day, so we threw more wood into the fireplace and hunkered down to get some writing done. When the rain slowed down in the afternoon, we took a break to pick up some things at the little "super" market in the village. We both walked out of the house without money or credit cards (maybe that Post-it is a good idea), so Tim dashed home for his wallet while I waited inside the market with our things. Of course, it started raining the minute he left. I was staring out the window feeling sorry for him when I felt a presence beside me. I looked around, then down to see a tiny elderly Portuguese woman standing at my elbow, carrying her groceries in two little plastic bags. I must have looked like a nine-foot Amazon from the planet America. She looked up at me and grinned. I smiled. She grinned some more. I smiled some more. She finally said, "*Sheirwrish msh durphlopishish parprikash dulneyetchki.*"

I said, "I am so sorry, but I do not speak Portuguese."

She said, "*Sheirishnaplak msh duphlopishishnyoa parparick-shmuchtin dulneyetchkipush.*"

I said, "I am so sorry, but I still do not speak Portuguese." I giggled at my own joke.

This continued for quite a while until she finally shook her head at my stupidity and disappeared with her parcels through one door as Tim arrived in the other. At that point, I had cracked myself up so much that tears were starting to roll down my cheeks. He looked at me with the same pitying expression as my new Portuguese friend, shook his head, and went to pay the bill. Guess you had to be there.

Lisbon is not only stunning, but also manageable. We never felt overwhelmed, except for our panting sessions after climbing one of its steep hills. A few days later, gifted by a sunny day, we caught the ferry to Belém, where we had landed with our friends on our first trip over to the mainland. It features the Tower of Belém, which looks like a baroque birthday cake. Originally located on an island in the middle of the Tagus, it is now attached to the mainland because the river was rerouted several hundred years ago after an earthquake. The Tower was built as part of the city's medieval fortification system, and remains one of the many wonders of the city. Also, the National Carriage Museum is within an easy stroll. Not only are the carriages astounding to see, but the building itself is breathtaking. It served as the royal riding arena for Belém Palace, and we could imagine members of the court perched above in the royal galleries on the second floor, watching the horses perform. As we were inspecting a lavishly gilded ceremonial carriage from the seventeenth century, Tim turned to me. "I wonder how much horsepower this baby needed. Leaded or diesel, d'ya think?"

Moving right along…

We walked through the lovely sunny afternoon to the nearby Monastery of the Hieronymites. We were fascinated with the sculptured columns that surround the cloisters in the monastery. We found their complex themes of sailing, exploration, and trade so interesting that we, who usually pay more attention to lunch than history, found ourselves slowly making our way around the huge courtyard, taking in the details. The church, chapels, museum, and monastery offered us a great treat. Since museums in Lisbon have free admission on Sundays, my banker was twice as happy. And you know that we found a nice lunch before we got back on that ferry, don't you? (Hint: It's a rhetorical question.)

The next bright day, we expanded our territory and drove to Almada to take the larger ferry, which lands at the huge terminal in the main part of the city. From there, we caught an easy tram ride up the hill to the Moorish Castle of São Jorge. The site has been inhabited since the sixth century BC. The ruins we visited dated back two thousand years and were rebuilt by Muslim forces in the tenth century. From the promontory, we caught a spectacular view of Lisbon's bridge, the monuments, the tiled roofs, and the river, with its constant activity.

As Tim snapped photos of the city, I finally said, "Okay, enough already with the photos. I'm going to have frostbite soon. I need to get out of here." When you consider this comment came from the one who loves scenery to the one who usually has the attention span of a gnat in the presence of natural wonders, you know it was really cold.

We rubbed frozen noses and aching fingers as we repaired to an Irish pub on the wharf where we fortified ourselves before facing the journey across the water. Throughout the twenty-minute trip the wind, whitecaps, and nasty chop didn't faze the ferry men, but we were forced to look intently at the horizon all the way across to keep our stomachs settled. It pleased us greatly to start a fire and tuck ourselves in for the evening as the beautiful day deteriorated into a howling, wind-driven storm, including thunderclaps and flashes of lightning.

We also needed our rest—company was coming! Our friends Rick and Margo Riccobono, our London pals, were on their way. We were so happy to have the chance to see them and thank Rick in person for the good advice he had so freely offered when the craziness around our story began. Since we hadn't lived in a house, let alone entertained house guests, in a very long time, our preparation became an event itself. We managed to get the supplies for a real dinner party for four together, and we decorated with flowers, fluffed up the guest bedroom, bought place mats and napkins, and pretended to be authentic residents. Of course, really comfortable furniture was not a possibility! We also managed to fetch them, on time, at the airport and felt like locals saying things like, "Now, look over there! That's the aqueduct that was built in the 1700s. And in front of you is the April 25 Bridge. We live right over there!"

Everybody likes to be a smart-aleck, even if they won't admit it.

Margo and Rick were overwhelmed with the suddenly mild weather, a big treat after their winter in London, the worst in many years (and for us after the preceding cold). Sunshine and temperatures in the 50-degree F range thrilled them. Rick enjoyed the hammock so much that he seriously considered missing his return flight to London! Our friends at the Kontiki beach restaurant showed off their fish cooking skills, and we took our guests on a whirlwind tour of Lisbon. Tim outdid himself, coming up with the quintessential Lisbon dining experience, the Café de São Bento restaurant. The classic 1900s-style brasserie steak house featured red walls and banquettes, decorated with large paintings of ladies and gentlemen of the period and photos of Lisbon in its golden days. Tim told us that it was rated the best steak in town and that the classic dish was the steak in pepper sauce topped with a fried egg. We all took his advice. Every time we've spoken since, Margo carries on about that lunch! What an outstanding treat for carnivores like us.

When the Riccobonos decamped, our house grew too quiet. We consoled ourselves with a visit to Sintra, an area just a few minutes outside Lisbon, that everyone says is not to be missed. It's easy to understand their enthusiasm, because castles and grand estates dot the entire forest area. It also offers some of the most romantic views in a country that's full of gorgeous things to see. Among the many treats we encountered was the Pena National Palace, one of the major examples of nineteenth-century Romanticism in the world.

May I tell you that it's also an example of one of the most difficult-to-get-to monuments in the world? I maintained complete silence so I wouldn't distract Tim as he inched our way up a road that seemed about six feet wide. We puttered past tourists who walked two and three abreast without apparent concern for their lives, through dense blankets of fog where said tourists were rendered invisible, and up steep grades that made our little car and its sewing-machine engine gasp and sputter. We were rewarded for our diligence by finding a parking lot near the entrance.

The palace itself was a riot of neo-Gothic, neo-Manueline, Islamic, and neo-Renaissance architecture, a fabulous hodgepodge of surprises. Truly a photographer's delight! King Ferdinand and

Queen Maria II did not hold back in expressing their tastes, so pink, yellow, green, and gray walls vied for attention, along with entirely different windows, decorations, and styles. It was like being at Portuguese Disneyland, but with a much better view than Anaheim offers! Best of all, descending the mountain was much less painful and dangerous, and we were home warming our frozen limbs within thirty minutes.

Finally, that day came. It was the moment when I could not continue at the furious pace I was keeping. My eyes and derriere were sore and my brain worn very thin from months of shaping our story. I decided that being the artiste was actually harder than being the support system. I wanted my old job back. I had reached the halfway point in the book, and I was so exhausted that editor Bob and my sweet Tim conspired, telling me that all authors hit this wall, and the cure was to take a week away from the project. Their made-up tale worked and I obediently allowed myself to be driven up the Portuguese coast over that huge bridge and north through the forests and mountains, relieved that this was an officially sanctioned time-out. The road climbed until vineyards began to appear below the pines. The views were magnificent, and even March rain couldn't spoil the day.

The showers stopped just as we drove through a set of elaborate iron gates leading to a cobblestone parkway that wound up through a forest along a tumbling stream, the rocks and banks covered in moss and vines. Beside it were exotic tropical palms and fern trees that looked more like Maui than Portugal. We learned that the two hundred fifty acres around the palace were planted by Discalced monks, beginning in the seventh century. Marvelous plants collected from all over the world filled the grounds.

We rounded the last hairpin curve. There it was: the Palace Hotel do Buçaco. The palace was over-the-top, wildly romantic in the neo-Manueline style prevalent in Portugal. It included curlicues and vines, chubby cherubs, plasterwork, huge tiled romantic frescoes depicting love tales and battles, stained glass, tapestries, carved wood, stone, concrete, and gargoyle rain spouts. That was just the outside.

We were greeted by a gracious chubby man wearing a uniform with epaulets (I'm a fool for a man with epaulets). I beheld a grand red-carpeted marble staircase, at least twelve feet wide, inhabited by a suit of armor, with great swaths of draperies hanging from thirty-foot ceilings, softening magnificent stained-glass windows. We were speechless.

The man in the shoulder gear took us to our enormous corner suite on the second floor. It was much bigger than our Christmas apartment base in Paso Robles. We looked up to fifteen-foot ceilings, elegant French windows, and a little balcony, its railing featuring carved ribbons and animals, with views of the elaborate formal gardens and the forest beyond. There was enough closet space for a whole family, with built-in velvet-lined drawers, mahogany shoe racks, and beautiful old wooden hangers to spare.

The spotless bathroom took up at least two hundred square feet, with the same high ceilings and Martha Stewart pale green fixtures, a tub long enough for Kobe Bryant to lie down and soak, and of course, big fluffy towels and robes. This was my kind of getaway.

Tim plopped himself in one of the super-comfy velvet chairs while I engaged in my customarily excessive "oohing and aahing." Even though he pretended to be blasé, I know that he was pleased with himself. The room could have used a little sprucing up, but I have a fondness for slightly threadbare aristocratic lodgings, and the bed was good, which is all that really mattered. We think it's much more interesting to have original furnishings than state-of-the-art number beds and too-hip decor!

My spouse smiled for another reason: the Palace Hotel do Buçaco is a seriously great bargain, particularly in the pre-season.

As usual, we were starving. When we entered the drop-dead-gorgeous baroque dining room, a wine-tasting group dominated the center of the elegant space. Another epaulet-encrusted fellow seated us at a romantic bay window table, where we could observe the swishing and spitting wine crowd while viewing the vast gardens. He presented us with a menu that would have made Julia and Paul Child come to attention. We were absorbed for quite a while by the dazzling choices.

Everything was delicious. The highlights included Tim's wild boar ravioli appetizer, and my duck breast accompanied by the best potatoes dauphinoise that have ever passed my lips. His steak over sautéed *foie gras* (as you may recall, Tim discovered his duck fetish in France) was remarkable.

As we relished our lunch, we had time to observe the goings-on at the big table. These were not folks who hopped off a tour bus expecting some crackers and free wine. This was serious business. We heard at least three languages, one of them an unmistakable American twang. They discussed, poured, tasted, and, from what I could tell, engaged in some large-scale buying.

I put down my very large empty wineglass. It had held a delicious Syrah, which I had polished off with pleasure. As I glanced up, I saw several of the wine guys standing near a gorgeous antique breakfront. An array of bottles commanded their attention. My eyes met those of a big man with curly hair, whose personality and enthusiasm I'd noticed during lunch. He smiled. I smiled. Then I raised my empty glass and my eyebrows. He grabbed a bottle and within seconds was standing over our table.

I apologized. "I'm sorry, but I just couldn't stand it," I said. "You were all having too much fun, and I know what you're tasting is probably delicious."

"Of course you should have some! We are having a two-day

conference to introduce international buyers to our regional wines." He poured a taste into my glass.

Next came Filipa Pato, a dark-haired, vibrant young woman who strolled around the room, offering wine sips as she talked with visitors. She brought another glass and poured a taste, elbowing her competition out of the way. "Now, here's something really worth tasting," she joked. And it was. Her wine was full bodied and delicious. Her label? "Authentic Wines, without Makeup!" Now that's audacity.

Within five minutes, winemakers surrounded us, vying for my attention, having fun demonstrating their art to an innocent bystander—one who happened to know a bit about wines. A willing accomplice, I enjoyed several varieties of delicious reds and even a nice white port, which is made from white grapes and is fruitier and bolder than the white wines I was accustomed to drinking. Dirk Niepoort, the man who first caught my eye, was a key player in the region. As well as producing some brilliant Douro wines, he acted as a catalyst by encouraging the leading wine producers to get together and spur each other on to greater things. By definition, port is made by taking a still wine and adding brandy to it. The name "port" is derived from the coastal city of Porto, Portugal's second largest city, and the key city found on the mouth of the Douro River. Through pure fortune, we had stumbled into one of his gatherings. For the rest of our visit, I noticed his label in the window of every wine shop I passed in Portugal!

We spent the rest of the afternoon wandering the gardens, waterfalls, paths, and woods on the estate. The sun cooperated at exactly the right moment, so we enjoyed the excesses of Portuguese architecture and horticulture, awash in perfect light.

After a sumptuous breakfast served by the same guys (is *Fawlty Towers* actually a European reality?), we drove up farther to Aveiro, a charming beach town centered around a series of canals. Despite the chilly wind, tourists lined up to be ferried around in motor-driven gondolas, ungainly compared with the Venetian originals they sought to imitate. Plus, I must say, the sight of a muscular gondolier surely beats that of an Evinrude motor! We skipped the boat ride but found a decent lunch, which is always our priority. Some Portuguese food is heavy on fish and olive oil and light on flavor, which was the case that day. However, I'm happy to report that our friend Dirk's wine was available. After a couple of glasses of his lovely Redoma, the bland lunch didn't bother me at all!

When we returned to our grand palace digs, we stopped in the hotel bar, with its heroic-size paintings, overstuffed, comfortable furniture, and high ceilings trimmed lavishly with layers of gilded crown molding. As we sat in the bar, Tim said, "I have something to confess."

Oh Lordy, no wife wants to hear anything like that. Ever. Thoughts like there's another woman, he wants to buy a Porsche, he really DOES think I'm fat, we've gone broke, tend to wander through a woman's brain when a man utters those five words. "Yeeesssss…?" I answered, trying to be casual.

"I'm looking forward to going 'home,' as in our Portugal 'home' on the beach in Caparica," he said.

I laughed inappropriately. "What's so funny?" he asked, puzzled.

"Nothing." I quickly pulled myself together as my fears dissipated.

He looked at me strangely for a moment, then went on. "What I'm saying is that I've begun to think of the places where we are staying as if they are really home. I mean, I'll be happy to get back to our bed, our kitchen, our little life in Caparica…like going home after a weekend away. I think that's interesting, don't you?"

I agreed. We had become so adept at adapting that we could now embrace whatever lifestyle we lived at the time, and feel so comfortable that it actually felt like home to us. I knew where everything was, from the vegetable peeler to my heavier socks, so none of the moving-in dance was necessary! We automatically knew where the light switches were and how the locks worked without skipping a beat. It was a restful change.

Sure enough, when we arrived in Caparica the next day, unlocked our gate, pulled in our luggage, checked emails, decided what to have for dinner, and went about our lives, it felt strangely like our own place in the world. Any place seems like home when we are together.

We lived in Caparica for five weeks, practically a record for us. We enjoyed the Portuguese people and the laid-back vibe so much that we started plotting a return visit as we packed. However, we wouldn't particularly miss the barking dog in the neighborhood… or the only unpleasant noisy neighbor, who lived right next door. The guy appeared every Saturday evening, played his television too loud, washed his car every week at 3:00 p.m.—rain or shine—and departed at exactly 9:30 p.m. every Sunday evening. Though he annoyed us, his schedule served as one of the ways we kept track of what day it was. It was pleasant to sink into the sameness of a routine, to rock along as we would at home for a little while, even the parts that weren't particularly fun.

One of the strange trade-offs of a home-free life is that we find it easy to ignore the irritations we might find unendurable in a permanent residence, like kids that yell constantly, traffic noises, partying neighbors, or loud motor scooters starting up every day at 7:00 a.m. We know we're going to move away soon, so they don't take up much space in our lives. Why worry about them?

On our final morning, Katarina appeared to say good-bye. She helped us stuff our gear into the toy-size car, and we were off again. We anticipated an easy trip to the airport because it was Easter Sunday, but when we arrived at the bridge, we were dismayed to see traffic bottled up in both directions. Of course, it was raining, as it had nearly every day for the entire five weeks. The ground was soaked, and people in the other cars didn't look very happy. We crossed the bridge, but traffic remained very slow, and we began to be concerned about running out of time.

We spotted emergency vehicles on the other side of the road. "Ahhhh, look," Tim said, clearly relieved, knowing the traffic would speed up on the other side of the flashing lights. "That explains the delays. They're stopped on that side because of a wreck, and our side is so slow because people can't help themselves. They have to have a look."

I followed his glance across the road. Instantly, we stopped breathing. A small forest of trees ran up the hill above the road. One of them, at least a hundred feet tall, began to move. Its top swayed drunkenly, and then it slowly began to fall, top first, down toward the road. It seemed to take forever to reach the ground— and then everything sped up. Within a nanosecond, the wreckage started crashing across the median. The tree landed on several cars, its top resting on the median railing, no more than a foot from us. Vehicles behind the smashed autos stopped at all kinds of odd angles, not at all where they should have been. People ran toward the scene from the wreck we had passed seconds before. I caught a glimpse of a woman standing beside the first car that had been hit, her mouth wide open. She was screaming. Since we continued to move forward, pushed by the traffic around us, we had no time to process what our eyes witnessed. Tim's knuckles grew white from his death-grip on the wheel.

Within moments, it was all behind us—the crash, the toppled tree, the smashed cars. Traffic moved along as if nothing happened. We were too shocked to speak for a little while, each of us sorting out the event in our own brains. When we regained our composure, we found that each of us had leapt from that moment of peril to thoughts of our own good fortune at being spared, and then to pondering the random nature of existence. The experience just served to reinforce our mantra: postpone nothing.

Epilogue
Postpone Nothing

O ur nomadic life caused us to postpone only one thing: feeling old. This is not to say that we have postponed *being* old.
Heaven knows that with each passing day we are surprised at the
changes we see in the mirror. We just do not feel old.

There is the difference. We cherish our excellent health and
financial stability—the two essential ingredients of what some
people call our "derring-do" retirement. We know that it's much
easier for a person to feel young when he or she is well. We looked
after our money and health throughout our lives, but we know that
we cannot claim all the responsibility for our good fortune. Luck
gave Tim and me good genes, and each other, both of which we are
thankful for every day.

Before we started our "home free" life, we were living in the
emotional place author Jess Walter termed "the vast, empty plateau
where most people live, between boredom and contentment" in his
novel, *Beautiful Ruins*. While not unhappy, we were bored. Old age
and ennui curled under the doors and around the windows.

Never again have we felt that threat; we have not looked back. We
are healthier, happier, and more in touch with our world and our own
selves than we dreamed possible. The boredom stands in a far corner,
kept at bay. As for contentment? In my opinion, it's overrated.

Some might find my view shallow, and they may be partially correct. Truth is, though, that I'd rather worry about how we will make
it from Charles de Gaulle Airport in Paris to our apartment at rush

hour next week than whether my napkins will match the tablecloth for a dinner party, if a gardener will fix the sprinklers before the roses croak, or if I will show up late for a club committee meeting. I am not espousing our lifestyle for everyone, nor do I think that our choices are superior in any way. I do know we are living exactly the way we want to live, and feel very lucky to have made the right decision for ourselves.

When we cast off on this adventure, we had no idea whether we were heading for years of regret and turmoil or a happy voyage. What would life be like without a haven where we could pull the covers over our heads and hide out until we found a better idea? The clock was ticking and we wanted to experience the last part of our lives without being bound to one place. This is where courage enters the picture. We needed a mixture of qualities, both admirable and unattractive, to conquer our fear of giving up our home, most of our belongings, and the good opinion of some of our friends and family to strike out, unfettered, for a new life. We were certainly old enough to know that our choice would be fraught with unforeseen consequences.

Now, the results are in. Life on the road suits us perfectly most of the time. Our minor upsets and mishaps usually have been conquered by patience, laughter, and flexibility. Sometimes, we solve the problem by simply spending a few extra bucks to pay for a more comfortable place, or to take a cab instead of the underground when we're lost or tired. There have been days when weather, illness, unpleasantness, frustration, or just plain bad moods plagued us. We have been frightened more than once, and I ache with longing for my family occasionally. I get sentimental about strange things like my garden, which some other woman fusses over now, or my great old cast-iron skillet, which waits for me in storage. Someday, I will have another garden, and that iron pot will produce another golden frittata when we finally decide to settle down again.

The trade-off for these discomforts and yearnings? Challenging our notions of what "old" means. We hold that specter at arms' length where it really counts: in our minds and attitudes.

Of course, we have to accommodate reality: we no longer sprint up the underground stairs in the London Tube or the Paris Metro; we step to the side and take our time. We don't frolic until the wee hours anymore; we take long, leisurely lunches instead. Red-eye flights or twelve-hour bus rides are no longer an option for us. However, we learn something every day, see something, plan something, meet someone, or solve some brand-new problem. For those reasons, we do not perceive ourselves as "old."

Not every older person can or wants to follow our lead by making radical changes in his or her life. However, we hope that our example can help others understand that "old" doesn't mean "finished" or resigned to a life of boredom and routine. Living home free is more than an action; it's a mind-set, an attitude. It allows one the latitude to embrace a new idea, change a long-observed pattern, or make a new friend. Those things can bring fresh life and excitement to anyone in any circumstance.

Many have written to tell us how they found their own version of home-free living. Some extended their travels farther afield. Others found places to live in other countries for months at a time. Several learned a new language or took an earlier retirement to buy more time to pursue their dreams. Some of our new friends are unable to travel or make changes. Yet, by riding with us through reading and interacting with us on our website, they enjoyed new pleasure, jogged their memories about their own forays into the world (however large or small), or pursued and rekindled interests they had abandoned because they considered themselves "old."

As I write this, Tim sits downstairs in our current home, a charming Irish cottage near the Ring of Kerry, looking into plans for the future. He mutters into his computer screen as he compares prices for a cruise we're considering for next year. Tonight our friends Maureen and Alan, who were our generous neighbors last year in Dublin, will be our dinner guests. Our dinner conversation will probably include a lively discussion about what we've learned since we last saw them, and our future plans. Right now, French Polynesia is of particular interest, and a more extensive exploration of South America is definitely a contender, which we want to see despite our experiences with those naysaying Argentines. Australia and New Zealand fascinate us, and Asia always sits on our table of primary consideration. We rejoice every day for being allowed this time to see the world together after so many years apart, and a major ingredient in our delight will continue to be sharing our experiences with you.

Ultimately, embracing the changes in our life's dynamics, finding the flexibility to temporarily switch roles (muse and writer, optimist and realist, dreamer and doer), and becoming acquainted with thousands of people also in the process of discovering new directions in their lives reinforced our belief in the power of saying "yes." To this day, it inspires us to postpone nothing because life is too short and too sweet not to savor it the way you want. We hope that you will, too.

The Learning Curve: Things the Guidebooks Won't Teach You

We've been asked by many people how to create a home-free lifestyle, and we'd be happy to oblige! For those of you who are interested, here are some of the essential tips, tricks, and lessons we've learned on the road.

Basic Chores Before You Go

- **Visas:** It's vital to do your homework about visa requirements for places you want to visit. Allow time to get it right. Not doing so could derail important plans. Also, some countries charge a significant amount for a visa, which could have an impact on your budget, so keep that in mind when picking destinations. Also, don't forget to check your passport. It should be more than six months before renewal time. You can find out more about all of that on this website: www.travel.state.gov.

- **Legal:** Make a trust or at least a will. It's a morbid thought, I know, but your family will thank you in case the unspeakable were to happen.

- **Money:** Arrange with your bank to pay bills online. It makes life so much easier abroad!
  - Acquire at least two major credit cards, preferably one that offers mileage points. Some also offer no currency exchange fees, which can be helpful when using them abroad.

- Get a PayPal account so you can deal with rentals while you are on the road. Phone them before you leave home to tell them your itinerary. Otherwise, they will not debit from your bank account and you'll be charged a substantial transaction fee.

- **Mail:** Ask a family member or trusted friend to receive your mail, if possible, and take time to stop the catalogs so they won't want to murder you when they have to dig through those tree-killing monsters that pile up every day.
  - Or try a mail service. USA2Me.com will receive and sort your mail, forward packages, and perform all kinds of tedious chores for a nominal fee, and you don't even have to write them a thank-you note or worry if they've forgotten to take care of your dentist's bill.

- **Health Insurance:** Medicare does not cover you outside the United States. It is prudent to look into international health insurance. There are a number of companies that offer policies to cover you for major emergencies. They will also evacuate you, if necessary. Many countries besides the United States offer excellent medical care to visitors for nominal fees. You might want to check the details of the places you plan to go as well to see what health services and insurance options are available to you.

- **Inoculations:** Check CDC recommendations for the places you will be going: www.cdc.gov/travel. Your local health department should be able to provide inoculations if needed. Give yourself enough time before your trip to get your shots and recover from them, because some of those puppies hurt!

Transportation

- **Cruising:** We highly recommend repositioning cruises to get where you want inexpensively. Twice a year, cruise lines reposition their equipment. These crossings offer big savings because they're not particularly popular routes. For more:
  - www.RepositioningCruise.com
  - www.VacationsToGo.com

- **Cars:** We have used two companies primarily:
  - CarRentals.com for general use
  - AutoFrance.net for rentals over seventeen days that commence in France. This is a terrific deal where you will get a brand-new Peugeot for much less than you would pay for a standard European rental car.

- **Housing:** We book apartments and houses far in advance with:
  - www.VRBO.com
  - www.HomeAway.com

And here are a number of other things we learned in the various places we went (organized by chapter below):

Chapter 3: San Miguel De Allende, Mexico

- **Watch Your Step:** Good walking shoes are essential in old cities. The sidewalks are paved with stone and held together unevenly with concrete grout. Narrow driveways and treacherous curbs lurk everywhere. Never look up while you are moving. Stop walking when you window-shop or stare at a wonderful church.

- **Take It Easy:** The elevation is 6,500 feet. Unless you are super-human, you will pant like crazy for the first few days, so don't push it. Remember, on any extended visit, you're not a tourist, you're a traveler. We move at a slower pace.

- **Plan Ahead:** Guanajuato International Airport near León is about an hour and fifteen minutes from San Miguel. You can save money by taking a shuttle. If you want to indulge yourself, send for a car, which will cost about $100. Either way, prearrange transportation. Just put it in the budget and start out happy. You may also fly into Mexico City and take a bus to San Miguel. It's a savings and those who do it often tell us it's just fine.

- **Health Issues:** Do NOT drink water from any tap unless you are certain that it is purified. Use bottled water—even to brush your teeth. Eat uncooked, unpeeled vegetables only in restaurants with good reputations. Restaurant ice will not hurt you, so margaritas are your friend.

- **Be Nice:** The Mexican people respond to courtesy. Do not shout. Greet people when you enter a store or restaurant, and use *gracias* and *por favor* liberally.

Chapter 4: Buenos Aires

- **About Long Flights:** You can make yourself so much more comfortable, even without springing for a higher-class ticket. For a much cheaper fare than business class, you can buy bulk-head seats. These offer more room and privacy. It's worth it! Also remember that drinking alcohol in-flight makes jet lag worse!

- **Car Pickup:** Our standard advice applies here, too. Spend a few extra bucks for a car pickup when you arrive. The driver will get you to your apartment without a hassle, and you can begin your home-free life with less drama! It's worth the extra expense. Economize on champagne to make up the difference.

- **Inspection List:** Make a list of all the things you'll need to know before you go. Politely insist that the agent or owner review it with you before he/she leaves the apartment. This includes: run-through on all appliances, how windows and doors work. Look at the pots and pans. Are they clean, usable? Is there a coffeepot? Note the location of closest stores, transportation options, and telephone, plus items particular to the country. You need a list because you will be too tired and excited to remember what to ask. Trust us. Take it to every new country. There is a good list on our website, www.homefreeadventures.com, which has been augmented with great ideas from our readers!

- **You're Not Special:** Remember that big cities are busy and people must lead their lives. Be prepared to fend for yourself and get out of the way. Don't take rudeness personally. Unless you stay in a hotel, you won't be treated with much deference in Buenos Aires.

- **Mexican Spanish:** This does you little good in Argentina. The dialect is difficult to understand and speak. Brush up on Argentinean Spanish before you go. Don't even try using Spanglish.

- **Unhappiness:** If you are too hot, cold, stressed, or unhappy, you have our permission *and your own* to leave early. You didn't start this life to be miserable, remember?

- **Ask the Right Questions:** In Argentina, the first answer to your every question usually will be, "No." Even locals will admit this fact. We're not being mean. Neither are they. Phrase the question so it leaves an opening to ask the next one. For instance, it's better to ask the waitress, "Do you have wine by the glass?" instead of, "May I have a glass of wine?" And before you enter a taxi, ask the driver if he or she will make change!

Chapter 5: Transatlantic Crossing

- **Pick the Right Cabin:** Pay attention to the season. For instance, a balcony cabin may not help you in winter, but staying in a lower deck room will reduce the risk of your having to tie yourself into your bed at night!

- **Choose Friends Carefully:** Watch and learn for the first day or so on your voyage. If you make pals too fast and change your mind, it will not be easy to avoid them gracefully in such close quarters.

- **Hide Out:** A night of room service (free on board), if needed, can be therapeutic!

Chapter 6: Turkey

- **Location, Location, Location:** If you plan a shorter stay in Istanbul, it is a good idea to rent a place close to the heart of the old city. You can walk to most major monuments and treat yourself to the real flavor of life in that marvelous country.

- **Match Your Attention Span:** Don't sign up for the in-depth, all-day tour if you're an overview kind of person. Sometimes, hitting the highlights and making time to wander is the better choice.

- **Keys!:** Always check your keys before leaving your apartment, especially if there is no supervisor or attendant. Otherwise, you can waste large amounts of time.

- **Read Reviews:** Take advantage of recent reviews before booking. Don't rely on memory or friends' recommendations from their trip ten years ago. Things change. If you're not careful, a diet of lousy European rock 'n' roll could assail you—or maybe inedible, all-inclusive fodder.

- **Make New Friends:** Talk to everyone. You'll learn from other travelers about places you might not have considered, and pick up all kinds of great ideas.

Chapter 7: Paris

- **Relax:** Enjoy the benefits of home-free life. Give yourself "down" days to read, cocoon, relax. This is your life, not a vacation when you must pack all the highlights you want to see into four days.

- **Shrink Your Ego:** Don't be afraid to look foolish and ask questions. People will usually forgive your ignorance and your lack of French if you ask for help politely.

- **Observe:** Avoid humiliation. Take a moment to watch locals in action. You'll learn the drills for the subway, grocery, movies, and restaurants by first observing how it's done.

- **Buy One, Toss One:** You can buy new clothes, but get rid of something in exchange. Otherwise, you will be traveling like a pack mule every time you move.

- **Grooming:** Ask a local about beauty salons and nails. You may get lucky; you may not. Be philosophical. Even the worst haircut grows out.

Chapter 8: Italy

- **Driving:** Buy a good GPS and take it with you. Your outbound and inbound drives will not follow the same route in a thousand-year-old city designed on goat paths, so you'll really need some help.

- **Invite the Kids:** Visits from children or grandchildren can double your fun!

- **Be Cool:** Do not live in Italy in July and August without air conditioning. The Italians have a different take on discomfort. Remember, dry heat cooks turkeys.

- **Get Out:** If you are unhappy, hot, and miserable, move on. You're a grown-up.

Chapter 9: England

- **Driving:** When you arrive, give yourself time to learn how to drive on the left side. Before putting the key in the ignition, also get a grip on the roundabouts concept—enter on the left and drive clockwise.

- **Side Trips:** Do not make a long trip to Cornwall or anywhere in the country the first day. Plan your country drives after you have settled into your "permanent" home. You will be too tired from traveling and too burdened with luggage if you tour first. Spring for the extra dough to take side trips while traveling light; leave your stuff at "home." Unless you're young and hardy, the extra lodging bill is worth it.

- **Say "Yes":** When someone offers you an opportunity to go somewhere, see something, do something new, say "Yes" whenever possible. Your best stories will come from things you never expected, but tried! Postpone nothing!

- **Keep in Touch:** Use your Internet connection to speak with friends and family via Skype or FaceTime. A thirty-minute chat can feel like a visit home and be a great tonic to you and the ones you love and miss. Best of all, Skype to Skype calls are free!

- **Shop Green:** Don't be shy. Charity shop browsing is considered chic in most countries. When seasons change, you can supplement your wardrobe without going broke, then recycle your purchases and enjoy the bonus of feeling righteous!

Chapter 10: Ireland

- **Housing:** When you're looking for a place to stay, do pay attention to all the things that are offered. This may be your chance to live in an authentic Irish cottage or have an apartment in a Georgian building!

- **Driving:** Tiny is better. Get the smallest car possible that will hold your luggage. Narrow roads are easier to negotiate with a little car. You'll save on petrol, too, a major consideration. It is much more expensive than U.S. fuel.

- **Side Trips:** Sometimes, it takes more than once for us to learn a lesson. We traveled around the country with all of our gear and were exhausted by it. Get settled, then travel.

- **Meet the Neighbors:** If you're lucky, your new neighbors will be interesting, informative, and own wonderful homes with comfortable furniture. If the people next door start to chat you up, do invite them in for a coffee or a glass of wine. The Irish love conversation and are interested in everyone's story. You may make friends for life!

Chapter 11: Marrakech, Morocco

- **Single File:** Don't consider walking side by side. A bicycle, motorcycle, or cart could ruin your day.

- **Don't Ask for Directions:** Expect to pay up when someone offers to show you the way. They will expect a tip. You WILL become lost in this labyrinth of a city, but it's half the fun. Don't panic, but be prepared to pay if you need help.

- **Everything Is Negotiable:** Don't consider paying full price for anything. Haggle over everything, including cab fare, and enjoy yourself while you do it because the natives will be having fun.

- **Eat Large:** Don't let the huge outdoor food stalls scare you into missing the fun. Plunk yourself at the paper-covered table and dig in.

Chapter 12: Break Time

- **Cruise and Schmooze:** After living on the road for such an extended period of time, use the voyage home to rest, reflect, and visit the gym to lose those extra pounds.

- **Make Appointments:** Take advantage of being "home." Deal with the documents, accountant, taxes, and all other boring but essential stuff, so that when you return to your next round of home-free adventure, you'll be worry-free as well.

- **Get a Visa:** As previously mentioned, take care of long-term visas while you are in the United States if you are going to go that route. It takes time to gather the necessary information, and a personal visit to the consulate may be necessary. Plan ahead.

- **Shop:** Use what you learned the first time out: pare down, replenish your wardrobe, and leave unnecessary gear at home.

- **Cruise News:** Before booking, check out the age and amenities of a ship, and whether it has experienced any mechanical or structural problems, or complaints about its voyages. Quality is more important than price. Eighteen days on an elderly ship is not necessarily a good bargain.

Chapter 13: Portugal

- **If Something Is Wrong, Speak Up:** If anything in your living situation is not up to par, correct it right away. The owner/manager wants you to be happy, so don't suffer in silence.

- **Succumb to a Checklist:** As we mentioned before (it's *that* important), make a checklist for use before leaving the house. It's really a good idea. Just a single omission, like house keys, money, or credit cards, can cause unnecessary havoc. You don't have to admit your surrender. We'll never tell.

- **Annoyances Fade:** Don't let minor irritations like barking dogs, noisy construction projects, or occasionally rowdy neighbors spoil your good time. You'll be gone soon. Buy some earplugs or a great set of headphones and tune them all out.

And last but not least, two essentials to do anywhere you go!

- **Remember to Laugh:** No matter how distressing your situation might seem at the time, inconvenient travel events make great dinner-table yarns later. Try to see the humor when you end up at the opposite end of Paris from where you intended to be or the bottle of capers whose German label you can't read turns out to be searingly hot green peppercorns, sending your dinner guests into gasping, red-faced anguish. Bad at the time, great stories later!

- **Write It All Down:** Be sure to take notes. Sometimes the most colorful parts of our experiences are found in the small moments, and you WILL forget them over time, so make a few notes every day before they get away from you. Trust us, you'll love yourself for them later.

Acknowledgments

My collaborators include every person who rode a bus, plane, train, ferry, underground, or ship with us, shared a laugh, gasped at a beautiful sight, ran from a storm, or gave a busker a buck. I thank every stranger who offered kindness, help, and their friendship as we stumbled along finding our way in the world. You are with us each day as our amazing journey unfolds. You have enriched our lives immeasurably!

We thank my parents, Wanda and Leonard Shomell, for their example. They were our inspiration and are always in our hearts. They blazed the international trail for us forty years ago, without the benefit of Internet or cell phones. Their courage and devotion to each other—and their determination to have fun and see the world together in their later years—drew the map for us. Daddy, how you would have loved all that has happened to us.

I am forever grateful to Jim Gray, a writer whose generous introduction to Glenn Ruffenach, editor at the *Wall Street Journal*, opened the door to a thrilling new opportunity. Working with Glenn was a privilege. He is a genuine gentleman and a distinguished journalist whose graceful editorial guidance and friendship made my experience with that celebrated publication pure joy.

Bob Yehling, a California writing, surfing, coaching, marathon-running dynamo, worked his editing magic with my first attempts, and not only piloted me through the task, but also gave me a private writing education. His patience, kindness, expertise, and counsel were the unwritten part of our contract and were just as valuable to me as his extraordinary editing job!

Dana Newman, my excellent literary agent/attorney, appeared

on the scene at exactly the right moment with just the qualities we needed: experience, tenacity, guidance, and the right connections. She smoothed our trajectory from concept to reality and continues leading us through the mysteries of the publishing business.

Which leads me directly to Stephanie Bowen, senior editor at Sourcebooks, who championed our story with her publisher, and whose editorial sensitivity, talent, taste, and enthusiasm shaped my manuscript into *Home Sweet Anywhere*. My affection and appreciation are boundless. Nicole Villeneuve, assistant publicity manager at Sourcebooks, invested her considerable talent and energy into seeing that *Home Sweet Anywhere* was given every opportunity to be discovered by its readers. Thanks to Heather Hall, Sourcebooks production editor, who made my words look luscious and inviting, and the cover design team, which created a charming, engaging book that thrills me each time I look at it!

And then there's the cheering section: Rick Riccobono, whose deep basso voice was always so welcome, and whose warm, positive personality piloted us through more than one moment of terror and panic as the project found its legs; Sarah McMullen, our extraordinary friend, who scooped us up and dusted us off when brushes with the big boys overwhelmed us; Maureen and Alan Grainger, whose warmth and wine gave us stability and comfort when we needed "family" abroad; Mark Chimsky, editor of *65 Things to Do When You Retire: Travel*, who gave me Colette's writing mantra when I was shredded with exhaustion and self-doubt; and Andie and Georges, who began as landlords and became friends forever. They handed us Paris on a plate garnished with pâté and love.

And, of course, thanks to our daughters, Robin Cloward, Alexandra Chamberlain, Alwyn Pinnow, and Amandah Goldsmith, and their families for their boundless enthusiasm, encouragement, and love. We cherish all of you, and perhaps one of these days we'll surprise you and make a Home Sweet Somewhere!

About the Author

In 2010, Lynne and Tim Martin decided to sell their home, disburse most of their belongings, and travel the world for the rest of their lives. Lynne's popular blog, www .homefreeadventures.com, chronicles their nomadic life, which was the cover article of the *Wall Street Journal*'s "Next" section in October 2012. It was the most commented-upon *WSJ* article of the month, was featured on the front page of Yahoo.com, and was picked up by the *Huffington Post*, Fodor's Travel Intelligence, Hacker News, and others. Her work

Photo credit: Kevin White Studios, Surbiton, Surrey, UK

has also appeared in Mark Chimsky's book, *65 Things to Do When You Retire*, International Living, the *Huffington Post*, and others.

Born in Texas and raised in Chicago, Lynne studied journalism in college and worked in radio and television for a number of years. She founded Maynor and Associates, a public relations firm in Hollywood, specializing in publicity for actors, television, and movies. Her firm's efforts resulted in *The Man Who Skied Down Everest* winning the 1976 Academy Award for best feature documentary. Later, she formed a gourmet cheese company whose products were distributed in upscale markets throughout the United States, and was co-owner of an equipment-leasing brokerage firm. She is the mother/stepmother of four daughters and grandmother of seven.

Lynne and her husband, Tim, a novelist, have lived in Mexico, Argentina, Turkey, France, Italy, Great Britain, Ireland, Morocco, Portugal, and Germany since they became home free. She now has no permanent address and intends to keep it that way until the wheels fall off sometime in the next thirty years.